D1615828

DARK HORSE

A Life of
ANNA SEWELL

Adrienne E. Gavin

SUTTON PUBLISHING

First published in the United Kingdom in 2004 by
Sutton Publishing Limited · Phoenix Mill
Thrupp · Stroud · Gloucestershire · GL5 2BU

British Library Cataloguing in Publication Data
A catalogue record for this book is available from the British Library.

ISBN 0-7509-2838-7

Typeset in Sabon 11/14.5pt.
Typesetting and origination by
Sutton Publishing Limited.
Printed and bound in England by
J.H. Haynes & Co. Ltd, Sparkford.

Contents

This book is dedicated with more love and gratitude than I can ever express to those who have always seen me through the things I take on and who give reason to my hopes and dreams: my parents Irene and John, my sisters Raewyn and Claire and my brother Scott and my husband Dewayne.

Preface

Anna Sewell, creator of the most famous black horse ever to exist in life or fiction, is herself the ultimate in metaphorical dark horses. During her life no one suspected that in her final years she would write a bestselling novel that would still be published, read, and loved over 125 years later. Neither was she lionized after her death, perhaps because *Black Beauty* was her only book, or because she died so soon after its publication. While her novel lives on as *the* horse book above all others, Anna herself has all but vanished from literary history.

Yet claims are made that *Black Beauty* was once the sixth highest selling book in the world and that it has outsold the collective works of Dickens.[1] Lesser claims would warrant more interest, but Anna's name rarely graces the lips of Victorian scholars or general readers. Works about her cluster neither shinily in the ranks of new publications nor dustily in the recesses of rare book shops. Even in the many towns she lived in across Britain little – usually nothing – is made of her in tourist brochures, where a mere lunch stop by someone whose achievements were less garners glossy promotion. Ask most people and they will say they have heard of *Black Beauty*, but the question 'Do you know who wrote it?' is often answered with twisted expressions of puzzlement and chagrin which dissolve into a drifting 'No, actually I don't', or a tentative 'somebody Sewell wasn't it?' Even those who confidently respond 'Anna Sewell' usually know little else about her: how she lived, when she died, or what nationality she was.

During a game of Trivial Pursuit™ near the beginning of my Sewell researches I recall the delight with which I received the victory-clinching question: 'What nationality was Anna Sewell, famous for her *Black Beauty* novel?' Imagine the utter glee of my opponent who insisted that the incorrect answer printed on the card, 'American', must be taken as absolute. Because of the enormous success of

Black Beauty in America the British Anna is sometimes thought to be American, but this reflects another fact of her afterlife: where there is knowledge about her it is not always correct.

The paradox of Anna's obscurity and her novel's phenomenal fame drew me to begin researching her life in 1995. I was fascinated by her also because *Black Beauty* fell into so many categories of my own interests: Victorian literature, children's literature, and women's writing and, too, because like so many who love her book I was once a girl who loved horses, and books, and books about horses.

Anna's is a life difficult to find, mainly because so little of it was recorded. It is a mixed blessing that her mother, Mary Sewell, was a Victorian author of some note and so accounts of her life exist which also mention Anna. Most important is Mrs [Mary] Bayly's biography *The Life and Letters of Mrs Sewell*, published in 1889, which is, in addition to the brief 1935 'Recollections of Anna Sewell' by Anna's niece Margaret Sewell, the source of most of what has been written about Anna since. In 1880 Mary also began her own unfinished and unpublished 'Reminiscences' for her grandchildren, much of which Bayly includes in her biography. Without these records of Mary's life there would be little left of Anna's, but this has also meant that Anna's own story has tended to hide behind the skirts of her mother's once greater fame. Because Anna and Mary's lives were for decades lived almost as one, this is not as problematic as it might have been in some cases; nevertheless, part of what I have endeavoured to do is to tease out as much as possible that is distinctively Anna.

Only two previous biographies of Anna exist. The first is a children's biography by Margaret J. Baker entitled *Anna Sewell and 'Black Beauty'* (1957), and the second is Susan Chitty's *The Woman Who Wrote 'Black Beauty'* (1971). When Chitty was writing, only a couple of letters by Anna had been discovered beyond the extracts from Anna's journals and other material that Bayly includes. Since that time additional letters by Anna and her family have come to light including over fifty letters bought by the Norfolk Record Office in 1986. These letters offer new insights into Anna's life and have given me many weeks of fascinating and often eye-strainingly frustrating transcription. Especially so given that many of them are 'crossed', i.e., a sheet is written over 'portrait' then turned and written over again 'landscape', then the same again on the reverse, in order to save paper and postage. All efforts to trace Anna's journals, the paintings and drawings she produced, and the manuscript of *Black Beauty* have proved unavailing.

Anna lived in many parts of southern England – Great Yarmouth, London, Brighton, Lancing, Haywards Heath, Chichester, Abson in Gloucestershire, Bath, and Old Catton near Norwich. Her local connections are most known in Norfolk which was the county of her birth, death, and family heritage, although most of her life was not spent there. Wherever I could find someone in the areas in which she lived who knew of her link with the locale, they were usually quick to tell me that the original of Black Beauty had grazed in a nearby field. Although the accuracy of such claims may be doubted, that they are made points to a deeper truth about the enduring power of Anna's equine autobiography. To her readers everywhere the field near their homes *is* always Black Beauty's, and equally he is their horse, and on another level he is them.

The great are often written about but not always the good. Anna strove successfully to live a life of practical altruism. Hers was not the life of fashionable society, love affairs, or dramatic action, but that does not make it any the less important. Anna led the life of an ordinary Victorian woman, but she also battled debilitating personal restrictions, and achieved, against painful odds, something extraordinary. She created a book of multiple capacities: horse-care manual, passionate protest against cruelty, novel of Victorian life, and children's classic. Hers was the life of a thinker of tenacious spirit and ramrod determination who was not afraid to live up to her own ideals. She lived quietly and without fanfare, but with a passion and endurance which touched the lives of those she knew and helped. Anna's was a life well lived, and in writing *Black Beauty* she did something that in its own way changed the world.

Canterbury, England
25 April 2003
(Written on the 125th anniversary of Anna Sewell's death)

Acknowledgements

One of the highlights of this project has been the opportunity of coming into contact with so many new people and meeting with such generosity of spirit in doing so. My thanks go first to those who have connections with, or interests in, the Sewell family or in Sewell-related properties, especially Charles and Avril Briscoe of Dudwick Cottage for exceptionally generous and gracious assistance. I also wish to thank Danielle O'Hara of the Anna Sewell Restaurant in Yarmouth and Robert Graham who ran the restaurant in 2002; Mark McArdle for his friendly tour of Anna Sewell's Bath home; Joyce and Robin Peachey of Blue Lodge, Abson; Anne Cryer of Dudwick House; and Sue and Robin Worden of Anna Sewell House, Old Catton. For genealogical and background information I am also grateful to Peter Foreman, Michael Metford-Sewell, Tim C. Ray, and Tracie Sargent (née Sewell). I am extremely grateful to Linda Large (and her mother I.V. Wright) and Linda Steward for their enthusiasm and abundant help. High gratitude goes, too, to fellow *Black Beauty* scholar Karen Crossley who has provided me with much interesting information and to Victoria Manthorpe who gave me Norfolk advice and whose Sewell newspaper article elicted for me many fruitful leads.

The help of librarians and archivists has been invaluable and I wish to thank especially the Norfolk Heritage Centre librarians at the Norfolk and Norwich Millennium Library, particularly Pat Gaisburgh-Watkyn, Clare Agate, Emma Lewis, and Amanda Sergeant. I am deeply indebted to Kim Leslie of the West Sussex Record Office who gave me very generous assistance on Anna Sewell's Sussex homes (I also thank R. Iden and Frances Lansley). Jackie Lewis of the Brighton Local Studies Library provided me, too, with very helpful suggestions and generous searching, as did Terri Goldich, curator of the Northeast Children's Literature Collection of the Thomas J. Dodd Research Center at the University of Connecticut. I wish also to thank Dawn Dyer of Bristol Reference Library; Helen Bradbury, Jean Price, and Janice Packham of the Gloucestershire Collection at the Gloucester Reference Library; Anne Thomson of Newnham College Archives, University of Cambridge; Stephanie Brownbridge of Bath Central Library; Sarah Hutcheon of the Arthur and Elizabeth Schlesinger Library on the History of Women in America, Harvard University; Sabra Ionno of the Harriet Beecher Stowe Center, Hartford, Connecticut. I am also grateful to the staffs of Bath City Record Office; Bishopsgate Library; the British Library; Cambridge University Library; Camomile Street Library; Canterbury Christ Church University College Library; Chichester Library; CLR James Library, Dalston; East Sussex Record Office; the Family Records Centre; Gloucestershire Record Office; Great Yarmouth Borough Library; the Harry Ransom Humanities Research Center at the University of Texas at Austin; Haywards Heath Library; Lancing Library, Library of the Religious Society of Friends, London; Norfolk Record Office; the Public Record Office; Stoke Newington Library; University of Kent Library; and Worthing Library.

I am also grateful to Bridget Collett, headteacher of Moorlands Infant School; John Cranston of BBC Look East; Rosemary Dixon of the *Eastern Daily Press*; Caroline Jarrold and Peter Jarrold of Jarrolds; David M. McDowell, Equine Veterinary Officer of the RSPCA; Diana Kennedy of the Sole Society; Robert Novak, Jr of the Derby Historical Society, Ansonia, Connecticut; Robin Phillips of the Chapels Society; Peter Salt, Jarrolds' former archivist; Marion Shaw of the Tennyson Society; Clare Wigmore of the British Driving Society; David Woodruff of the Strict Baptist Historical Society. I also wish to thank Terence Burchell for photographic work done on my behalf in Norfolk.

My appreciation goes, too, to the many people who replied to queries or offered information including Barbara Baskerville, Eve Collishaw, Robert Daines, Joyce Eaton, Virginia Freed, David Little, Lianda Martin, John Marriott, Debby Matthews, Tom Mollard, Brian Mumford, Marcos Gago Otero, Andrew Roberts, Lilian Rogers, Malcolm Spiers, Gavin Thorpe, Louise van der Merwe, Neville Way, and Paul Winstanley.

I am grateful to Canterbury Christ Church University College for granting me a term's research leave while I worked on the project and to my colleagues in the English Department, especially Terry Clifford-Amos who enabled my leave, Carolyn Oulton, and the ever generous Peter Merchant who has offered me advice on topics ranging from corsets to Episcopalians. I also wish to thank the many students who over the years have discussed *Black Beauty* with me.

Winning the Biographers' Club Prize 2000 for my proposal for this book gave me great encouragement and I am very grateful to the judges and the Club. I also wish to thank my agent Andrew Lownie and my editor Jaqueline Mitchell together with assistant editor Jane Entrican.

My thanks go, too, to those institutions or individuals who have granted me permission to quote from or reproduce material (which is specified more particularly in the text) including 'anonymous owner', Susan Chitty, Graham Clark, Tony Hall, R.E.F. Pegg, James Pepper, Linda Steward, EDPpics, the *Eastern Daily Press*, Norfolk County Council Library and Information Service, Norfolk Record Office, and the Syndics of Cambridge University Library.

Friends and family who have encouraged me in so many ways during my years of 'Sewelling' have given me the greatest help of all and I wish to thank in particular Laurette Carter-Locke, Shu-Huei Henrickson, Karen Keres, John Marriott, Helen McClelland, Catherine Sinasac, and Susan Watson for keeping the faith. Most especially I thank Lee Hodder for her unwavering support when it was needed most. I am grateful beyond measure to Claire Gavin for 'kindest cut' editing of the first draft, to Raewyn Gavin for medical research and advice, to Scott Gavin for inventing the invaluable word 'Sewelling' and to Irene and John Gavin for advice, encouragement, and constant support. My greatest debt is to Dewayne Crawford who has travelled every step of this journey with me and whose contribution to every stage of this book is, quite simply, incalculable.

Note on the Text

In order not to interrupt the flow and 'voice' of quotations from manuscript sources, where the spelling is often idiosyncratic, I have not added *sic* nor made alterations in square brackets except where not to do so would cause confusion. Punctuation is sparse and/or not always legible in manuscript sources so I have occasionally added it silently where it was likely to have existed originally or is needed for clarity.

Some letters quoted from have multiple writers, dates, or recipients. The dates and names used here are those for the specific writer, date, and recipient for the section of letter quoted.

Quotations from *Black Beauty* are taken from the World's Classics Edition edited by Peter Hollindale (Oxford, Oxford University Press, 1992).

ONE

The Little Stranger

1820

You have been well bred and well born; your father has a great name in these parts, and your grandfather won the cup two years at the Newmarket races; your grandmother had the sweetest temper of any horse I ever knew, and I think you have never seen me kick or bite.

(*Black Beauty*, Chapter 1)

'I fancy you would be interested to know a little about the author. There is no doubt most persons will have imagined her a robust young woman, mostly in the saddle with the reins in her hand.'[1] Mary Sewell paused in the letter she was writing to an early admirer of *Black Beauty* and looked over at the novel's author, her daughter Anna, who lay frail and exhausted on a water bed in the drawing room. Her eyes closed and her fists clenched, Anna shifted slightly. Distressing pains in her back and chest made even slight movements difficult, and a wracking cough thieved what little strength she had. Sighing silently, Mary dipped her pen in the inkwell and continued her task. 'Instead of this,' she wrote, 'for the last seven years she has been confined either to her bed or couch, and has not in all that time passed beyond the garden-gate.'[2]

On that winter's day early in 1878, while she lay powerless and her mother wrote to *Black Beauty*'s first devotees, Anna Sewell was experiencing her novel's initial success. Fan letters were arriving at the Sewell residence and the *Black Beauty* phenomenon had begun. Admirers wrote of their amazement that a lady could know so much about horses; surely only grooms, horse-dealers, jockeys, or veterinary surgeons had such accurate equine knowledge? They testified to the heart-wrenching impact of Black Beauty's misfortunes and to weeping over the death of 'poor Ginger'. They urged widespread promotion of the book and universally praised its indictment of cruelty to horses.[3] Enthusiasts proclaimed *Black Beauty* 'the best book in the world',[4] while others lauded its provocation to action: 'You have so filled my mind with the thought of what these poor animals suffer from the bearing-rein . . . that I feel quite breathless as I look at some of them, and only my sex, and fear of the police, prevent my cutting the leathers and setting them free.'[5]

During the years when all that lay beyond the garden gate had been denied her, Anna had achieved that rarest of feats: she had written a classic. Overjoyed at her book's reception, she could never have dreamed of the success it would become. In the 1890s it would be pirated by a promoter whose goal was that every American home should have a copy. By 1924 it would be the 'sixth best seller of any books in the world',[6] and by 1995 its worldwide sales would be estimated at 40 million compared to 50 million for Dickens's entire works.[7] Anna's story of a black horse and the injustices he witnesses and endures would transform attitudes, capture hearts, excite tears, and inspire sequels, movies, television series, comics, spoofs, and figurines. Over 125 years after its appearance not only is it still published and read, but it is still loved.

This is the life story of *Black Beauty*'s author, Anna Sewell, a story in which indomitable spirit conquers adversity, in which self-control and the drive for truth succeed, and in which a fearless woman of passionate beliefs produces one of the most famous novels ever written.

Anna was born into a family that on both sides had been Norfolk and Quaker for generations.[8] Norfolk, the prairie-like eastern county of England with its magnificent skies, agriculture, and nonconformist traditions, and Quakerism with its habits plain in dress, word, and deed were, even when she was far from both, profoundly important in Anna's life.

Her mother, Mary Sewell (née Wright), had her own Quaker upbringing on Norfolk farms before moving to Yarmouth where she met Anna's father Isaac Sewell. Mary was the daughter of Ann Wright (née Holmes) and John Wright who had met when John, aged about seventeen, was sent by his guardian, another John Wright known as 'Cousin Wright', to learn farming on Ann's father's farm, Tivetshall Hall in Tivetshall, Norfolk. To Anna Sewell's gentle grandfather the household of her great-grandfather, John Holmes, seemed a harsh one. The women of this very strict Quaker home –

Anna's great-grandmother and two daughters – were kind and friendly, but cowed by the head of the household. Tall, gaunt, irascible John Holmes was a gentleman farmer and Quaker minister whose crabbed temper made him difficult to live with and also engendered obstinacy in his six 'stalwart' sons.[9] Once, while the Holmes men were stacking wheat in the barn, a horse had to be lowered down afterwards. Impatient at his sons' inability to get the horse down speedily, John ordered them 'to let it off', and the horse then fell and broke its neck. 'It will throw some little light upon the scene', Anna's mother recollected in her 'Reminiscences', 'to know that, on the part of the sons, there was no decided lamentation.'[10]

These scabrous men became John Wright's in-laws when in 1792, aged twenty-two, he married twenty-year-old Ann Holmes, a comely young woman of good moral sense and a kind heart.[11] While Ann did not have John's education, theirs was a love match which produced over sixty years of happy marriage. John's guardian, Cousin Wright, a banker and landed gentleman who drove a carriage with four magnificent black horses,[12] settled the couple on a series of his farms over the ensuing years. At Buxton, about ten miles from Norwich, John and Ann's first child, Anna Wright, was born in 1793, followed a year later by John (names were repeated in almost every generation on both sides of the Sewell family). When Anna Sewell's mother, Mary, was born on 6 April 1797 the family were living at Sutton in Suffolk. On New Year's Day 1798 Cousin Wright died, oddly leaving his property not to the John Wright he had raised from the age of six or seven, but to John's then three-year-old son, John, to be held in trust until he came of age. Nevertheless, provision was made that the burgeoning Wright family (another child, Elizabeth, would be born that December) should have another of Cousin Wright's former properties, Felthorpe Farm, at Felthorpe in Norfolk where in 1801 Maria was born, followed by Richard in 1804.[13]

Mary spent a happy childhood growing up in Felthorpe, about seven miles north-west of Norwich, where the family regularly drove for Quaker meetings. Most of Felthorpe's roughly three hundred inhabitants were agricultural workers, and Mary's mother was by default the 'lady' of the village. Now renamed Church Farm, Mary's childhood home still stands on Brands/Bilney Lane and is a large, white, comfortable two-storeyed farmhouse with outbuildings and a lawn and open views over fields. A small orchard is situated beside the house just as it was when Mary and her siblings raced out on summer mornings to feast on overnight fruit fall.[14] In 1997 Felthorpe commemorated its connection with Anna Sewell's heritage by erecting a village sign depicting Anna and Mary driving a trap drawn by 'Black Beauty'.[15]

Growing up on this busy 800-acre farm, Mary developed a love of rural life and the natural world that would never leave her. Nature also, significantly, brought her to God, as she recalled of one calm summer evening when she saw a tree silhouetted against a sunset: 'it seemed as if all the beauty and the stillness flowed into my little heart and filled it . . . and I felt God there.'[16] She was a responsible, lively, confident child, her sisters taunting her by saying: 'Mary always thinks she can do everything.'[17] In the constant company of her sister Elizabeth she took pleasure in the farm animals, explored fields and swamps for flowers and plants, and was absorbed by the farm's seasonal activities. She helped her mother, sisters, and the servants cure bacon, sew clothes, wash laundry, churn butter, bake bread, brew beer, and prepare meals for farm workers and family. Every shearing season she watched in paroxysms of excitement as her very own sheep was shorn, its fleece weighed, and the exact market price counted out for her. At harvest time she begged to go in the cart to deliver meat, puddings, bread, beer, and harvest-cakes to workers in far-off fields. Worldly pastimes like music, dancing, fiction, art, and fashion were forbidden in this Quaker home, so it was an unusual thrill for Mary and her siblings to peek through their glass kitchen door at the annual dance the harvesters held when the season was over.[18]

The more idyllic qualities of Mary's countryside childhood were streaked by fears of imminent invasion during the Napoleonic wars. Hearing her father read out news of dramatic war events, Mary recalled, 'sent the blood through my veins with quickened speed'.[19] Her father's zealous patriotism (including prophetic dreams about battles, devastation when Nelson died, exultance after Waterloo, and a dog called 'Briton') infected Mary: 'though I was a little Quaker girl, and my father was a good Quaker, nothing availed to temper us down.'[20] Her father's Quaker principles were soon tested when he was 'drawn' as a solider. Although the pacifism with which twentieth-century Quakerism became so closely associated was not then as clearly evidenced, bearing arms was against Quaker principles, and a number of Quaker shipowners who armed their ships or chartered them to the government for war use were expelled from the Friends.[21] John Wright's refusal to enlist would have led to his imprisonment had he not been allowed the principle-stretching option of paying £40 (equivalent to £2,000 in 2003) for a substitute to take his place. Owning horses and wagons, he instead stood poised to take women and children to safety should Bonaparte's army land, and the household was packed ready for instant flight.[22]

Invasion did not come but financial strain did when, during a pause in the conflict, corn prices plummeted. The Wrights' land being poor, they were hard hit and John made the heartbreaking decision to sell the farm.[23] On a chilly autumn day in 1809, twelve-year-old Mary moved with her family to Yarmouth on the flat, watery east Norfolk coast, where her father entered into partnership with a prosperous shipowner. In Yarmouth Mary would meet her husband, Isaac Sewell, and their daughter Anna would be born.[24]

Now a fading resort town with an illuminated parade and a sideshow pier, Yarmouth at the time of Anna's birth and her parents' youth was entering its heyday as a site for seawater cures and summer holidays and was an exciting, thriving seaport. Many of its 18,000 residents,[25] who proudly termed themselves 'Yarmouth Bloaters', worked in shipping or the herring fisheries, but this was a fatal coast and shipwrecks were frequent.

The Wrights settled in the Southtown or 'Little Yarmouth' portion of Yarmouth, on the western side of the River Yare from the main town. It was a comfortable, well-furnished, newly built home, Mary remembered, with 'a Laundry, Washhouse and Dairy detached also Stable and Chaisehouse', as well as a large kitchen garden, 'a good sized meadow which ran down to the marshes',[26] and two 'competent servants' to help with the work.[27] The Wrights were accepted swiftly into the local Quaker community, Mary and her siblings exhilarated by the company of so many other youngsters.

One of these young Friends was Isaac Sewell whose parents, Hannah Maria Sewell (née Fuller) and William Sewell, were the leading Quaker Elders in Yarmouth and were esteemed both within and without Quaker circles.[28] 'The one family somewhat dominated the meeting,' wrote one of their descendants, 'William and H.M. Sewell . . . were strict Friends, but with wider intellectual interests than might have been expected.'[29]

Isaac, born in Yarmouth on 25 September 1793, was the youngest of their seven surviving children, four or five others having died in childhood. He and the brothers and sisters he knew – Hannah Maria, Fulleretta, William, Sarah, Abraham, and Edward – grew up during exciting times in this Neptune-flavoured town. Ships foundered, bodies were washed ashore, battleships were launched, smugglers landed under cover of darkness, pirates were captured and tried by admiralty, press gangs roamed the streets by night, Norfolk hero Horatio Nelson disembarked or sailed with great fanfare, guns were emplaced, and from 1803 troops took up duty.

Isaac's father ran a large grocer's shop situated at the marketplace entrance of Sewell's Row (Row 46), one of the arm-span wide Rows through which narrow troll carts drawn by one horse trundled with goods between the river quay – 'the longest and finest in England'[30] – and the bustling marketplace. This shop would remain in Sewell ownership for generations. There William trained his progeny in business skills from an early age, but they did not, Mary stated, 'at all becom[e] what is commonly called shopmen and shopwomen'.[31]

As Quaker Elders, Isaac's parents watched that worldly attractions did not divert any of the young Friends. William founded in their home the Demosthenian Society for the young Quaker men, at which they discussed issues and annually read aloud their essays to the young women and other interested Friends. The Agenorian Society, which Mary and her sisters attended, was also duly founded for the young Quaker women.[32]

The Yarmouth Quaker Meeting was large and worship involved quiet, contemplative sitting for two hours in the morning and again in the afternoon on First Day (Sunday) as well as a mid-week meeting. The Sewells were stricter of Quaker habit than the Wrights, and one of Mary's first encounters with her future mother-in-law concerned the matter of dress. Although she followed Quaker precepts, Mary's mother liked to see her children well turned out, and for her daughters ordered from a fashionable Norwich dressmaker 'cloth pelisses of a very pretty sage green colour with capes' trimmed with swansdown at neck and wrist. Mary and her three sisters felt very stylish wearing these to Meeting for the first time, but their striking appearance caused consternation: 'all eyes were upon us,' Mary remembered, 'especially the dear Elder's whose silent cogitations were very painful and perplexed. When we went again in the afternoon, she passed us without speaking.'[33]

Hannah Maria Sewell's silence spoke volumes, but she clearly felt that some admonition was in order. The following morning she came to the Wrights' home and explained privately to Mary's mother that her daughters' worldly dress might lead other girls into the temptations of fashion. To Mary's deep chagrin the pelisses were sent back to the dressmaker and the swansdown replaced with 'a trifling little cord'.[34]

Mary's formal education had been started when the family was still in Felthorpe, initially by her mother, next at a dame school, then was taken over by an eager and intelligent young governess who, Mary recalled, flew 'over the ditches inciting us to follow her, and d[u]g up primroses and violets to plant [at] the sides of our long bower'.[35] This governess also ignited Mary's love of literature by teaching stirring poetry and telling the Wright children 'little romances' which, in the absence of fiction in the house became, as Mary put it, 'the little Quaker girls' Novels'.[36] The children also had French and drawing lessons. After being 'finished' for a year at Abigail Frieth's Quaker boarding school at Tottenham, her sister Anna had become, not entirely happily for anyone involved, her sisters' teacher.[37] Now fourteen herself, Mary was sent from Yarmouth for a year to the same Tottenham school where her learning, much of which she regarded as 'dead seed', was largely by rote. On her return she and Anna shared the teaching of Elizabeth and Maria, and Mary continued her self-education where she could.[38]

Mary adored poetry, especially the Romantic poets of her day – 'Moore, Southey, Byron, Scott and others' – and memorized whole volumes of poems which she recited to herself during tiresome Quaker meetings.[39] With Elizabeth she sometimes borrowed forbidden fiction from the library, devouring it clandestinely in their little bedroom which, Mary revealed, 'being far away from the others admitted of secret practices'.[40]

In 1814, ten years after their last child, Mary's parents had an unlooked-for final baby, Ellen, who arrived at a time of financial hardship and anxiety for the family precipitated by an escalation in food prices and an episode of business fraud. In 1813 John Wright's adventurous younger brother, Richard, had started running the first steamer on the River Yare between Yarmouth and Norwich. John became his partner, then took over the running completely, but a new partner he took on cheated him out of much money.[41]

Yet 1814 did bring cause for celebration when Napoleon's government was overthrown and Louis XVIII was restored to the French throne. On 19 April the Wrights and the Sewells joined in the celebratory Grand Festival held at Yarmouth.[42] Flags flew, floats processed, and houses and boats were decorated. With around eight thousand others they sat at tables along the quay partaking in a dinner of roast beef, plum pudding, penny loaves, ale, and (for men) tobacco, and afterwards saw Napoleon's effigy burnt on a huge bonfire. William Sewell and John Wright served as stewards on separate tables while Isaac Sewell, then twenty, and Mary's brother John, then nineteen, served on another together.[43] Mary, newly seventeen, may well have sat at this table with her brother and future husband. It was certainly while she was seventeen that Isaac first made serious romantic overtures to her, but she was not interested, and the disappointed Isaac left his father's shop and went to London for two or three years to work in a 'Manchester' (linen) warehouse.[44]

On the sunny Good Friday of 4 April 1817 Mary's life changed through a tragedy that occurred on one of her father's now two steam packets. The fire on *The Telegraph* had been stoked up to outrun a rival packet, but as it left Norwich the engine exploded instantly killing eight of the twenty-two people on board and seriously injuring many others.[45] John Wright, who travelled to Norwich in the other boat, was horrified when he saw the bodies of the dead lying side by side on the river's edge, and a pall of shock and sorrow fell over everyone in the area.[46]

These were doleful days for the Wrights. Not only did they have to come to terms with the tragedy, but in their attempts to compensate victims' families they were also financially ruined by it. Mary and her two eldest sisters now had to seek work as governesses, an onerous, poorly paid job, but the only respectable option open to middle-class women. Anna and Elizabeth became governesses to families (Elizabeth working for Isaac's sister Fulleretta and her husband Joseph Hunton),[47] while Mary found a job teaching reading, writing, and (what she feared most) arithmetic at an Essex school. Her days there were spent teaching, making and mending around forty quill pens every writing day, and engaging in extra duties including 'a quantity of mending of stockings'.[48]

Mary coped well with the work, but adjusting to her steep social descent, marked by the servants calling her familiarly by her first name, was more difficult. She discovered respite in literature, finding silent repetition of Byron's poetry an effective palliative for the drudgery of school life.[49] She also befriended the Mistress's sister who introduced her to the works of Shakespeare.

Mary's brother, John, had the previous year married the talented and charming Anne Harford. Having also come into Cousin Wright's properties when he came of age, he had settled with Anne at one of these, Dudwick House at Buxton.[50] He now moved his distressed parents and the younger children, Maria, Ellen, and probably Richard, into neighbouring Dudwick Cottage and gave his father control of the small farm, roughly 100 acres.[51]

At this time of financial ruin the situation must have been very awkward for the senior John Wright who had not inherited and the junior John Wright who had, but Mary maintained that they both accepted the situation and 'no jars no jealousy ever arose'.[52] The first years at Dudwick Cottage were, however, very hard for what Mary termed the 'little crushed company' who moved in. Her mother found the small farmhouse a place of 'irksome drudgery', and having suffered before with nervous illness fell again into a period of 'mental depression' which worried the family.[53] That first Buxton Christmas was, however, gladdened by the trio of governessing daughters coming to visit, their parents doing their utmost, Mary recollected, to conceal the 'straitened resources of the house'.[54]

Now twenty, Mary had a troublesome decision to make. Isaac Sewell had returned to Yarmouth after his years in London and was involved in the social world of the Yarmouth Friends. These young Quakers were less rigid than their parents on matters of music and dancing, Isaac even hiring a hand-organ for a ball they held which he and Mary's sister Elizabeth both attended.[55] His heart, however, was set on the Essex schoolteacher and that

Christmas of 1817 he tried again to win Mary's heart and hand. Mary stated that she was 'obliged to consent to see him'. She felt this period a 'great trial'; 'my heart had never been entangled', she wrote, 'and was not at all ready to put on chains.'[56] Nevertheless, when she returned to Essex she and Isaac began, as she put it, 'a very uninteresting correspondence which led nowhere'.[57]

During the summer holidays they again spent time together but, as Mary remembered, 'the way did not seem to clear up, there was no spark upon the tinder'.[58] Mary's poetical nature, her observation of her parents' happy marriage, her involvement in a friend's passionate elopement with a non-Quaker,[59] and her own hopeful nature had given her a belief in romance. She was filled, she said, 'with the idea that a very rare atmosphere was needed for wedded life',[60] and did not want her freedom taken away by a loveless match. Young, 'enthusiastic and sentimental',[61] and hungering for depth of feeling, she vacillated while Isaac patiently waited. As a Quaker of good standing from a respected family – on 8 July 1818 he was even admitted as a Freeman of the City of Norwich[62] – and with good prospects in a drapery partnership he was entering into in Yarmouth, Isaac was a worthy suitor, and besides, he was kind-hearted, selfless, and very fond of Mary.

However extensive her dreams, Mary's realistic life choices were limited. Unless she continued in the genteel poverty of teaching, marriage was the only other viable option, particularly as her father could no longer easily support her. There was also no guarantee that she would ever receive another offer – indeed three of her four sisters never married. Accepting Isaac Sewell made financial, social, even spiritual sense, and sense, something Mary did have, was then often reason enough to marry. Mary knew, too, that 'the friends on both sides approved & wished for the connection & they could not see anything to hind[er] it'.[63]

Isaac's suit finally was sealed around Christmas 1818. Mary felt she must leave her teaching post because the Mistress had grown jealous over Mary's friendship with her sister. New situations were hard to find and Mary did not want to burden her father; effectively she had no choice. 'I had a vivid imagination', she recalled. 'I made beautiful pictures of a home of my own where my father mother & sisters could come & I thought I might be able to be some help & so

I wrought myself up to saying yes.'[64] Her engagement period was not that of an excited fiancée anticipating life with the man of her dreams, but rather that of a convict awaiting sentence: 'I did not repent whilst I kept my castles in view', she wrote. 'When there came a fog, the wheels dragged heavily but they did drag on till they came to the wedding day.'[65]

On 15 June 1819, aged twenty-two, Mary Wright married Isaac Sewell, aged twenty-five. The wedding was held in the tiny Quaker Meeting House at Lammas near Buxton where generations of Wrights had been married and buried, and a wedding supper followed at Dudwick House hosted by Mary's brother John. The newlyweds, accompanied by Elizabeth, set off in a chaise for a week's honeymoon at coastal Cromer.[66]

On the north-eastern corner of Yarmouth's expansive market-place a little home was prepared for the young couple. A skinny mid-seventeenth-century cottage wedged between other houses, 26 Church Plain[67] was to be Anna Sewell's birthplace. Standing behind rows of lime trees associated with its neighbour, the imposing St Nicholas's church, it had only one small room on each of its three storeys: a living area on the ground floor, above that a bedroom, and on top an attic. The kitchen and washroom with a small loft space above were in the small gardenless rear yard.

Ten minutes walk west from the sea front, and five minutes east from the river quay, Anna's birthplace still stands. In 1932 a mock Tudor façade was added, and alterations within the last thirty years have made the kitchen integral. In recent decades the house has served variously as a photographic studio, furniture store, gallery, and as a tiny Anna Sewell museum. After a period of neglect it was restored and reopened on the 156th anniversary of Anna's birth in 1976 and in 1984 became the Anna Sewell Tea Shoppe. In 2002 the 14-by-16-foot downstairs room was home to the Anna Sewell Restaurant, whose walls displayed newspaper clippings and memorabilia related to her connection with the house, and a decades old sign above the door still commemorates her birth. In 2004 her birthplace will reopen temporarily as a bridal shop, but the longer-term uses of the house are unknown.[68]

Mary was very pleased with the house into which she and Isaac moved. 'The little house in the church trees, close to the large church, was very diminutive,' she recalled, 'large enough to be happy in, and able to take in a friend and to enter upon my first experience of housekeeping.'[69] Mary set her home in order and Isaac worked in the drapery while they adjusted to married life and got to know each other better. Mary was vivacious, literary leaning and energetically hardworking. Isaac was more reserved, and although he had an excellent sense of humour and an unselfish disposition, he was business-oriented and, like his parents, stricter in his following of Quaker teaching on worldly things. Mary may have been reluctant to marry Isaac, but looking back sixty-two years later she believed that she had made the right decision: 'I am sure I made no mistake, a kinder husband or better Father would rarely be found. Our dissimilarity has probably introduced much more variety and interest into our lives, which have been anything but dull.'[70] Their marriage may not have been one of great physical passion – both from fecund families they only produced two children – but by nineteenth-century standards it was a sound one.

The young couple was soon preparing to welcome its honeymoon baby. Quakers eschewing 'baby linen shops', Mary sewed all the necessary babywear by hand with the help of 'friends ever ready to "welcome a little stranger"'[71] On 30 March 1820, on the cusp of spring, in the first-floor bedroom of the Church Plain house, this 'little stranger', Anna Sewell, was born.

TWO

Walks with Mamma

1820–32

Whilst I was young I lived upon my mother's milk, as I could not eat grass. In the day-time I ran by her side.

(*Black Beauty*, Chapter 1)

Anna's future seemed bright with possibilities as she lay for the first time in her mother's arms, but her days as a Yarmouth Bloater were already numbered. Unexpected shifts of fortune meant that her life took on early the peripatetic quality it would retain. Just days after her birth Isaac discovered that the draper's shop could not support two families and that he, as the younger partner, must leave.[1] For Mary and Isaac the 'for worses' of marriage had begun, and with a baby to support, few savings, and no social welfare system to fall back on, this was a worrying time. Isaac could not find a new position in Norfolk, so despite Mary's abhorrence at the idea, they were forced to head for the largest city in the world, London, dark magnet of opportunity.

This move proved a costly mistake. Led, as Mary put it, 'by some unlucky genius', Isaac's eldest brother William found a small London house for them, the ground floor of which they could use as a Quaker draper's shop.[2] William's brothers admired his business acumen, but Mary thought there was little sense in the plan, and when Isaac set off for London to see to the expensive shop alterations she took Anna to stay with her parents at Buxton.[3] Anna spent her first six months surrounded by fresh air, farm life, horses and doting relatives, while Mary struggled to accept that not only could her marriage not help her family as she had hoped, but that her own married life was going to be far harder than she had envisaged. In late September 1820 she took Anna to London accompanied by Isaac's parents who left Yarmouth to settle in Hackney.[4]

Anna's new home was tall and narrow with a basement kitchen, a street-level room used as the shop, and four single-roomed storeys above.[5] The calm address of 38 Camomile Street belied its nature.

Lying near Liverpool Street Station in the ever-changing heart of London where the City meets the East End, the former site of Anna's home is now absorbed in a district of polished office blocks and wine bars. In 1820 there was much to fascinate Anna's infant senses. Although Camomile Street had little traffic and no shops apart from the Sewells' own, the house stood almost on the corner of Bishopsgate Street, one of London's busiest shopping strips, then recently gaslit by night. Pedestrians, horses, carriages, donkeys, and carts steadily streamed along this thoroughfare into the financial centre of the City or out to Shoreditch and beyond. Street hawkers cried pitches for everything from ballads to gingerbread, chair repairs to knife sharpening. Fruit and vegetable odours wafted from nearby Spitalfields Market, even closer fluttered the second-hand clothes along Petticoat Lane, and across from the house was a hackney-coach stand whose horses may have stirred Anna's equine affinity.[6]

Nothing here fell gently on Mary's lonely soul. She loathed London. The area was dark, dingy, dirty, busy, and their house caught all the noise of traffic and the raucous pub opposite, which Mary termed 'a dirty disgusting looking place . . . often resound[ing] with oaths, songs, and quarrels'.[7] That Anna had to spend hours in the underground kitchen wearing a 'dark print round-about slip' so as not to show the dirt[8] did not help Mary's depression, and she mourned her lost ideals for her daughter's infancy:

> I thought it would be impossible for me, to bring up my little girl amongst black houses, and dirty streets, with never a flower for her little hand to gather, nor a bird's song for her to hear; I used to sit, and look over the roofs of the opposite houses, at the floating clouds, and the bits of blue sky, and cry like a child. Great London, was to me like a huge cage, with iron bars.[9]

Although they had been recommended officially by the Yarmouth Monthly Meeting into the 'Christian care' of the Devonshire House Monthly Meeting, Mary never settled.[10] She had frequent 'recourse to a strong cup of coffee' to raise her spirits,[11] but as she recalled, the lack of 'fresh air, the high stairs, the noise, and incessant work began to tell upon me'.[12] Financial worries were constant, and the business was a failure from the outset. Being close to the Meeting

House, the shop seemed well placed to attract Quaker custom, but Anna's Uncle William had not taken into consideration the nearby presence of a well-established competitor upon whose business the Sewells' small, side-street shop made little impact. Isaac soon dismissed the young man he had brought with him as an assistant and had 'a boy' instead. After hours Mary helped Isaac tidy up; during the day she made what she termed 'little fancy things' for window displays, and even did the sewing that a customer assumed she had sent out to a needlewoman. It was getting harder and harder to make ends meet and one day no customers at all came to the shop.[13]

As was usual at times of crisis in Isaac's family, a Sewell family council was held over a nice dinner and a good bottle of wine (temperance not yet touching their lives).[14] The upshot of this was that Isaac became a partner in a larger drapery business, and Anna and her parents moved into 'a large house with a large number of assistants',[15] at 1 Bishopsgate Without,[16] just around the corner from Camomile Street. They probably again lived over the shop, the larger size and assistants likely referring to the business rather than their own home, but there seems to have been a nurse for Anna.[17] The move eased life slightly, but they were still mired in the depths of London, and Mary's anguish soon was exacerbated by the knowledge that the second child she was now expecting would also be reared in the city's dark climes. 'I *was* rebellious at having to live in that dingy place in London,' she wrote, 'I only existed on the hope of its coming to an end . . . how I hated it! I blotted my lesson-book with my tears.'[18]

Yet Mary well knew that the distresses of London life were measurable by degrees. Anna's infancy was one of genteel hardship, not that of a ragged, starving street child, but evidence of poverty and crime was close at hand. Outside a pub opposite, in all weathers, sat a wan woman selling fruit and nuts. Mary regularly watched as the fruitseller's little children made their way through the streets alone to bring her the baby to whom she gave alcoholic as well as motherly comfort.[19] A few streets over, near the Bank of England, prostitutes stood 'in rows like hackney-coaches' and half the hackney coachmen in London were said to be in league with thieves.[20] The modern police force would not be established until 1829, and fear of crime was palpable. Dirt and desperation were even more prevalent. The poor were badly clothed, fed, and

educated, and toiled long hours in harsh conditions at whatever
work they could find, living in overcrowded alleys and slums.
Smoke blackened buildings, clothing, and lungs and contributed to
the dense choking London fogs. When it rained the roads were
viscous with dung-mixed mud, and with none of the sanitary
reforms of the 1840s yet instigated the risks of disease – cholera,
smallpox, typhus, scarlet fever – were high.

Appalled at the conditions she saw, Mary offered help where she
could. One Shoreditch woman she regularly visited, at times to jolt
herself out of her own 'fits of misery', impressed Mary deeply through
the contentment she displayed despite living in one room with an
irregularly employed husband and several children. When this woman
died in a cholera epidemic Mary continued to help her children.[21]
Living in London gave Mary an acute understanding of what the
working classes had to endure, and by the time Anna was two years
old a determination to help the poor had settled like steel in Mary's
soul. The alleviation of suffering was to become the *raison d'être* of
both Anna and Mary's lives, but first there were more personal trials
to bear. The Sewells' London life was about to fall apart.

Just as Anna's birth had been followed immediately by financial
setbacks for her parents, so too was the birth, on 14 January 1822,
of her only sibling, Philip Edward Sewell. Isaac's business partner
proved to be 'very reckless and unsound in his trading principles',[22]
and this second London enterprise also failed. The business 'was
broken up', wrote Mary, 'and so was I'.[23] London, once undesirable,
was now literally intolerable and the doctor advised Mary to leave
immediately. She relocated with Anna and Philip to lodgings in
Hackney. Isaac stayed behind to see what might be salvaged, but
they had lost everything.[24]

Quakerism and business often went together, and financial failure
could have religious as well as financial consequences. Bankruptcy
was grounds for 'disownment' (expulsion) from the Friends,
sometimes even when the cause of the business failure was not the
bankrupt's own.[25] Although Isaac seems not to have been declared
bankrupt officially,[26] the risks to his Quaker reputation of failing to
sustain a living from three businesses in as many years must have
weighed on his mind. To pay their debts most of the family's
possessions were auctioned off, including their furniture and

wedding gifts over which Mary grieved. Mary's brother John and another Friend bought back some of their furniture for them, but, without capital, life had to begin anew.[27]

Despite her parent's ongoing financial woes, Anna's childhood was a happy one, mainly spent at 12 Park Road[28] in Dalston, where the family moved in 1822. Their new home was five minutes' walk from the centre of Dalston, a peaceful village (now part of greater London) which offered respite from the noise, bustle, and effluvia which had overborne Mary in the City. The Sewells had a few neighbours, but otherwise fields and nursery gardens surrounded them, and a footpath ran from the end of the road through open land to London Fields nearby. Mary's health improved and the family established friendships in the neighbourhood, although none of Anna's own are recorded.

Mary wanted Anna and Philip to be raised happy and free from either 'carking care' or over-abundance.[29] There was no risk of excess at Dalston; money remained tight[30] and there was none to spare for anything but the simplest in food and clothing and 'one little servant'.[31] Laundry was done at home rather than sent out, and as they grew older Anna and Philip helped run the household. Isaac became a traveller in Nottingham lace and was often away from home, but when Anna was about five, he took up a position in his brother William's warehouse. He worked long hours and was still away from home from at least eight in the morning until eight at night six days a week, so Anna saw little of him except on Sundays which the family enjoyed together.[32]

An 1825 letter provides a rare insight into Anna's parents' marriage in its seventh year. Isaac was in Yarmouth helping his brother Abraham who, with his wife Dorothy and another brother, Edward, still ran the grocery shop there. Mary and Dorothy were very close, and during the years of Anna's infancy Dorothy filled the role that Anna would later take on as Mary's spiritual confidante and soulmate.[33] Mary offered to take in and educate one of Dorothy's sons for a while if it would be of help, and expressed concern over three-year-old Philip who was with Isaac and 'very much troubled with a humour' following a vaccination.[34] She asked Dorothy to send Philip to be cared for by her family at Buxton, but advised that there was no rush for Isaac's return:

I can quite well spare him, thou knowest it best I am no very tender mate, and a slighter thing than serving you might reconcile me to a longer separation but do not understand me as thinking disrespectfully of my husband. I acknowledge his kindness and affection to me fourfold more than I deserve from him and often do I take shame to myself that I return it so imperfectly.[35]

Mary and Isaac were nevertheless making a go of things and family life seems to have been peaceful, although Isaac's working hours grew longer. On 14 November 1826 – two days before Anna's grandmother, Hannah Maria Sewell, died – Mary rounded off a letter to Dorothy by telling her: 'Isaac is now returned and bids me put away my desk and as he is now off to business at 6 in the morning and does not return till 9 at night I feel myself rather bound to make the short time he has at home pass agreeably.'[36] Isaac was well, she reported, she herself had had toothache for three weeks, Philip was 'sadly pulled down by the scarlet fever', and six-year-old Anna was 'as fat and boisterous as ever'.[37]

Anna, affectionately known as Nanny within the family,[38] had begun her education at home under Mary's tutelage. Although Mary once claimed she was 'a very dolt at teaching',[39] she was clearly anything but. She took her role as her children's teacher very seriously, so much so that in later life friends asked her to produce a manuscript setting out her advice on education.[40] Mary believed that a 'free, active happy childhood is the best foundation for a happy life', and that giving children 'as much responsibility as they can carry without anxiety', produced in them enjoyment and strong character.[41] One of her most important lessons for Anna was that the 'soul must be trained to govern the body, and not to be its slave'.[42]

Young children's demands, 'What shall I do?' 'I don't know what to play at', 'Give me this or that',[43] as Mary phrased them, were as common to Anna and Philip as to any young children, but Mary's strategy was to prevent this by setting up an 'invincibly regular' routine for the day. Regularity in playing, learning, sleeping, rising, and eating, in a 'humane' way, Mary stated, made 'obedience a virtue through habit' rather than trial.[44] Anna's routine is likely to have included periods of an hour once or twice a day when she could learn self-restraint and independence by being, as Mary advised, 'set up at the table to amuse [her]self quietly, without any assistance except being furnished with [her] amusements for the time'.[45] Too much variety in 'amusements' Mary avoided as unnecessary for children and a waste of parental resources. Anna probably amused herself with the pastimes Mary recommended for all children: 'stringing beads, putting different kinds of seeds or beads into different divisions of a box, drawing, cutting, &c'.[46] In developing these skills she was encouraged towards 'a degree of perfectness . . . even something approaching to business habits' because, in her mother's view, 'Perfect play [was] the anticipation of perfect work'.[47]

Enforced frugality meant that there was no money spare for educational books, so Mary turned to authorship to earn the sum needed. Although her literary career would not be established fully for another thirty years, in 1824 her first book, *Walks with Mamma, or Stories in Words of One Syllable* was anonymously published. It was one of the first children's books ever bound in cloth and joined titles such as *Cock Robin*, *The House that Jack Built*, and *The Rational Alphabet*, in publisher John Harris's 58-title *Cabinet of Amusement and Instruction*, a collection of 'the most appropriate novelties for the nursery'.[48] For Mary the book served a dual purpose: it earned her, as she put it, the 'little fortune' of three pounds,[49] to buy books for Anna and Philip's lessons, and it also surely served as one of their own early readers.

What is read early lasts long and Anna must many times have pored over this Beatrix Potter sized book with its eight hand-coloured woodcuts which were mainly of animals, including an ostrich, a wild boar, and a horse being saddled. Using one-syllabled words – some advanced, like 'gauze', 'haws', 'veins', 'helm' – the book tells five stories of a young girl, appositely named Anne, who accompanies her mother on walks during which the wonders of God's natural kingdom and other more quotidian things are explained to her. These fictional walks detail much of what Anna herself observed under Mary's guidance on their own walks around Dalston, Anna often toting a little basket to collect treasures.[50] The weather, seasons, plants, the skills and needs of animals, the hard work and cooperative nature of ant colonies, the habits of moles and bees, and the eating and nesting customs of birds are all discussed. The book also warns against fearing or harming animals and repeatedly propounds the anti-cruelty message that would be paramount in Anna's life and art. Hopping frogs, Mamma tells her charge, 'will not hurt you. We could soon kill them if we chose; but we will not do it, for they can feel, and do not like pain more than you or I . . . Do not fear, poor frog, Anne will not hurt you; she will just look at your bright eyes, and the nice spots on your back, and let you hop home.'[51] Mary herself was always proud that Anna and Philip were 'never afraid of any kind of insect, would handle earwigs beetles and spiders with pleasure & were much amused if any one was afraid of them'.[52] She taught them that everything living was part of God's family and 'that all cruelty or injury inflicted is displeasing to Him who made His creatures to be happy'.[53]

As well as observing nature, the fictional Anne, like Anna, learned about human activities: breadmaking, sailing, shipbuilding, the circulation of the blood, and the ubiquity of child deaths. Story III, in which Anne and Mamma observe the burial of a child, teaches that the child is 'now more blest than we are' adding the message:

> In a short time we shall all be dead, and those who are good are glad to die, that they may be with God . . . I hope Anne will try to be a good girl; but then she must not cry, nor be cross, nor do what she is told not to do; but she must speak the truth, and be mild and kind, and mind what her friends say to her, and love them for the care they take of her, and try to please them.[54]

Obedience – to parents and to God – was a trait Mary sought to instil in Anna by referring 'constantly to the happiness and obedience of the insect and animal world',[55] and by holding up Christ as the perfect exemplar of obedience to God's will.[56] Yet Anna learned more than obedience from Mary's book, she also experienced the thrall of narrative. Like *Black Beauty*, *Walks with Mamma* contains both didacticism and adventure. Story IV interpolates the tale of a small girl, unable to swim, who falls overboard. A kindly man jumps in to save her, but a ferocious shark is heading straight for them. Seeing this, the man's son leaps into the water with his sword and slashes at the shark while the man and girl are rescued. The boy is almost hauled aboard when 'the fierce shark, who could not bear to lose his prey, sprang up, and bit the poor boy's legs both off, and [ate] them up'.[57]

The other key book of Anna's early education was the Bible, and she is reported as saying in childhood: 'Mother's Bible was read to make everybody happy and good.'[58] Although Mary believed that religious conversion could only be performed by God, she believed that it was important to build in Anna 'a beautiful natural temple which the Blessed Master may irradiate with His own light . . . at whatever time He may please to enter'.[59] This was not the fire-and-brimstone approach to faith experienced by some of Anna's contemporaries. Mary believed that children should not be impressed too early with the idea that they are sinners nor, as she put it, need they 'come to a considerable development of sinfulness, before they can be converted'.[60] When Anna was not yet old enough to understand the concept of Christ's atonement for sin through sacrifice, Mary asserted that self-denial, 'the milder form of sacrifice', could be taught through examples 'from the animal world, by facts and anecdotes, and whenever possible, from living human example'.[61]

Because Mary regularly used the Bible as Anna's lesson-book,[62] it is surprising that the educational work she most valued was Maria and Richard Edgeworth's *Practical Education* (1798), which dealt with moral and intellectual education while excluding religious training.[63] The Edgeworths favoured and wrote rationalist, secular, and realist literature for children. Following those precepts it is unlikely that fairy tales or fantasy were part of Anna's reading fare, but it is improbable that Mary, with her own secret literary consumption in youth, would have banned Anna from reading novels. Those with a moral or religious purpose were, however, always encouraged, and Mary would later exclaim: 'Oh that the rising generation that are learning to read might be taught to read God's Works and not trashy novels!'[64] Although hoops were popular Anna probably had few toys, not just because they were expensive, but also because the Edgeworths approved of toys only with scientific or practical applications.

Anna had her 'little feet [brought] within the charmed line' of science before she could read,[65] as Mary wrote: 'it would be almost ridiculous to mention the number of sciences into which [she and

Philip] took the first steps'.[66] They performed 'little chemical experiments',[67] probably including testing the various effects of water on quicklime, sand, and clay which demonstrated effervescence, absorption, and pliability. They learned about the effects of acids on alkalis and experimented with colour extraction and dyeing. Before she was eight Anna was likely to have practised all kinds of measuring, and Mary was convinced that the 'relative weights connected with the bulk of different materials would amuse children for many an hour'.[68] They planted seeds, used hammers and nails, took care of animals and were taught to keep an accurate account of expenses.[69] Anna also acquired the skills involved in good domestic management including never-ending sewing.

Anna did not have a 'hothouse' education as Mary believed in letting her children learn naturally, but she also regarded high parental expectations as essential to moral training. The imbuing of virtue was the end goal of her teaching,[70] but she also required articulacy, and advised parents: 'Do not be content with confused description. Let the child do his very best first, then supply him with the words he needs to make his detail accurate and complete.'[71] She strove to make Anna and Philip's education 'stimulating, animating, affectionate, nothing depressing',[72] and wanted them to look back on childhood, as she did, as a time of summer joy and love of nature. 'What little things will make fairy days of enjoyment for children!'[73] she wrote, and she encouraged them to explore their worlds in minute detail. On long summer afternoons she challenged them to try to build birds' nests by ferreting out their own twigs and scraps.[74]

Animals were one of Anna's greatest and earliest loves, but she also adored all kinds of nature including insects, flowers, and shells. Natural collections were then in vogue: butterflies, birds' eggs, stuffed animals, but Anna and Philip were taught to be selective in what they collected and to do no unnecessary harm simply to gratify what Mary called the 'greedy spirit of acquisition'.[75] After one experiment they never again 'compassed death to make a collection'.[76] Mary later wrote that 'The accounts of naturalists' murderous tours have been often very revolting to my mind',[77] and she regarded killing to collect as having an especially dire effect on children's characters.[78] Entomology, however, fascinated them and

they certainly captured butterflies and other insects, closely observing
them for a short while, often drawing or painting them, before
releasing them.[79] Anna, especially, showed an early talent for art
which Mary encouraged. They also collected shells which Isaac
brought home for them and made visits to the British Museum to
identify them and look at the other wonders there.[80]

They may well also have been among the first wave of visitors to
London's Zoological Gardens in Regent's Park which opened in
1828 and housed the biggest collection of animals in the world.[81]
With her already firm views on kindness to animals, Anna
undoubtedly approved of the zoo's rule that whips must be left at
the gate and disapproved of the ladies who tried to poke their
parasols through the bars at the animals.[82] Even in childhood Anna
was not afraid to speak out against cruelty. She was especially
indignant over the people she dubbed 'bobies'[83] who shot birds for
pleasure. One day such a man appeared at the front gate seeking to
retrieve a blackbird he had shot which had fallen in the Sewells'
front garden. 'If you please miss will you let me take my bird?' the
man asked Anna, who had rushed out. 'No,' she told him, 'thee
cruel man, thee shan't have it at all.'[84]

Prevention and alleviation of all forms of cruelty was a strong
Quaker principle, and Quaker beliefs and habits were central to
Anna's early life. With family roots stretching back to the Friends'
seventeenth-century origins, she had a pedigree prized by Quakers.[85]
During her childhood many of the traditional ways still persisted,
and she followed Quaker rules on speech and dress known as
'peculiarity' or 'plainness'. She referred to months and weeks
ordinally as 'First Month' and 'First Day' rather than by their
'heathen' referents, January and Sunday. She used the otherwise
archaic second person singular 'thee' and 'thou', as 'you' was
thought flattering when referring to a single person and not in
keeping with the Quaker belief in the equality of all people under
God. For the same reason Quakers frowned upon honorifics, titles,
bowing, and hat doffing, but unlike most denominations allowed
Quaker women as well as men to preach.[86]

Friends wore plain, unornamented clothes with broad-brimmed
hats for men and a Quaker bonnet with a brim that covered the
sides of the face for women. Reflecting Mary's own girlhood

attraction to swansdown trimming, Anna probably had some freedom to gravitate towards the 'gay Friends' end of the clothing spectrum rather than be restrained at the 'very plain Friends' end.[87] Although her childhood (and indeed adult) clothes were plain they were not completely austere; nevertheless, because Quaker clothing was a sign of faith, any bows, frills, or lacy extras had to be considered carefully.[88] In childhood Anna probably wore low-necked, short-sleeved, long dresses in sober colours, with an added pinafore when playing or doing chores. Underneath this would have been white cotton stockings and cambric ankle-length 'trousers' whose gathered flounce or lace trim showed below the hem of her dress. Indoors she may have occasionally worn a white cap, but outdoors she would have always worn a bonnet.[89]

During their early Dalston years Anna's family continued attending Meeting in London, probably at Devonshire House,[90] which required a walk of about an hour in each direction. Without mass public transit until horse-drawn omnibuses proliferated in the 1830s, and given the prohibitive cost of keeping a horse and conveyance, walking was, for all but the wealthy, the primary means of getting about. Devout Quakers were expected to attend two meetings on Sunday and one on Wednesday, but it is not clear whether Anna's family met these ideals. In 1828 their Sabbath commuting was shortened by almost a half when they started to attend the new Friends' Meeting House in Yoakley Road, Stoke Newington, a village just north of Dalston. The new Meeting House was a 'three-bay house with three-bay loggia on square piers', with a plain but elegant interior, its 'gallery supported by pillars with Grecian capitals'.[91] Attractive as this sounds, the meetings for Anna seemed intolerable.

No sacrament or other forms of outward worship were used in Quaker meetings; instead members communed together in inward spiritual meditation. The silence was broken only if an adult felt moved by the Spirit to speak in an inspired 'sing-song' voice using biblical phraseology.[92] Separated from Philip who sat with his father on the men's side of the room, and feeling the eyes of the Elders slide over her as they sat on their dais facing the rest of the Meeting, Anna sat for the two hours on a numbing wooden bench, among the women Friends who looked, as fellow Quaker Mary Howitt put it, like 'images in marble'.[93] Anna found her own struggle for marblehood excruciating at times; required not to move, talk, fidget, read, or sleep, she always, Mary recalled, 'chafed against' silent meetings as 'purposeless'.[94] These meetings did help imbue Anna with the self-discipline and self-control that marked her life, and as she matured she displayed many traits that were regarded as particularly 'Quaker': gravity, determination, tolerance, humility, a calm demeanour, and extreme kindness.[95]

Mary later maintained that Anna and Philip were 'nice little toward children',[96] 'fine, attractive . . . [and] very intelligent',[97] with 'very happy dispositions and fine tempers'.[98] Having a tendency to timidity herself, Mary deliberately fostered courage in her children, wanting them to have 'dauntless, persevering, independent' characters.[99] 'As very little children', she wrote, 'I accustomed them to playing in the dark. Many a game of hide-and-seek I have played with them in a room which had a dressing room and two closets and admitted of all kind of surprises.'[100] Anna's boldness emerged early. She 'had a great deal of courage and independence of character', Mary reported, 'never burdened with any kind of fear'.[101] She also discovered the fortitude she would so need in later years when she dislocated her elbow. Ominously foreshadowing later events, Anna's arm took a long time to recover, but as she professed to an aunt, 'I bored it well.'[102]

A child of such spirit and confidence as Anna, even though schooled in her mother's curriculum of charity, frugality, and faith, could not have been passively obedient. She had a wilful streak and displayed all the usual childhood recalcitrances, as is revealed by a report of her progress that Mary wrote on her ninth birthday. Anna was 'in many respects a delight and comfort to her mother', Mary recorded, and was truthful, full of candour, and learning well in some areas, but she was also:

> Much disposed to idle over lessons and work. She needs to get the habit of a cheerful surrender of her own will – to give up entirely telling tales of her brother. She begins to be useful to her mother, but is not tidy. In *everything* her mother hopes she will be improved by another year.[103]

Twelve months later, however, Anna's errors and imperfections had increased.[104] Probably around that time Mary told Dorothy:

I feel a little discouraged about my children for at present I see no evidence of religious feeling I mean no effect of the spirit working within and producing conviction of sin. Anna says candidly that she does not see that she is so very naughty though she appears also concerned that her own righteousness would never save her. Her mind is particularly simple and unaffected but self denial has taken but very slender root.[105]

Mary was adamant that Anna and Philip should love God and nature, be charitable, and have all the skills necessary for respectable life, but she was not overly harsh in her discipline. '[W]e knew nothing about punishments,' she wrote, 'to have a kiss withheld was too severe for either of them',[106] and 'was enough to send them to bed with tears and sobs'.[107] This was the way in which Mary herself had been raised, delighted in but not indulged by her parents, rarely physically punished,[108] but instead reasoned with and allowed to develop naturally. Like the Edgeworths, Mary believed that children should bear to the full the natural consequences of either their wrongdoing or their ignorance, but should suffer no additional penalty.[109] She successfully inculcated in Anna a sense of personal conscience and self-control and in adulthood Anna was a firm self-chastiser.

Throughout their childhood Anna and Philip took regular holidays at their maternal grandparents' farm in Buxton, making the jostling fourteen-hour journey between London and Norwich by stagecoach, with pauses every twelve miles or so for a rapid change of horses and longer stops at coaching inns for meals. Generations of the Wright family had close connections with the villages of Buxton and its neighbour Lammas (now often spelled Lamas), situated about ten miles north of Norwich. In Dudwick Park at Buxton were two homes Anna knew well. Her Aunt and Uncle Wright (Mary's brother John and his wife Anne) lived in Dudwick House, 'an ancient mansion, with a well-wooded lawn and good estate',[110] and her grandparents and aunts lived, as Mary put it, in 'comparative poverty' in the smaller flint-built Dudwick Cottage.[111] It remains a lovely spot, little changed since Anna's early visits.[112] The lane which divides the two properties meanders in from Buxton village through the tree-speckled park where mellow cattle graze, and open fields stretch out beyond. It is a peaceful, pastoral place which enchanted Anna throughout her life.

Buxton was, Mary declared, 'the Paradise of children', and here Anna and Philip 'found the unfettered joys & freedom of the country'.[113] Their relatives delighted in them, especially as, until 1829, they were the only Wright grandchildren. Anna and Philip chattered to their beloved grandfather as they walked with him on the farm, enjoyed time with their Aunt Ellen who was only six years older than Anna and with whichever of aunts Anna, Elizabeth, and Maria were currently not away governessing. They were also fascinated by their Aunt Wright, a semi-invalid who was much loved in the family and a favourite in Buxton society. A self-educated, cultivated woman, she had no children herself but displayed great affinity with youngsters and delighted Anna and Philip with her enthusiasm for natural history.[114]

At Buxton Anna learned to ride and drive horses. Following the nineteenth-century female norm she rode side-saddle, a more perilous and skilled method of riding with both legs modestly placed on the near (left) side of the horse. Requiring a keen sense of balance, it would have taken a little practice before she found her 'seat', but she was soon off, spending exhilarating hours on horseback exploring the surrounding lanes and parks.[115] She surely rode along the banks of the River Bure which divided Buxton on the west from Lammas on the east, seeing the large mill on its banks near where on hot summer days children still swim. Anna herself learned to swim at Buxton and, astonishingly given her opinion of 'Bobies', to shoot. Hers was not nihilistic pleasure hunting, however, but was, Mary thought, 'confined to garden thieves – the blackbirds & sparrows', who were regarded as pests.[116]

Links with Buxton continued when the children returned to Dalston through letters and the eagerly anticipated Christmas hamper. Anna and Philip exclaimed as each of the contents was unpacked. Mary recalled that their grandmother sent 'ducks and sausages & mince meat', their grandfather 'apples, pears & walnuts'. There was something from each aunt then at Buxton and what Anna and Philip most rejoiced over: the special gifts labelled 'For my little maid' or 'For my dear boy'.[117] Christmas Day was always Anna and Philip's special day when they could choose all their own entertainments and their own pudding.[118]

Through halcyon Buxton visits Anna developed a close knowledge
of the countryside, but she also learned about the seaside on a
holiday the family made to Sandgate on the East Kent coast when
she was nine. Mary had been scrimping towards this long-
anticipated vacation, when news came of the suffering of the Irish in
a potato famine in 1829 that preceded the Great Famine some
twenty years later. Mary gave the children a day to make their
decision: to go to the seaside or to send their holiday fund to help
the starving Irish. Although disappointed, the children adamantly
decided for Ireland.[119] Their good deed was rewarded when,
knowing nothing of their sacrifice, their Uncle William Sewell
decided to send them all to the seaside for several weeks, together
with his daughter, Lucy, a cousin and close friend of Anna's who
was just a few years her senior.[120]

Directly across the English Channel from Boulogne, Sandgate had
been a centre of shipbuilding and Martello towers during the
Napoleonic Wars, but by 1829 it was a pleasant watering hole. It
was not a place of balls or any great pomp, but this suited the Sewell
party who found plenty that charmed in this peaceful village. There
were sea-bathing machines, warm and cold baths, reading-rooms
and a library, donkeys and ponies, and plenty of walks available
along the long pebbly beach, across the top of the cliffs above the
village, over the Downs, or to nearby Cheriton.[121] Anna explored
with Philip and Lucy, collected shells, and walked and talked with
Mary. Her lifelong love of flowers was cultivated when she met
Gerard Edward Smith (1804–81), a botanist who was collecting
specimens for his best-known work, *A Catalogue of Rare or
Remarkable Phanogamous Plants Collected in South Kent* (1829).

They also visited Folkestone a couple of miles up the coast, where
they explored one of the great fossil areas of England, the coastal
Gault clay cliffs.[122] In this blue-grey Cretaceous clay they searched
for spiral-shaped ammonites, belemnites, fossilized wood, fool's
gold, fish teeth, and other fascinating plant and animal fossils to add
to their collections. As one nineteenth-century writer reported, 'not
a clod of [this clay] can we break without disclosing dozens of the
glittering irridescent [*sic*] shells of the crawling things that perished
ages since in the oozy bed of an antediluvian sea'.[123] All kinds of
exciting discoveries were open to Anna as she dug through the clay

and fossicked along the shore. In 1811, when only eleven, Mary Anning, reputed inspirer of the tongue-twister 'She sells seashells on the sea shore', had near Lyme Regis discovered the first complete fossilized ichthyosaurus, and ichthyosaur and plesiosaur bones also lay where Anna picked.

Around this time Philip was enrolled as a day pupil at the new Hackney Grammar School, built in 1829, while Anna continued her education at home under Mary's careful guidance. As well as education, play, chores, and religion, assisting Mary with charity work became increasingly important as Anna matured. Although Mary claimed, 'I fill myself to the full whilst I know others to be starving and hug myself under plenty of blankets whilst I know others to be shivering under a bundle of shavings',[124] she was involved in a range of beneficent activities. During one harsh winter, with the assistance of two or three others, she visited every house in the Dalston area. Finding 'every variation and gradation of misery', she helped set up a soup kitchen and established a clothing society to provide flannel and bedding to the poor.[125] As well as regular poor visiting, she raised ten pounds for the purchase and introduction in Dalston of a broom that sweeps could send up chimneys in place of tiny suffering boys.[126] She was also involved with the Anti-Slavery Association and, probably influenced by the famous Quaker prison reformer Elizabeth Fry (who was one of the Norfolk Gurney family who Mary's own knew well), became a penitentiary visitor in Shoreditch.[127] Anna herself can never have known a time when she was not at least conscious of some philanthropic occupation or concern.

When Anna was twelve the family were harrowed by fears of what the cholera epidemic of 1831–2 might visit upon them. Half of those who contracted cholera died, often within hours, beset by muscle spasms, severe diarrhoea, dehydration, inability to retain body heat, and blue-hued skin. Transmitted by contaminated water or sometimes tainted food, cholera's cause and cure were then unknown, but theories abounded. Mary told Dorothy on 18 July 1832, 'the disease here does not appear to be contagious, but in the atmosphere, and the infected air appears to travel in streams, where it listest, baffling the power and the wisdom of man. I never felt before what it was to draw in the air with distrust fearing it might be charged with death.'[128] Mary confessed that the family could think of little else:

> it is impossible to feel apathy, or indifference, or to help thinking about it, as no one speaks upon anything else . . . the care we have to take in our diet is bringing it constantly to mind. I can assure thee I never felt so strongly the ne[c]essity of being in a state of preparation and having my house in order and my business done.[129]

She warned Dorothy not to let her sister Sarah Stickney come to Dalston for a planned visit by quoting her doctor's words:

> As you value her life . . . prevent her coming up at present – from my experience I should say she would be almost certain to be attacked with the disease without the probability of recovery that there is for residents, by no means I would advise you allow her to come – the disease goes on rapidly spreading my cases yesterday were 15 today they are 29 God knows how many they may be tomorrow[130]

Sarah Stickney, who, under her married name Ellis, would later become a noted writer, was a friend of Mary's and of her generation, but Anna also enjoyed her company, in part because she and Sarah shared a fascination with animals. Mary told Dorothy that Anna had been counting on Sarah coming but upon hearing the doctor's opinion had turned to her at once and said, 'Mother write to her directly, I would rather never see her again, than have her come here and die.'[131] Anna's decided reaction reflects her determined nature and foreshadows the role she increasingly would take on as her mother's trusted advisor. As she entered adolescence Anna's horizons would expand, but they would also change in a way no one could foresee.

THREE

Sunshine Before Rain

1832–6

I stumbled, and fell with violence on both my knees. . . . I soon recovered my feet and limped to the side of the road . . . I was suffering intense pain both from my foot and knees.

(*Black Beauty*, Chapter 25)

Anna's connection with horses took a residential turn when she spent her early teens living at Palatine Cottage, formerly the stables of Palatine House, one of the eighteenth-century Palatine houses built for German refugee families in Stoke Newington.[1] By 1832 the Dalston house was feeling cramped, and Isaac, who had a proclivity for altering and improving houses, had discovered an empty stable and coach house which could be converted into their next home.[2] Situated down a lane and long driveway at 109 Stoke Newington Road, Palatine House still exists, and immediately beyond it is a double-storeyed dwelling now containing two semi-detached houses that is the likely site of Anna's former home.[3]

When Anna, Philip, and Mary saw the derelict site with its old damask rose rambling wild, they were enraptured, for although rooms needed to be fitted and heavy alterations done, the surroundings had heavenly potential.[4] The tenant of Palatine House kept only a small garden, so the rest of the land was the Sewells'. As Mary recalled, there was a sizeable fruit and vegetable garden, 'a very fine Acacia and Tulip tree, besides Walnut, Apple, Pear, and plane trees', outhouses, and a wide goldfish pond divided the garden from their four-acre meadow.[5] The improvements took about six months, paid for through a loan from Isaac's uncle, Philip Sewell. Anna and Mary papered and painted the house, and set the garden in order. 'We never thought we could not do things that wanted to be done', Mary wrote. 'I often wonder now at the difficult things I trusted and encouraged [Anna and Philip] to attempt.'[6] When Sarah Stickney paid her cholera-postponed visit in September 1832, she described it as a 'delightful spot, where . . . I am happier tha[n] in any other place and with any other society'.[7]

Now a trendy district of Hackney, Stoke Newington's heart in Church Street is dappled with bookstores, alternative therapy shops, and cafés. In the 1830s it was a highly respectable village of 'dreamy walks . . . immemorial elms, and . . . mouldering dwellings',[8] with 'numerous neat detached residences, and some extensive nursery grounds'.[9] Since the seventeenth century it had been a centre of religious dissent[10] and was in particular attracting Quaker residents when the Sewells moved there. Linked with its dissenting ethos, Stoke Newington also had literary credentials. Daniel Defoe had gone to school and written *Robinson Crusoe* there, and a string of eighteenth-century children's writers, many of whom Anna had probably read, had lived in the area, including Isaac Watts, Thomas Day, Anna Laetitia Barbauld, and Mary Wollstonecraft.[11] Edgar Allan Poe, educated at the Manor House School from 1817 to 1820, described Stoke Newington in his story 'William Wilson' as a 'misty-looking village of England, where were a vast number of gigantic and gnarled trees, and where all the houses were excessively ancient. In truth, it was a dream-like and spirit-soothing place, that venerable old town.' He recalled the 'refreshing chilliness of its deeply-shadowed avenues . . . the fragrance of its thousand shrubberies' and the 'deep hollow note of the church-bell, breaking, each hour, with sullen and sudden roar upon the stillness of the dusky atmosphere'.[12] The sound of the bell from St Mary's old church must have been as familiar to Anna as the route of her own dreamy walks. She often strolled to visit her many Hunton cousins who lived around the corner in Church Street itself where her Aunt Fulleretta (Isaac's sister) and Uncle Joseph ran a haberdashery and draper's shop.[13]

With Isaac's income insufficient to sustain a comfortable middle-class lifestyle, especially with the house loan to be repaid, Anna's youth continued frugal. Mary soon dismissed their only servant, taking on all the work herself with the help of Anna and Philip and, as she put it, 'a little assistance in the morning'.[14] Palatine Cottage was, nevertheless, a rapturous place for the children. They raced around the meadow, played in the garden, and expanded their knowledge of animals and domestic economy by tending to their cows, ducks, chickens, rabbits, and pigs. Anna took on special responsibility for bee-keeping, an activity in which she retained a lifelong interest, while Philip oversaw the measuring of the milk in the morning, often helping to milk, and sharpened knives or cleaned the family's shoes.[15]

These chores soon had to fit in around school hours. Philip had left Hackney Grammar and had enrolled at a Stoke Newington Friends' school,[16] and Anna, aged about twelve, was now also for the first time let out from under her mother's supervisory eye, and began attending 'a good day school' within a mile of the house.[17] Mary's younger brother Richard, who had suffered what Mary termed a 'painful history', probably involving depressive illness and financial mishaps, had taken some land at Enfield and had come to live with the family. As a result, Mary found that she no longer had time to teach Anna.[18]

No evidence survives of Anna's friendships, but she would at school have expanded her curriculum and her circle of friends and she mixed regularly with her Hunton relatives and her cousin, Lucy Sewell, who lived in nearby Lower Clapton. There were also local Friends she knew from the Quaker Meeting. The highlight of the Quaker year was the Devonshire House Yearly Meeting held each May, to which Quakers from all over the country and representatives from across the globe came. It resembled a huge family reunion as most Quakers knew each other, at least by name.[19] Mary and Anna would have each year attended the Women's Yearly Meeting, which Mary described as uniquely pretty: 'no colour was to be seen in it except the varying shades from white, silver grey and every gradation of dove colour, drab, fawn, brown up to black, which usually was confined to the bonnet'. The Friends' bonnet then being widespread, she recalled, the occasional woman who sported a 'straw cottage' was 'not considered genteel'.[20]

As a teenager Anna was now entering among the young Friends, who Mary termed 'far from indifferent to their dress', and who sat in 'quiet rows on the forms with their sweet, pure faces and modest manners'.[21] The best of the yearly gathering for Anna must have been the many excursion parties for the youngsters to visit art exhibitions and the sights of London.[22] As long as they avoided stepping over into worldliness, there was much to see: the British Museum, the Royal Academy of Arts, the National Gallery, and the Egyptian Hall in Piccadilly with its 'upwards of Fifteen Thousand Natural and Foreign

Curiosities, Antiques and Productions of the Fine Arts'.[23] There were panoramas and dioramas including The Colosseum in Regent's Park, which offered 'a vast panoramic view of London as seen from the top of St Paul's and had in addition, a Hall of Mirrors, a Gothic aviary, and a Swiss Chalet with a panorama of Mount Blanc'.[24] There were walks and talks, companionship and laughter. Anna, however, did not have many years of attending these happy, outward-looking, social events, for when she was about fourteen a sequence of harsh setbacks and unexpected changes were visited upon her family.

The Sewells had been experimenting with keeping cows to sell milk for supplementary income, but, like so many of Isaac's previous business ventures, it failed through no fault of their own. Trusting their neighbours who bought the milk as 'thoroughly respectable persons and many of them Friends', the Sewells were not unduly worried when the milkwoman – who had been hired with her husband to tend the cows and deliver the milk – told Mary that the regular customers had not yet paid. Given Quaker particularity about paying debts, however, Mary found ongoing non-payment curious and soon discovered that their customers had in fact paid on time. Catching wind of Mary's detection of her thievery, the milkwoman and her husband vanished, leaving the Sewells bereft of a sum they had been counting on for necessities.[25] Mary tried taking in an American couple as lodgers, but ended up losing money in trying to meet their discontented requirements, and had to ask them to leave.[26] The family could no longer make ends meet, but worse was to come. An event Mary's biographer, Mary Bayly, describes as 'so shrouded in mystery that it scarcely admits of comment',[27] was about to change Anna's life for ever.

Walking home from school one day Anna was caught in a heavy rain shower. Having no umbrella she ran as fast as she could to avoid getting drenched. Turning into their carriage-drive she pelted down its steep slope towards home but, just outside the garden gate, she slipped or tripped, her ankle twisted violently and she fell. In the seconds of silence before she cried out for Mary, with the rain rushing down over her collapsed form, Anna's destiny imperceptibly shifted.

This was the moment that Anna's 'life of constant frustration' began,[28] and as Mary rushed out to help her fallen daughter inside she little suspected 'that her dear life was to be henceforward coloured by this event – *not dis*coloured'.[29] Anna's ankle was badly sprained, but it was assumed that, like her arm, it would heal in due course. The words Black Beauty hears about his own condition – 'The foot is a good deal hurt, and the lameness will not go off directly'[30] – were to apply even more permanently to his creator. Anna's foot never completely regained its strength and she was lame for life.

Walks with Mamma had advised the fictional Anne not to go too near the sails of a windmill or she might be tossed up in the air and on landing 'might break an arm or a leg, and that would give us great pain'.[31] It was strangely prescient as injuring her ankle would not only give Anna pain of many kinds but meant, too, that her own so frequent walks with Mamma were now over. What caused this ongoing lameness is mystifying, especially as it was an ailment that would vary in its intensity, but it is possible that it was an insidious early symptom of a disease that would later have an even greater impact. Anna seemed at times to have had some ability to walk, but for most of her life walking or standing for any length of time was not possible. It is also not entirely clear whether one or both ankles were injured. Mary describes the initial injury as being to one ankle, and some later references also comment on Anna's 'lame foot', but after the first few months Anna herself and her family begin to write of the problems with her 'feet' in the plural.

The ankle may have been mismanaged in its early treatment; certainly Mary believed so, later wishing: 'Oh! If I had done *this*! – Oh! if she had not done that! – Oh if the Doctors had been wiser! – or perhaps if we try this or perhaps if we try that she may be cured'.[32] Typical treatments of the time included rest, bleeding (with leeches or 'cupping' with lancet and a glass), blistering, embrocations, plasters of various types, poultices, application of hot or cold water, bandaging, and recipes such as this 'oil for a sprain':

Take of oil of John's wort, oil of swallows, oil of worms, oil of whelps, oils of camomile and spirits of wine, each half an ounce; mix them together, and apply them to the part affected, with a feather, by the fire side, when going to bed; keep it moist with the oil as fast as the fire dries it, for half an hour; and, in the most obstinate case, it will effect a cure in a few days.[33]

Anna's case was beyond obstinacy and the family's search for a cure would continue for years: 'we tried every thing,' Mary wrote, 'as far as our circumstances would allow'.[34]

Anna's fall marked the end of her free-running schooldays, but in the months following there was hope of recovery and Anna was bright-spirited and resilient. In the summer of 1835 she seems to have visited Ridgmont,[35] the large farm in Holderness, east Yorkshire, that was Sarah Stickney's family home. She probably travelled there via the 25-hour boat journey from London to Hull that unfailingly induced seasickness in Sarah. Like Anna, Sarah was a great animal lover and as a girl, her nieces recalled, she had been given 'presents of hawks, magpies, jackdaws, a raven, a snake, a weasel, a fox, and once a full-grown badger' which she tamed.[36] More recently she had kept a monkey, but her greatest passion, like Anna's, was for horses, and she was said to be a 'fearless rider' who 'could manage almost any horse'.[37] Although all her exotic animals can no longer have been at Ridgmont, there were still plenty of creatures for Anna to spend time with as well as horses to ride, so it is not surprising that the place was a little heaven to her. There was also the companionship of Sarah's younger half-siblings who were near Anna's age, and she doubtless also met Sarah's nieces who lived at Lancaster and also kept pets. 'Oh it is a brave place', she wrote to Mary, after she had travelled on to Buxton:

> When I went away I felt as if I had left my home, a half mother, two sisters and a brother. I hope I have not seen the last of it. I should be very unhappy if I thought I had. Even with a lame foot it is a Paradise. Perhaps I was too happy there, but I never was so happy in any place in my life.[38]

Anna now spent at least six months living at Dudwick Cottage with her grandparents, her Aunt Ellen, and her Uncle Richard who had also left Palatine Cottage. Being away from home so long was not only for recuperative reasons, but surely also because the time (given her lameness) and money saved by Anna's absence could benefit her stressed parents while they attempted to stave off penury. On 23 September Anna wrote to Mary, wryly apologizing that 'the postage of my letters will almost ruin you'. 'Dost thou not find a great many I's in my letters?' she added, 'I [am] afraid thou willt think they are quite Egotistical.'[39] Landscapes that she had painted at Ridgmont, particularly one of Lancaster, had fired her passion for painting scenery: 'I am now always looking for something to make a picture of; what tints will harmonise together, what colours will do for this oak and ash and what for the distances. In fact I never enjoyed looking at the country so much before. It seems like another sense.'[40] She confessed that she 'heartedly repented' of a resolution she had made to give up oil painting after she saw the autumnal elms and oaks at Buxton and told Mary she would send her three oils and would try and 'conjer up several letters if so be that I can create out of nothing anything worth the trouble of reading'.[41]

She was taking full advantage of her grandfather's horses, regularly riding the local lanes and byways and over to visit friends at nearby Rippon Hall on Bob who she found a rough mount after the smoother Balaam.[42] She also spent time over in the big house with her Aunt and Uncle Wright, visited Aunt Wright's family, the Harfords, and travelled, too, to Yarmouth along the route of her grandfather's tragic steamer. She took little relish in her birthplace, as she told Mary: 'On first day I awoke with an obstropolous cold and sore throat which so increased in the evening that I felt quite poorly and went to bed early and found it worse in the morning so that I had not much pleasure in Yarmouth. But what with wine, whey and treakle posset it is better to-day.'[43]

Anna was the particular charge of Ellen, then only twenty-one, who determined much of Anna's routine. 'Aunt Ellen have laid me out such a power of work for the winter', Anna told Mary, 'that I do not expect I shall have time for what I had laid out for myself which is no little.'[44] With winter approaching she asked Mary to send her 'trousers for I want them now with the flannel shifts Aunt Ellen made. I began yesterday to make my stuff frock. . . . Aunt Ellen has pronounced in a very decided manner that my green peleese is to be kept as it is for me to ride out in.'[45] She also wanted Mary to send her materials for one of the popular crafts of the day, wax-flower making, and her 'recipe book and if thou chances to see anything of mine that I shall want. For when I write a letter I forget everything.'[46]

She advised Mary how to care for her precious bees who had experienced some calamity: 'Now for the poor bees. I think the dairy would be a good place for them in a few more weeks if they can be kept dry. Aunt Ellen feeds hers. I cannot yet think calmly on that sad affair with those dear little industrious Bees.'[47] Like many bee-keepers Anna assuredly felt that her bees came to know her, but with her stance against cruelty she is unlikely to have been among the bee-keepers who then commonly killed their bees by sulphuring, burning, or drowning, in order to collect their wax and honey. Come harvesting time, she probably used smoke to stupefy them only temporarily, a method promoted by books like *The Bee Preserver* (1829) and Thomas Nutt's *Humanity to Honey Bees* (1832).

Anna's schooldays had ended prematurely, but she kept up her self-education in Buxton by doing 'French exercises'[48] and reading, including 'Don Juan – Van Halen's imprisonment & escape from the inquisition it is very interesting'.[49] She missed her schoolfriends and her cousin Lucy, and in September asked Mary to send her love to 'all the friends, at the school particularly'.[50] The following February she asked her, 'hast thou heard anything about School lately and I very much want to know about Miss Lydia will you give my very dear love to Lucy I often think of her'.[51]

During Anna's months away important changes were taking place both in the family and in Anna herself. One of the unhappiest was that Mary and Isaac realized that they could no longer afford to live at Palatine Cottage. They rented the house out for £20 a year – 'not much – but something then' – to a friend who was getting married, and they moved into cheaper accommodation at 5 Down Cottages in nearby Shacklewell where they would live for almost a year.[52]

By mid-February 1836 Anna was making vague plans to come home. 'I do not know whether you think of my coming home on the top or inside of the coach,' she asked Mary, 'if you thought of the former I should not exactly like going alone in my presant rather lame condition on account of getting up & down but the inside I should not care a straw for going alone indeed if I had a book I had rather be alone as there is nothing any one could do for me'.[53] This remark about a fourteen-hour coach journey reflects Anna's dauntless practicality, but also shows her awareness that inside travel was almost twice as expensive. Her lameness continued, but she claimed some improvement: 'my feet are better and I have very little bandage on'. Perhaps alluding to an illness that had affected the Dudwick household she also stressed, 'I am now *quite* well in *Every* [triple underscored] *respect* is that not a good thing and have not felt at all poorly except on the first day.'[54]

As well as this account of her health, she also reassured Mary about her dress habits and frugality: 'the frock which thou wast so kind as to send me is made up it is very pretty Ellen likes her's very much my old Tuscan bonnet which was hardly deacent for [a] beggar has been done up & lined . . . so that I take it for my best & save the other – so thou sees I am provident'.[55] Anna's straw Tuscan bonnet, a fashion of the early 1830s with a low sloping crown and a broad square brim,[56] reveals that Anna was not wearing the Quaker bonnet. This surely reflected the spiritual sea change that was transforming the family and causing awkwardness with Anna's grandmother. '[A]lthough I should like to come home & see you all I do not', Anna told Mary:

> better than anything I am exceedingly happy here & do not wish to hurry away & for this reason because Grandmother has got an idea that I do not like being here so I have to be very cautious in saying anything about going home and if when she asks me if I should not like to see you I say yes very much indeed she says Ah, I think so thee'll be glad when thee get away from thy old Grandmother & such things as that she says . . . it is sometimes quite distressing. She says we don't care anything about her and all such things as those. She turns everything we say into something against herself so that she is almost more difficult to deal with than Uncle Richard was. However she thinks I should go home as soon as there is an opportunity because you are now settled want me home & I want to go home too though I should be very sorry at leaving Buxton.[57]

Ann Wright's over-sensitiveness may be indicative of the spells of depressive illness that had earlier afflicted her and from which her irascible father, John Holmes, and her son Richard also seem to have suffered. Even Anna, the now cheery, thoughtful granddaughter whose companionship she longed to retain, would in her turn experience emotional darkness. Her grandmother's anxiety was also, however, provoked by the sharpening religious differences that were about to cleave the family.

In a postscript to Anna's letter her Aunt Wright added some paragraphs to Mary about Anna's health and Ann Wright's state of mind:

> I have begged a corner of thy dr girls letter to say no Mother could desire to see her child in better health than dr Anna is – her ankles also strengthen. She has no doubt told thee all things are right in the constitution . . . She seems in excellent spirits I do not see half as much of her as I should like – it is difficult for her to leave the house over the way & I am such a poor cobweb of a creature that I have barely power to go through my small home & village duties . . . we are on sad touchy ground with our dr Mother she went on 7th day to consult with Lucy Aggs what she ought to do with her family & as far as I learnt she gave her good advice that as it was not from lightness they thought differently to her she must be comforted in the belief they acted from principle.[58]

This 'sad touchy ground' with Anna's grandmother was caused by the shocking realization that six of her seven children were on the verge of leaving the Quakers. Until now whoever was at Buxton, including Anna, had attended the nearby Friends' Meeting House at Lammas. With its stable and its steps outside from which women Friends mounted their horses, this meeting house was a fixture in Wright family life and had once had a large enough attendance to hold the 'Half-Yearly meeting'.[59] That this was now falling rapidly away upset Anna's grandmother. Like Anna's grandfather, she would remain a staunch Quaker to the end of her days, punctiliously attending First Day as well as mid-week meetings, even when in later years she was the sole worshipper.[60]

Probably soon after Anna had left Palatine Cottage for Ridgmont, her Aunt and Uncle Wright had visited Mary and Isaac. During this time Mary had many religious discussions with her brother John whom she described as 'full of joy and peace in the blessed realization of salvation through Christ's atonement'.[61] For a long time Mary had been spiritually uneasy, and although she was rather annoyed by her brother's daily expatiations on his new 'stronghold', the doctrine of Justification by Faith, she also saw that it had instilled in him 'rest peace and joy overflowing' that she did not have.[62] This evangelical doctrine held that righteousness or sanctification could only be received through true belief in Christ's atonement for sins and effectively required a conversion experience. Quakerism said little about doctrine, did not emphasize Scripture as evangelicals did, and, as Mary put it, was '*silent*' concerning Justification by Faith.[63]

As early as 1826 Mary had confessed to Dorothy Sewell that she was uneasy about Quaker practice:

I have greatly feared that we are degenerating either into careless or formal professors who make clean the outside of the cup but leave the interior defiled with worldlymindedness, uncharitableness and greediness after wealth who array themselves in formality rather than simplicity and rigidity rather than humility I think we are glorying in the estimation in which we are held by the world & do not enough consider how very far short we fall short of the high spiritual profession that we make & I fear that our bonnets and coats which mark us out from the world increase our pride rather than our humility.[64]

Her religious discontent had bubbled on and in 1830 she had told Dorothy that she imputed what she saw as Anna and Philip's spiritual deficiencies to herself.[65] More recently she had been impressed with the works of William Ellery Channing (1780–1842), the American Unitarian minister and writer.[66] She found that 'the very reasonable and attractive views of the Unitarians were very difficult to escape from', but as she put it, 'through God's exceeding mercy I did make a clean escape'.[67] After her brother's visit she spent months closely reading the New Testament, praying and trying to discern 'the *exact truth*', eventually finding her own belief in Christ's atonement.[68]

Mary was not the only Quaker to alter her religious beliefs at this time. Dissension developed between quietist Quakers who emphasized the 'Inward Light' of the spirit and evangelical Quakers who stressed Scripture. Manchester Quaker Isaac Crewdson's unintentionally schismatic book, *A Beacon to the Society of Friends*

(1835), labelled the doctrine of inward light a 'delusive notion' and criticized Quaker mysticism and silent worship.[69] Anna's family were especially influenced by these ideas because in 1828 Mary's eldest sister Anna had married Crewdson's brother Joseph, a Manchester widower with six children. Crewdson's book caused tearful ructions in the Manchester Meeting, provoked a flurry of pamphlets on both sides, and at the 1835 Yearly Meeting in London was the subject of a committee of enquiry. A decision was made not to 'proceed against Crewdson for doctrinal unsoundness', but that, although a Quaker minister, he should remain silent in meetings.[70] The Beaconite controversy raged on until after the 1836 Yearly Meeting in May by which time Anna was probably home. This was the last annual Quaker gathering Mary, and Anna if she were able to go, ever attended, and they were not alone. Roughly three hundred Quakers would resign later that year,[71] including Mary, Anna's aunts Anna, Elizabeth, Maria, and Ellen, her Uncle Joseph Crewdson and her Aunt and Uncle Wright. Isaac Crewdson also resigned, followed by fifty Manchester sympathizers, and set up the new schismatic 'Evangelical Friends' Meeting which Anna would later visit.[72]

Mary's decision to abandon Quakerism was concretized through her wish to take communion and be baptised. Considered empty external rites, Communion and Baptism were against Quaker precepts, and to be baptised meant resignation or disownment from the Society of Friends. Mary spoke with a visiting pastor, Benjamin Wills Newton, who told her it was her duty to follow her convictions. 'But I do not know where to go . . . and I have no one to be with me', she told him. 'I would baptise you', he reassured her, 'and my wife could be with you, if you liked.'[73] Mary's baptism by immersion was arranged, but first she had the painful task of telling Isaac.

Isaac still worked long hours and was very late home the night Mary chose to tell him. She left his supper ready for him and went up to their bedroom where she sat alone in the dark waiting and listening for him to arrive. Ten o'clock came and went but still he did not come home. Finally she heard the door open and the sounds of her husband settling to his supper. Then his footsteps on the stairs. Isaac knew as soon as he heard Mary's voice in the depths of the shadowy room that something was wrong:

'What's the matter?' he asked.

'Let us kneel down together beside the bed and I will tell thee.'

Kneeling side by side Mary told him of the life-altering decision she had made. Of his response she many years later recalled 'with streaming tears, "His kindness to me I shall *never* forget."'[74]

Isaac preferred that Mary withdraw from the Quakers rather than be expelled so she sent in her resignation to the Gracechurch Street Monthly Meeting which governed Stoke Newington. 'Then', Mary wrote, 'I ceased being a "Friend" in *name*.'[75] Isaac cannot have been happy about Mary's resignation, especially coming on top of their financial woes and Anna's laming. His father also died that year (1836) during a visit north to see Dorothy and Abraham Sewell who had recently moved to Malton, Yorkshire to take up a grocery opportunity, the Yarmouth shop no longer being able to support two families.[76] Mary maintained, however, that 'never bigoted or pronouncing harsh judgements upon any one, [Isaac always] had a truly catholic and charitable spirit', and was 'exceedingly kind and patient' about her decision.[77] This may have been so, but as Mary admitted, 'not to be fully united in external practical religion is a matter, if possible to be avoided in a domestic family. I made many mistakes through ignorance which I remember with much pain.'[78] The fissure ran down the centre of the family. Isaac remained a lifelong Quaker, with Philip for the time being continuing to attend meetings with him. Mary experimented with other denominations while Anna, still officially a Quaker, accompanied her when able. This was not often, Mary reported, as 'dear Anna being lame seldom could go anywhere'.[79]

Although her baptism gave her great joy and a wonderful sense of peace,[80] Mary sorely missed the security, calmness, and serenity of Quaker meetings. 'It was heartbreaking work', she wrote, 'not going with dear [Isaac] to Meeting.'[81] Although she might have remained a 'habitual attender' without being a full Quaker, her plan to attend both a Friends' meeting and another church or chapel service on a Sunday was quashed by Isaac's disapproval.[82] Mary also felt deeply the forfeiture of Quaker community and knew she had fallen in the estimation of Quaker relatives and friends[83] who thought that she wanted 'more liberty', or was 'impatient of the little distinctive peculiarities of the "Friends"' or 'wished to get rid of the Quaker bonnet'. Forgoing the bonnet was for Mary, in fact, a regret rather than an emancipation, for she believed that Friends' dress was the 'prettiest a woman can wear'.[84]

Mary did not have any clear plan about what form of worship was to replace the old one, and she started church- and chapel-hopping, discussing options with Anna. The Church of England proved unsatisfactory as the Prayer Book was puzzling, and the quick movement between prayer, praise, and confession seemed to mask the spirit of worship. She was also shocked at the hypocrisy of making choir children, in sight of the congregation, 'go through the whole of the service in an audible voice, whilst a man with a long stick kept touching them up to their duty'.[85] Next she tried the Independent Chapel, which, with its greater peacefulness and 'extempore prayer and preaching', was similar to the Friends' method of worship, but what she saw as its 'high Calvinist doctrine' and 'stern dogmatism' replaced the spirituality she sought.[86] The Plymouth Brethren whose unworldliness she liked were, she felt, too narrow.[87]

For Anna, Mary's resignation opened up wider horizons but also stripped away certainties about her way of life and the future. It also brought a division, however lovingly handled, into her family and a sense that she had to negotiate allegiances to parents and grandparents. This religious flux, together with adapting to her disability, came at a time when she was also undergoing the more typical changes of adolescence.

The Anna who had come home to Shacklewell had blossomed into womanhood. In September 1835 she had written proudly: 'I was measured this morning and am 1 inch and ¼ higher than Philip. I believe I grew all this at [R]idgmont and I gained 8 pounds in weight.'[88] The ideal for belles of the 1830s was to be 'short and plump' with a 'well-rounded face' so Anna's pleasure in her pounds may reflect popular taste as well as signalling health and adolescent growth.[89] A portrait of her at about this time shows her with curly brown hair, hazel eyes, a peaches-and-cream complexion, looking well-nourished, with a sweet solidity of features. She strikes a serious pose as befits a portrait and is wearing a brownish-maroon, high-waisted dress with a ruffle of plain white lace along its wide neckline.

Anna is likely to have reached menarche during the then British norm of between fourteen and sixteen,[90] and is unlikely to have had it brought on early by perceived contemporary accelerants such as 'high living; by the whirl and bustle and excitement of city life; by reading novels which are full of love-incidents; by attending balls, theatres, and parties; and by mingling much in the society of gentlemen'.[91] Certainly her Aunt Wright had noticed her new womanliness, as she told Mary in February 1836: 'as [Anna] brought this letter over just now I was amused to see how the girl was changed into the young woman by having last night turned up her hair it is rather an improvement for she is almost outgrown the child'.[92]

Menstruating signalled her entry into womanhood but also carried practical and restrictive consequences. Practically she had to grow accustomed to wearing the bulky cloth napkins made from flannel and a little smaller than babies' napkins, which had to be washed and reused.[93] There was also the discomfort of menstrual cramps exacerbated by the corset that, although fashion-minded mothers laced their daughters into them as young as seven or eight, Anna, with a more sensible mother, doubtless had only more recently begun to wear.[94] Perhaps her emphatic 'I am now *quite well* in *Every* [triple underscored] *respect*', to Mary reflected these new aspects of her life.

As Anna settled in at Shacklewell what was most practically restricting to her was her lameness. Her parents must have felt keenly that if they had a greater income they could better provide for her needs. It is unlikely that Anna or her family yet owned their own horse, even though Palatine Cottage had a meadow for grazing.[95] When guests came they probably hired a job horse and vehicle from a livery stables. The cost of buying and keeping a horse and its accoutrements was high, and even by 1848 only around 100,000 out of a population of over 18 million owned their own horses.[96] This is one reason why places like Buxton and Ridgmont were such a glory to Anna, especially after the onset of her lameness: they offered her horses, and horses offered her freedom. Sarah Stickney (Ellis) would soon write in her popular *The Daughters of England* (1842) that young women should 'let one hour every day, generally two, and sometimes three, be spent in taking exercise in the open air, either on horseback, or on foot'.[97] Exercise was widely seen as crucial for health, and, in lieu of the walking now denied her, Anna needed horseback exercise. Back at home in a pedestrian-propelled world, her lameness often held her captive and even simple walks to visit cousins or to assist Mary were rarely possible. Given that her lameness was lifelong it is surprising that no mention is ever made of Anna having any mobility aids such as a walking stick, crutches, or a wheeled chair. Possibly she did not have strength enough for crutches or need enough for a wheelchair. She seems to have often had some power to move around her house or garden but apparently enough for only a few steps at a time. Some local transport may have been available – perhaps short-stage coaches, or the twenty-seater horse-drawn omnibuses which had been introduced in 1829, or the hansom cabs from 1834 – but it cost money the Sewells simply could not spare.

Despite the shift to Shacklewell, financial constraints continued. Anna's Uncle William, who had employed Isaac for about a decade, seems to have been taking familial advantage of Isaac's skills while not increasing his salary. Anna, who had worried for some time that her father 'gets quite worn up' with work,[98] was decidedly of this opinion, as she had written from Buxton:

> how does the business go on – has father got anything given him this stock taking Grandfather often speaks about it I do not think Uncle William will ever rise in his opinion again if he does not advance Father's sallery & no more he ought I think father might strike for wages with good success for they could not do without him & could better afford to pay him more than loose him.[99]

In Mary's words, Isaac 'was considered a thorough man of business' because he had 'seen a variety of business was scrupulously upright and exact in everything, exceedingly industrious and persevering [and] never saved himself trouble by throwing it on others'.[100] His Quaker credentials were an asset in business as it was 'an advantage, and no slight one either, to be a member of a Society so highly esteemed and respected'.[101] While at Shacklewell some of this esteem bore fruit when he was appointed manager of the Brighton branch of the Surrey, Kent and Sussex Joint Stock Bank founded in 1836. Like his former positions in drapery, sales, and in his brother's business, banking was a common Quaker occupation. Friends' perceived quest for wealth was both admired and criticized by non-Quakers. William Cobbett, for example, excoriated Quakers as 'the pestiferous sect of non-labouring, sleek and fat hypocrites',[102] but none of these epithets are in any way apt for the honest, hard-working Isaac Sewell.

In October 1836 Isaac found a 'very pleasantly situated', 'convenient', and yet 'retired' house in Brighton which with some expense could be altered into a bank.[103] Anna was by then away from home again and would not return until the Brighton house was ready. She first went to stay with her Great-Aunt Elizabeth (her grandfather Wright's sister) and her Great-Uncle William Curtis in Alton, Hampshire just two miles from Chawton where Jane Austen had live two decades before. Mary, busy with the impending move, wrote to Anna at Alton apologizing for her tardy reply to Anna's 'long looked for most welcome & acceptable letter', stating that she was always happy to 'sit down and have a little chat with' her daughter. Mary's newfound evangelical zeal was uppermost in her mind but, as she told Anna, it was having no effect on her brother Richard, back living with them, who was 'so thoroughly impregnated with quakerism that it appears impracticable to fix him upon the simple unadulterated truths of the Gospel for five minutes at a time. I never saw such an extraordinary instance of the cleaving effect of traditional prejudice and error.'[104] Mary had higher hopes of helping a friend who seems to have been an ex love-interest of Richard's who wanted to come and stay before the Brighton move and who she would have readily put off, 'had she not told me that she had received evangelical views of the atonement & that she wanted a friend to confide in and consult – I bless our Heavenly Father so humbly for this, that I am willing to take up with my portion of trial which it certainly will be to me just now to have an additional inmate.'[105]

This extra inmate was probably Sarah Stickney who did come to stay in November 1836. If Richard had harboured romantic feelings for her he was to be disappointed for during her visit Sarah became engaged to widower William Ellis, a Congregationalist minister who was secretary of the London Missionary Society. Like Mary, Sarah had been looking for a non-Quaker spiritual home and although she felt she could 'live separate from every religious sect, and just glean up a little good from all',[106] in March the following year when she became a wife and stepmother she also became a Congregationalist.

Mary informed Anna of recent family religious intrigue: 'Uncle & Aunt & Lucy are returned from Appledore. Lucy, I believe has been baptised but this is a secret at present – Aunt Bessey [probably Anna's Aunt Elizabeth] has been baptised at Uncle Crewdson's not by immersion but I understand it was a very solemn & impressive time Uncle & Aunt Wright were there.' She urged Anna to read the 'most admirable' and 'unanswerable' publication on baptism by Elisha Bates, a strongly evangelical American Quaker.[107]

Anna relished her time away from home, as she often would in her later teenage years, but Mary reminds her, as *she* often would, 'Thou must tell me what thou thinks of the propriety of staying longer be sure not to remain *till* thy welcome is worn out or it may be inconvenient to our kind relations to accommodate thee longer.'[108] Mary was also always keen for 'kind relations' to offer thoughts on Anna's lameness. 'I am very desirous to know if thy prognostics have in any way been verified', she asked Anna. 'I am quite amased to find that neither my uncle nor cousin Wm have seen thy feet. Wilt thou ask thy uncle to look at them if he has not yet done so and say that thy mother very much wishes to know what is his opinion of them . . . write in a very few days as we are anxious to hear of thee.'[109]

Mary also confessed to Anna that 'A most alarming catastrophe happened to thy bees last week.' An old man who was beating the Sewells' dining-room carpet had toppled Anna's 'bee house' and the bees went into a stinging frenzy, Mary wrote:

Sarah who was soon upon the scene of action had several upon her forehead and asked the old man to put them off but he manifests somewhat of the selfish propensity of our nature by running away and letting her to *shake herself* Uncle Richard was fortunately at home. I dressed and perfectly secured him so that he went courageously to the work and replaced them in the stand much of the comb was displaced and the wooden hive broken.[110]

Mary admitted she could not restrain her 'almost immoderate laughter' at seeing the 'luckless author of the damage running about with a blue apron over his head and looking as if he apprehended the end of all things was at hand'.[111]

The end of Anna's life in the orbit of London was at hand. Now sixteen, she would soon join her family in glittering seaside Brighton where she would enter into some of its gaieties and test her newly fledged wings on more frequent visits away from home.

FOUR

Experience and Information
of All Sorts

1837-8

I must not forget to mention one part of my training, which I have always considered a very great advantage. (*Black Beauty*, Chapter 3)

In a pattern emerging since her laming, Anna was not with her family when they moved to Brighton in the icy December of 1836. After her Alton visit she had probably spent Christmas in Buxton, and in January 1837 she travelled on by snowy coach journey – Mary hoping she had the sense to ride inside – to Stoke Newington. Here she stayed at her Aunt Fulleretta's 'comfortable and hospitable fireside' until the Brighton home was ready.[1]

They were yearning to see her, Mary wrote, but everything was still in a state of 'dust and confusion' as they were knocking 169 and 170 North Street into one residence.[2] As yet without servants, Mary was doing most of the housework herself and her hands were, she told Anna, so 'stiff chapped & red that they are not fit to be seen . . . only think of thy Lady mother'.[3] She had, however, hired a 'very nice charwoman' to scrub the house, something essential in her view as 'the last servant was the quintessence of indolence'.[4]

Mary sent Anna mixed messages about her Brighton home. Although it was in a convenient location for Isaac's bank just two doors down at 167 North Street, she confessed that she had 'not yet been able to discern any agreeableness in the situation'.[5] Mary felt like a stranger and did not take to the town environment of this little London-by-the-sea which offered little nature besides the ocean, which never assuaged her longing for the countryside.[6] North Street now as then is a busy thoroughfare of banks, shops, and businesses about five minutes walk from the seafront and near the historic twisting Lanes. The thrice widening of North Street since their day[7] means that the Sewells' house would have stood in what is now the roadway or pavement. Isaac's bank was on the south-east corner of Prince's Place, the cul-de-sac that houses the Chapel Royal and abuts the grounds of the opulent oriental-style Royal Pavilion. Next east, at 168 North Street, were the publishing quarters of the *Brighton Gazette*[8] and next door to that the Sewells' 'double house'.[9]

Mary told Anna that their furniture fitted 'to admiration' and that all that was needed to make it 'a very nice comfortable house' was 'a basic common carpet cover to hide some very dirty boards',[10] which she asked Anna to arrange. She also directed her to pay a string of social calls in Dalston and Stoke Newington, but advised pecuniary delicacy while doing so: 'Joseph Cooper has not paid for his bees so if he offers to pay thee thou canst take the money also 4/ for some pigeons of Philip's but do not mention it if he do not.'[11]

After fulfilling her social obligations Anna made the fifty-mile, four-to-five hour coach trip to Brighton, following Mary's advice about cost: 'If thou canst borrow amongst thy friends enough money to take thee as far as the Brighton Coach thy father will meet and pay for thee at the end of the journey.'[12] London–Brighton was 'the giddiest route in the country for competition',[13] and Anna had plenty of brightly coloured coaches to choose from, with names such as *The Age*, *The Alert*, *The Emerald*, and *The True Blue*.[14] Popularity, however, led to increased risk of accidents on the route caused by reckless drivers attempting to be speediest and to horses sometimes being whipped on well beyond their limits, even to the point of exhaustion and death. Seeing any such equine cruelty, Anna, vocal in the face of injustice from childhood, was unlikely to have kept silent.

Arriving safely in the most fashionable watering-hole in Britain, sixteen-year-old Anna must have felt a thrill at seeing the fashions, seaside, and glamour of the beau monde. Formerly a fishing village, Brighton had been popularized as a health resort by Dr Richard Russell whose 1750 advocacy of bathing in and drinking seawater had led to the craze for seawater cures. The Prince of Wales, later George IV, had further accelerated the town's popularity by his many visits which attracted the rich and famous to vacation there. In Anna's day this clement-climated town had a population of about 40,000 which almost doubled during the 'season'.[15]

When her fluctuating lameness allowed her to do so, Anna surely took keen enjoyment in exploring what contemporary guidebooks described as the shops 'richly stored with every article of taste, fancy and use',[16] and the town's 'places of amusement [which] are various and select'.[17] She knew the Regency splendour of the crescents and squares, and watched glamorous visitors promenade along the seafront, milling amongst stylish equestrians, invalids in bath chairs, and children being pulled in goat carts. She must have often gazed at the Royal Pavilion and its adjacent domed stables which were touted as 'decidedly the most magnificent pile ever erected for such a purpose in Europe'.[18]

Just five months after Anna reached North Street, the Victorian era dawned when Victoria, her senior by just one year, became sovereign of what would become within their lifetimes the greatest country, indeed empire, in the world. Anna must have taken fascinated glimpses of her regal contemporary and near neighbour when Victoria made a five-week visit to Brighton in October 1837. On 28 June the following year Anna may have seen Brighton's celebration of Victoria's coronation which involved a dinner for two thousand of the town's children at which each was given half a pound of roast beef, plum pudding, and a glass of wine.[19] 'You will be sure & give my love to the Queen when she comes if you have an opportunity', she asked Isaac in October 1838.[20]

Anna, of course, did not move in queenly circles, and there is no evidence of her attending balls or society events. She did attend lectures, meetings, and talks and went for walks and excursions with friends, whose names are again unrecorded. She must also have frequented libraries and reading-rooms. Whether she went to the Royal Marine Library to sit in its bow windows overlooking the sea, glancing occasionally through one of its 'capital telescopes', before selecting from 'popular work, especially such as are calculated for the fair sex' is not known.[21] Possibly a library more studious and wide-ranging might have been chosen for a Sewell family subscription.

She must have many times walked out along the magnificent Chain pier with its little shops in the towers selling trinkets and sweets, and listened to the summertime bands playing on the pier head. Standing under the swooping, skirling seagulls she would have gazed back at the views of Brighton and along the Sussex coast and let the crash or calm of the sea charge her spirit or soothe her soul. The Sewells probably had an annual subscription to the pier as Mary habitually took pre-breakfast strolls along it. Early rising not being the Brighton norm, she wrote, 'I was commonly the only occupant, and had the lessons of the winds and the waves all to myself.'[22]

Even before Anna arrived in Brighton, Isaac had opened his bank successfully. It was a branch of the new Surrey, Kent and Sussex Joint Stock Bank, which had headquarters in London, and was one of the proliferating joint stock banks then entering into competition with the older private banks. In 1839 it would change its name to the London and County Bank to highlight its link with the London money markets, and in the twentieth century would become part of National Westminster Bank.[23] Mary later wrote that Isaac was 'very kind and considerate to all he employed and never made an enemy. He was so skilful in training young men in the conduct of Bank business that clerks intended for other Banks were often sent to him first.'[24] His first clerk was his own son, fifteen-year-old Philip, who had now left school.

Banking had its risks: failure or robbery, and although Isaac escaped both, the bank did go through a shaky opening phase during the financial panic of 1837. Anna told him the following year: 'I am very glad indeed that the bank gets on so much better & that thou hast not so much anxiety as formerly it must be a great relief not to be always expecting an uncomfortable letter from London every time you discount a little.'[25] By November 1838 Philip could report: 'We are getting on famously lots to do & well paid for it.'[26]

In banking Isaac finally found a financially successful niche. Although Mary always claimed indifference 'to wealth as an adjunct of refinement',[27] and eschewed luxury, she did naturally enough desire security. Isaac's increased income after so many years of hardship was very welcome, especially as in later Brighton years medical expenses for Anna would increase.

Mary was already becoming an expert in available remedies, and it was not only Anna for whom she sought treatment. In January 1838 Dorothy Sewell fell seriously ill and travelled from Malton to stay at her sister Sarah Stickney Ellis's house in London, while seeking medical advice.[28] Mary dashed to London to help the woman who was probably her closest friend. 'I have walked till my feet are

blistered, and talked till my tongue is tired and spent money till I am
almost pennyless', she told Isaac on 5 February of her search for
treatments for Dorothy.[29] Nothing could be done. Mary paid Dorothy
what she knew would be her last farewell and in spring the news came
that Dorothy had died.[30] Now Anna became Mary's truest soulmate,
and although Mary's search for a cure for Dorothy had proved
unavailing, she never gave up hope of finding one for Anna.

When Anna came to live in Brighton she was still a Quaker, but
unlike Philip rarely accompanied her father to the Friends' Meeting
House in nearby Ship Street. Like Mary, and soon Philip, she was
searching for a new spiritual home, and could have been in no better
place for doing so. Brighton was a religious smorgasbord laid out for
the sampling, and sample they did. Methodist, Unitarian, Baptist,
Independent, Salem, Bethel, and Bethesda chapels, and a string of
Anglican chapels were all nearby and they tried most at least once.
The Chapel Royal was closest but its exclusivity was unlikely to meet
their egalitarian taste. It was the first of many proprietory chapels in
Brighton that were businesses as much as places of worship with
attendees having to rent or purchase a pew or pay a shilling for a
seat.[31] The Countess of Huntingdon's chapel was on North Street,[32]
but Mary, who had tried it before Anna's arrival, found it 'a very
unprofitable mixture of the Church with dissent'.[33]

Anna, Mary, and Philip developed their steadiest connection with
the Anglican St James's chapel, on the corner of St James's and
Chapel Streets. A chapel-of-ease to Brighton's then parish church St
Nicholas's,[34] it held services at 11 a.m. and 6.30 p.m. on Sundays.[35]
Given Mary's dissatisfaction with the established church – she wrote
to Anna in 1838: 'I heartily pity [the Church missions] for having
that cumbersome church service to drag about with them'[36] – the
attraction of St James's seems to have been more the man than the
method. Before Anna arrived in Brighton, Mary had told her she
had attended a service at 'Mr Maitland's whom I liked exceedingly
and where from all I can hear I think we shall be most likely to find
our place – everything I hear of him and his congregation makes me
incline more to them than any others I have yet heard of'.[37]
Reverend Charles David Maitland was perpetual curate at the
chapel and took an interest in the family. He had served twenty

years in the Army and had been an artillery lieutenant at the Battle of Waterloo before taking orders and was regarded as 'a saintly man' whose congregation was 'quiet and to some extent old-fashioned'.[38] Bayly states that he 'was truly a pastor as well as a preacher, and watched over these members of his flock'.[39]

St James's became a focus of activity with Anna, Philip, and Mary soon becoming deeply involved with Sunday school teaching in the 1836-built schoolroom attached to the chapel. Around 250 boys and girls were taught there each Sunday and 130 girls were taught daily.[40] Mary and Anna also oversaw an infant school, whether at St James's or elsewhere is unclear. In the 1830s and 1840s Sunday school teaching was aimed largely at working-class children. For the swelling evangelical movement literacy was next to godliness as personal access to the Bible was thought essential to faith, and Anna would not only have taught her pupils religion and moral virtue, but reading, writing, possibly arithmetic, and practical skills such as sewing. She probably taught for a minimum of three hours on a Sunday and may have also worked on weekdays, undoubtedly following Mary's dictate that Sunday school teachers should never dress gaily lest it distract pupils from the lesson in hand.[41]

Teaching was the cornerstone of Anna's charitable endeavours in Brighton, but she was also involved, either practically or as a moral support, in Mary's other philanthropic projects. The fashionable flounce of Brighton swept over depths of poverty and hardship, so much so that a shocked Elizabeth Fry after holidaying there in 1824 had set up the Brighton District Visiting Society which became a template for others across the country. Mary and Anna for the rest of their lives engaged in regular district visiting among the poor, their particular aims being to help the poor help themselves and – but never at the expense of practical help – to encourage faith in God.

Courtyards off North Street then housed some of the worst slums in Brighton,[42] and conditions for poor inhabitants were dire. Open cesspools, slaughter-houses, poor drainage, a deficient water supply and overcrowding increased disease as well as malodorous surroundings, and epidemics repeatedly hit the town: whooping-cough in 1839, smallpox in 1841, and scarlet fever in 1842. As the 'hungry forties' rolled forward there was much for Mary and Anna to do.

Mary herself recruited philanthropic help. Of an acquaintance planning to visit Brighton, she told Anna: 'if she is pretty well I mean to make her useful in visiting amongst the poor & I dare say shall find her long purse useful in that way'.[43] Similarly, paying calls was not always simply a social nicety: 'I called too upon Mrs Ellis the wife of the Wine merchant – I wished to revive her interest about the Penitentiary as she is on the committee but her health & many children will not allow it.'[44]

Mary's biographer Bayly records that in Brighton more than anywhere else Mary comforted 'those who were crushed' and writes that she had a ready empathy with the oppressed who seemed to confide easily in her.[45] One place at which she regularly gave succour was the Brighton workhouse on Church Hill. During the Sewells' first two years in Brighton, Dickens's *Oliver Twist* was appearing serially. In it Dickens attacked the controversial 1834 Poor Law Amendment Act which instituted a system whereby relief-seeking paupers had to live in workhouses with deliberately abysmal conditions where spouses were separated from each other, children could be taken from parents, entry was shameful, and rations were meagre. *Oliver Twist's* asking for 'more' accurately reflected the situation Mary regularly saw on her visits.

Undaunted by reluctant authorities, Mary battled for access to the 'bad' ward in the workhouse which she described as 'the general receptacle for the miscellaneous cases of sin and poverty, which could not readily be classified, and admitted into the other wards.'[46] This ward was rarely visited by the chaplain who gave Mary 'alarming accounts of window-smashing, of fighting and swearing . . . and the governor and matron fully corroborated his statements, and advised me not to adventure myself into it'.[47] Adamant that she would take the risk, Mary began visiting this ward weekly, providing practical help, a friendly ear, and more than once sitting with culprits on the floor of the ward's bare underground punishment cell known as the 'black hole', which confirmed her in her belief that 'penitence [was] more apt to follow upon kindness, than upon correction'.[48]

Mary also, in their own home, started training up servants from among the needy, plucking likely candidates from wherever she spotted them and schooling them in practical skills, tractability, and

Christian duty. She once brought home a desolate Irish Catholic widow from the 'bad' workhouse ward and trained her up as a cook. 'Perhaps you will think me rash,' Mary commented, 'but this poor destitute mother threw herself upon my sympathy, and I could not leave her there.'[49] To modern minds it might be tempting, but is too simplistic, to see the charity work engaged in by Mary and Anna as busybody do-gooding that did more for the giver than the recipient. In Mary's, and later Anna's, case it was a vocation. It gave them purpose and activity in a period when middle-class female activities were limited, but they also saw it as God's will and were truly moved by the very real horrors they saw about them. Their Quaker background, which urged the alleviation of suffering wherever it was seen, as well as their now evangelical religious leanings, encouraged active charity. In confluence with their faith and writing this became their life's work and would absorb them both utterly. It was, however, still more Mary's task at the moment while Anna enjoyed something of the expansiveness of youth.

Around the time of her eighteenth birthday Anna literally took the plunge. Entering what she called a 'formidable' yet welcoming 'dark pool' in nearby Bond Street,[50] probably at the Salem Particular Baptist chapel,[51] she was baptised, according to Bayly, 'by immersion, the Church Service not being used'.[52] Coming on top of other perceived infractions, Anna's baptism caused a stream of official comment in Quaker records that gave rise to consequences that must have caused her staunch Quaker father some pain and mortification. Unlike Mary, who had already left the Friends, or Philip, who in February 1844 would do so, Anna was to end her Quaker days not through resignation but by disownment.

Expelling someone from their Society was not something Quakers took lightly, yet when regulations were breached expulsion was at this time readily enacted.[53] Anna's predicament cannot have surprised her and was probably more a case of having neglected to resign than anything else. Possibly Isaac had wanted her to continue her membership and letting herself be expelled was a passive form of teenage rebellion, but it seems clear that in her heart, and well before her disownment, Anna's Quaker allegiance was already over. There were official procedures, however, that had to be gone through.

On 11 May 1838 Anna came up for special consideration at the
Lewes and Chichester Monthly Meeting, which oversaw the
Brighton Quaker Meeting. The Clerk Susannah Kemp reported:

Anna Sewell – The following communication was received from
the women's meeting and the further consideration thereof is
deferred until a future meeting – 'This meeting believes it right at
the present time to inform men friends, private labour having
been unavailing, that our young friend Anna Sewell has attended
our meetings for worship but seldom since her residence amongst
us, that she has frequented other places of worship, and has
recently submitted to water baptism.'[54]

Clearly Anna had already had discussions with concerned
women Friends who had questioned her neglect of Quakerism in
favour of new religious practices. At the next monthly meeting on
15 June, after 'mature consideration' of the previous month's
report on Anna, it was decided that 'Grover Kemp [should] unite
with a committee of women friends in visiting her thereon' and
report further.[55] That very day Anna was visited by a delegation
comprising Grover Kemp, and Sarah Rickman and Susanna Beck
from the Women's Meeting. They reported to the following
monthly meeting on 20 July:

We, your committee appointed to visit Anna Sewell report that we
have had an interview with her. She received us in a friendly
manner, and afforded an opportunity for a free interchange of
sentiment, but expressed herself perfectly satisfied with the step
she had taken and had no wish to be any longer retained as a
member of our religious society.[56]

The Meeting decided that Testimony of Disownment should be
prepared and 'issued against her'.[57]

At the monthly meeting of 17 August the duly prepared
Testimony was twice read over, a few emendations were made, and
soon afterwards Anna received her official expulsion paper which
recounted the steps taken by the Meeting in considering her case and
advised her:

In thus taking leave of our young friend, as a fellow professor with us, we would remind her of the apostolic declaration that 'the natural man receiveth not the things of the spirit of God, for they are foolishness unto him, neither can he know them, because they are spiritually discerned.' And of the language of the Royal Psalmist that the meek the Lord will guide in Judgment, and the meek he will teach his way – And we would also express an affectionate desire that she may be faithful and obedient to the humbling, contriting operations of Divine Grace in the secret of her soul, and dwell under the inward teaching of that Holy Annointing which the Apostle John declares to be the truth and no lie, that thus she may become a true believer in Christ, not only in his outward appearance in the flesh, and in all that he has done and suffered for us on the cross, as 'an offering and a sacrifice unto God for a sweet smelling savour' but also in his inward appearance by his Holy Spirit, in the heart, as that true light which enlighteneth every man that cometh into the world.[58]

With these sonorous words of farewell Anna embarked on the next stage of her spiritual journey. Philip, too, was baptised at this time, but he was not subject to expulsion perhaps because he was only sixteen and because he for a long time, out of 'affection and admiration for the Society', continued to attend Quaker meetings with Isaac.[59] Mary and Anna would always remain Quaker in nature and habits, and like many Quakers by birth who left the Society, neither of them ultimately found a replacement denomination to which they could give their hearts completely.[60] Over time they effectively became a church of two, and Mary stated at the end of her life, 'If I ever joined any religious body again . . . it would be the Friends – though I've left them.'[61]

Less than two months after her disownment Anna paid a long visit to her Aunt Anna and Uncle Joseph Crewdson's home in Ardwick Green, Manchester, arriving sometime before 2 October 1838 and staying on till around Christmas. She got on well with her aunt as she told Mary: 'She is very kind to me & I like her more & more.'[62] Being reserved by nature yet never afraid to speak out, Anna Crewdson shared some characteristics with her namesake niece. Mary described her older sister as having also had 'a great deal of character as a child',[63] and in adolescence, yearning 'to be something', she had secretly taught herself Latin.[64]

Anna also enjoyed the company of her aunt's stepchildren Susannah, Robert, Elizabeth, Isaac, Rachel, and Joseph, aged from twenty-two to thirteen, Elizabeth being eighteen like herself. She also got to know her aunt and uncle's young children John, Anna, Alfred, and Theodore, aged from nine to three. She adapted to the Crewdsons' habits, telling Isaac, 'we are such a long time over [breakfast and tea] . . . they often lay down their knives & forks & talk',[65] and was, she told Mary, 'quite settled & very happy'.[66]

Her Uncle Joseph and his Beaconite brother, Isaac, were silk and cotton producers, and Manchester was already a burgeoning manufacturing city saddled with the desperate poverty, child labour, and choking factories that writers such as Elizabeth Gaskell would portray graphically in the following decade. A.B. Granville described it at the time as a 'region of red-brick mills, seven stories high, of factories and warehouses, with a suffocating atmosphere, and grubby faces'.[67] Anna told Isaac she was unimpressed:

I am often struck with the difference between Manchester & our town, here everybody seems sound and florishing substantial calculating slow thinking men that go on on on till they get sick not like the frothy shopkeepers about us that go for a year or so & then brake and as to rank the only titled person in Manchester is just dead & the rest are chiefly merchants & people who have risen from nothing, thou sees it is very different is not it, it is a most disagreeable town just like London without the amusement of shops on account of the factorys & warehouses.[68]

Her allusions to 'frothy' Brighton and its titled inhabitants indicate Anna's interest in fashion, which she pursued to the extent that economy and ingrained notions of 'plainness' would allow. Like many eighteen-year-olds away from home, she wrote to her mother begging for more money while emphasizing her frugality:

and now for divers casual matters. I am going next time we go to town to get a black marino frock which I think is necessary because it will soon be too cold for prints in the morning so I shall have to take my mousline de laine & it would never do to take my black silk for afternoon because thou knowst it would be worn up almost in a fortnight and then I should have no gown for best but I have not got money enough to buy it with. Yes I have enough to buy the marino with but not enough for lining & pipings &c & one or two little things that I want but I have not been extravagant or got any thing that I do not want 2 prs of shoes came to 11*s* flannel 6*s* paint brush 3*s* it is a very good one pocket handkfs 1*s* stockings 3*s* 6 and gloves sewing silk cotton braid tape hooks pins ribbon comb & velvet cuffs bonnet ribbon waistband tooth brush tooth powder & fly to McGraffs so make up the 2£ that I have spent so thou sees I am short.[69]

To accentuate her request she advised, 'Aunt Anna has kindly given me a bonnet ribbon & payed for my bonnet being turned dost not thou think that you had better send me a little money & wilt thou write what thou writes to me about money & frocks & such like so that I read it out to Aunt Anna.'[70] She asked Isaac, 'will thou ask mother to put into the parcel the pattern of my frock perhaps she will find 2 I should like them both as I do not know which is the right one also the pencils'.[71]

Anna's dress fabrics – mousselaine de laine and merino – were *à la mode* in 1838.[72] Bonnets, which she mentions several times, were also very *in* in the 1830s as were the voluminous cloaks on which Mary advised her:[73] 'I will just say if thou shouldst think it needful to get a cloak do not get one of those blue *cloth* plaids. They look so very shabby the second year I have seen several looking miserably.'[74] Anna's request that her 'furr tippet'[75] and 'the tail of my boa'[76] be sent also shows that she followed the then recent vogue for wearing boas, otherwise known as tippets, made from furs such as ermine, sable, or grey squirrel.[77] Her wearing of fur, like her eating of meat, reveals that, typically of the time, her anti-cruelty to animals stance did not condemn the use of animals for food or apparel. It was probably also now that she began to wear her hair in the fashionable central parting and ringlets which she retained for life. She felt some guilt at her self-concern, asking Mary, 'will you pray for me for I am sorry to say I get very vain & thoughtless'.[78]

Anna's Manchester sojourn seems to have been intended in part as a finishing school for the soul and she was encouraged by her mother and her aunt to broaden her experience and knowledge of the world, particularly the religious world. The longest letter of the very few still existing in Anna's hand dates from this visit. Including sections to Philip, Mary, and Isaac, it is one of the rare places we find unadulterated Anna. In it she outlines her Manchester days which consisted of sewing, painting, reading, listening to others read aloud, writing letters and probably a journal, walking in the garden, charitable activities, outings with her stepcousins, and attending a slew of meetings and sermons, some connected with the Crewdsons' central role in the new Evangelical Friends. In an experimental 'journal system' section to Philip, as always graced by her idiosyncratic spelling and punctuation, she detailed these activities more fully:

Tuesday 2nd [October 1838] . . . in the morning I went to town with Aunt Anna to buy some silk &c for some fancy things we were going to make for a sale for the penitentiary we then went into a print shop and Aunt A hired for me a very nice drawing it is done on coloured paper with coulor chalk & white it was the inside of Chatres Cathedral quite a new stile to me – afternoon I worked in the evening we went to tea next door . . .
      Wednesday 3rd I read my chap in Isaiah Elizabeth is reading it too went to meeting . . . after that we went to the school room to help in giving out clothing came home at 1 . . . in the evening I went to the bible meeting at the Corn exchange the first I have been to.[79]

At this meeting she listened to one man whom she described as 'a little lush man just like a glass of champagne' and another 'who told us an interesting tale about an interview he had with a tribe of Bedouin Arabs & how they wanted him to stay and teach them'.[80]
      Two Crewdson relatives, Margaret and Hannah, came to stay adding to the lively household and Anna reported that on Thursday 4 October: 'I began my drawing at 12 we all of us set off in an omnibus full of us inside & out to see the new zoological gardens which are very nice we came home tired.'[81] The following day, she wrote:

Friday 5th washed my handkfs & darned my frock afternoon drew &c in the evening I went with Uncle & Aunt I R & E[82] to a kind of church meeting at Grosvenor St to consider about the propriety of drawing up a short history of the rise & progress of the Evangelical Friends & of the way in which it is to be done also about making themselves a body and the terms of membership the last subject was not determined being very difficult but there is to be another meeting in a fortnight at ½ past 6 on Friday 19th to consider further of it so you can imagine me at that time the meeting itself was not interesting but the subject was very important too so I shall go to all the meetings they have about it I intend as long as I can be admitted not being one of the congregation I think it will very much meet mothers view that I should get experience and information of all sorts & truly I think I am come to the right place for it Aunt Anna sometimes says 'Well Anna thou must go because thou knows thou wilt get experience here.'[83]

The previous year the Evangelical Friends, led by Isaac Crewdson, had built the 600-seat chapel in Grosvenor Street that Anna now often sat in. A contemporary visitor described it as 'plain and unassuming with a low platform and rostrum, but no pulpit. There were seats on the platform and in the room, and from the rostrum one of the leaders conducted the service, which was rather tame and frigid.'[84] Anna shared this view of Beaconite worship as unadventurous, telling Mary: 'they are a body that I should never think of joining although I respect them very much I do not think they will last in this present form longer than IC & WB[85] live . . . the communications are always upon rudiments much in friends style and you never get a new light upon a subject'.[86] She also witnessed the baptism of one 'Samuel Loyd', a Quaker minister for fifty years, who gave an account of his life that Anna found tediously long, except for the fact that he confessed to having broken '*every one*' of the ten commandments.[87] Her prediction that the Evangelical Friends would not endure was borne out when members soon drifted to other denominations, and when Isaac Crewdson died in 1844 the movement was effectively over and Baptists bought the chapel.[88]

Anna was actively looking for 'a new light' on spiritual subjects as the deliberate eclecticism of the meetings she attended illustrates. As well as regular Evangelical Friends meetings, she went with Robert and Elizabeth to a sermon by the prospective pastor 'of a persecuted church of the Waldenses', to other chapel services, and to a Methodist missionary meeting which had a range of speakers, she told Philip, who addressed:

> the thought of the 2nd advent & millenium and spoke of the time when the Jews would all be converted & we should see the tears of penitance stealing down their cheeks whilst kneeling at our altar one thing struck me especially they many of them seemed expecting some great though indefinite change & overturn & spoke of the expectation being general both in the world and the church. On the same evening we found afterwards there was a meeting of the Jews society at the corn exchange . . . if we had known we should surely have gone there.[89]

On the morning of Sunday 14 October she heard 'a nice sermon but nothing striking – I was very much troubled by my enemy drowsyness. Indeed I almost always am when I sit still it is very trying.' In the evening she went to another chapel and heard 'a very beautiful sermon' by a preacher who 'talked about the Millenarians baseless notions'.[90]

Millenarianism, the belief that Christ was about to reign on earth for one thousand years before the Second Coming, was in the air. Anna told Mary that her 22-year-old stepcousin Susannah was 'quite a Millenarian'.[91] Although she seems not to have shared this belief, Anna always preferred people and ideas with depth and felt she had found this in Susannah: 'I like Susannah very much she is I think very good I find more in her than in Elizabeth though I like E very much indeed.'[92]

Anna and Mary were currently interested in biblical prophecy and Anna's daily Manchester reading of chapters from the book of the prophet Isaiah was surely connected to this. 'I find prophecy very difficult', she admitted to her mother, 'but what can be clearer than that the Jews will be restored &c &c from Isa?'[93] She and her Aunt Anna were also reading a book on biblical types, that is, the foreshadowing in the Old Testament of future events, persons, or episodes in the New Testament. Anna may also have been experimenting with Plymouth Brethrenism. Founded in 1827 the Plymouth Brethren were puritanical evangelicals who emphasized prophecy, the millennium, and the belief that anyone might preach or celebrate Holy Communion. The Brethren enjoyed a very successful period before splitting into Open and Exclusive camps in 1849. 'I think I get on very comfortably,' Anna told Mary, 'I never speak about prophecy or Plymouth views unless I am spoken to I find that the best way . . . I do not see how a person can get bigotted here I endeavour to hold my own sentiments only so long as they can not be proved incorrect with regard to the Evangelical friends.'[94]

Of Anna it can truly be said that she had a mind and will of her own and used them. Although strongly influenced by her family, particularly Mary, she never followed opinion blindly and her beliefs were her own. Her mind was strong but open, which would later lead to painful wrestling with faith and doubt. At this stage of her spiritual journey she was listening to and pondering over new views, opinions, and denominations, but none of them entirely met her post-Quaker needs and her religious thinking was unsettled. 'I observe what thou says about going back in spiritual things,' Mary advised her, 'I seem unwilling to believe it is the case though to thyself it may appear so. We are often quite ignorant when we are growing most especially when we are seeing something of our vain, indolent and cold natures if thou keeps up prayer through all it will be well we do not cease to remember thee in our prayers.'[95]

Religious matters often featured in Anna's letters but so also, naturally, did health. Although she seems to have been able to walk at this time, her feet were still bothersome. On Monday 8 October she had visited a print works, probably her uncle's, and had, she told Philip, 'look[ed] over them . . . very minutely they are very interesting. My feet got very tired with so much standing about and going upstairs & downstairs. After dinner . . . I painted and rubbed my feet.'[96] Her current foot treatment seems to have been a prescribed method of rubbing – perhaps sometimes professionally done – together with applying lotion and plaster to them. '[N]ow I do not know what thou wilt say to me', she warned Mary:

but I must ask for a parcel for my lotion will not nearly hold out my plaister is almost done & my feet are worse thou knows chillblain time is come again & I have several which help a good deal to inflaim my feet wilt thou or Philip be kind enough to see Harrop about my feet perhaps he can give me a little advise how to treat them I am not at all disconcerted at their getting a little worse & hope you will not be because I have always found that whether my feet have got better or got worse it has been for my good & so I have no doubt it will be now but probably they will get better soon as the weather is very much against them I hope they will . . . I should like a quart bottle of lotion please & a good stock of plaister if the plaister is not part of Harrops quackery & he could give me the prescription to get it made up here it would be very convenient because I find that when it gets a little old it will scarcely stick.[97]

'I shall anxiously look for the next account of thy feet,' Mary wrote to Anna in November:

I am afraid the rubbing will be a heavy expense as well as trouble, dost thou think thou hadst better return before the specified time, so as to have the trouble & expense at home, I just mention this because I am not willing that we should burthen our friends and not because I think thou shouldst be better cared for at home.[98]

Anna's Manchester life remained happy and during the week of 9–16 October she lined her bonnet 'very nicely', made a flannel petticoat, 'fathfully' darned lots of stockings, did some worsted work, painted, walked in the garden, and supervised her youngest stepcousin's drawing. Her stepcousin Robert was reading them Boswell's *Life of Johnson* in the evenings, and they were all enjoying 'Todds Student' – 'what a capital book it is', she told Philip.[99] This was *The Student's Manual: Designed by Specific Directions to Aid in Forming and Strengthening the Intellectual and Moral Character and Habits of the Student* (1835) by the Reverend John Todd, pastor of the First Congregational church in Philadelphia. A much-reprinted self-help manual and moral guide, it included chapters on Diet, Exercise, Reading, Time,

Conversation, Politeness, Economy, Discipline of the Heart, Object of Study, and The Object of Life. In late November Philip told Anna, 'At tea time now Mother reads to us Todds Students Guide & we hope we are improving by its advice.'[100]

Anna desired detailed news from home. 'I hope thou wilt write me a good long letter,' she implored Philip, 'I want very much to know how my plants are mother has not mentioned them once about how high are the accacia's.'[101] 'I think thou hadst better write the whole of thy foolscap sheet to me,' she advised Mary, 'art thou reading anything particular why didst not thou tell me about that sermon about Noah's day & ours I want so much to know about it.'[102] She begged Isaac to send her 'a great deal of news by the parcel'.[103]

On 20 November Philip updated her on Brighton events including an account of the Sunday school society tea where he was asked to sit next to Mr Maitland and near 'Sir Thomas', 'quite in the best place'.[104] He described examination days at the school and reported: 'Last Sunday 2 boys were suspended & one degraded & I had a turnout with one of my boys . . . because he was uproarious & disobedient & set a bad example.'[105] He also told Anna, 'Thy Hop Picking and Basket boy is just gone by crying most musically "any fine young spring watercresses" it sounds quite musical.'[106]

Accounts Mary and Philip gave Anna of a recent sermon on Justification by Faith highlighted religious differences in the family. Philip told Anna it had been 'a most excellent sermon . . . the best on that I have ever heard'.[107] Mary, who agreed, revealed, 'Philip has not told thee that father went to St James on Sunday evening . . . and did not like the sermon at all, it was the most admirable clear and well argued sermon on the subject that I ever heard. I think I never felt so fully convinced that the doctrine of Justification by Faith is an odious doctrine to a quaker.'[108] Philip further relayed to Anna the comments of a 'very nice fellow' named Pennyfeather who 'pulled [the Friends] to pieces right and left, among other things, he said that when Christ came into Jerusalem & the people cried Hosanna & the Stones were like to cry out that if there had been a parcel of Quakers there they would not have said a word "because of their objections to singing"'.[109]

'Dear Philip is not looking very robust now,' Mary told Anna in November:

I think he has not sufficient exercise, he is frequently standing and leaning over the books all day long sometimes till late at nights, and gets neither walking nor fresh air I cannot cause father as yet to make an arrangement which could be easily done by altering his time for reading the newspaper for his having a good walk directly after breakfast – but I mean to go at it again . . . & thou knowest I can make out a case when I try.[110]

Isaac was immovable in his Quakerism and usually dictated why and when the family would move homes, but in most other matters he was no match for his dear Mary. Within the month she reported to Anna that Philip 'has had a good long walk every day since I wrote last'.[111]

Mary kept Anna apprised of the progress of their charitable activities. The most recent batch of servants she was training had now gone up to London to seek employment: 'I have still Mary Anne Hunter in the house who improves exceedingly & I hope if she remains with us a little longer "*undriven*" she will learn to use her hands and head together and be able to take a place.'[112] One of the Brighton families Anna regularly visited was, Mary reported, 'wretchedly poor . . . I have been giving them a few clothes and am lending them books as the young lady [Anna] did whom they will be very glad to see again.'[113] A string of other people also 'desired their love' to Anna, Mary told her.[114] '[W]ith respect to the Infant school,' Mary wrote, 'I should like that we should teach the little girl who now is allowed to mismanage the poor little things and pretty frequently visit it ourselves.'[115] At the Sunday school Mary had introduced patchwork: 'it is sufficiently exacting and amusing to keep them industrious indoors which is a habit I want so much to establish amongst the little girls as it will save them from bad company and idleness and as I withhold my grant of pieces if they are not sewed neatly I oblige them to work well'.[116] Of Anna's own Sunday school pupils she revealed: 'the children have left off telling stories and stealing which surely is something'.[117] The teacher filling in for Anna, Mary reported, 'tells me that thy displeasure is the rod she holds out over them. She always finds it effectual with Mary who cannot bear that thou shouldst know she is naughty. I told her I should not mention [her] little relapse to thee'.[118]

For all the serious subject matter discussed by Anna's family, laughter and good humour were just as much part of their daily life and familial bond. Mary, who must have cherished Anna's often wry observations, told her on 26 November that she was missing her companionship and humour:

I am again sat down to write to my own dear Nanny Oh that I had her by my side for a long cosy chat ... I am sitting ... with a bright cheerful fire and everything nice and comfortable only I am alone, how very slow the weeks go, it hardly seems nearer to Christmas than when we parted. I never knew such months as these have been, they seem to have a double number of weeks in them Father and Philip quite laugh at me for they constantly catch me saying 'I wonder what Anna is doing now' 'I wish dear Nanny was here' and many other such things but I do not mind them I think I could nearly perform Philips remarkable wriggle when I think of thy being with me again. I was saying at breakfast this morning that I should grow quite dull if I had not somebody to laugh and make merry with and father proposed that I should have Philip out of the Bank for one hour every morning to crack jokes with but I think this would not do.[119]

Although still expecting maternal chastisement and seeking Mary's approval, Anna nevertheless, in small but clear-sighted ways, was now increasingly 'mothering' and advising Mary. 'I am very glad that thy cold is nearly well,' she told Mary, 'pray take care of thy self well till I come back.'[120] She also expressed concern over some of Mary's associates: 'I am sorry the Elwins are so indiscreet & peculiar it is a good job that poor Mr Lane is quieted for a little while do pray beware of Miss Bull I am frightened to hear of thy close contact with her.'[121] The bond between mother and daughter was clearly strong. While Anna signs off sections of her longest letter to Philip and Isaac respectively, 'farewell dear, thy very affectionate sister AS' and 'With very dear love to thyself I remain thy very affectionate Daughter AS', to Mary she ends 'so farewell dearest mother thy every loving word put togeather AS'.[122]

Anna returned to Brighton soon after Christmas. She paid visits to a series of friends and relatives en route including Sarah

Stickney Ellis in London, the Huntons in Stoke Newington, and some relatives in Croydon. Philip after his own 'gad[ding] about in all directions', met her there before they travelled home to Brighton together.[123]

During her first two years in Brighton Anna expanded her horizons both geographically and intellectually, experimented with spiritual perspectives, met many new people, developed her teaching skills, and showed enthusiasm for knowledge and optimism for the future. Although many of her regular activities would continue, her remaining Brighton years were to be marked by bleakness. In Bayly's words, Anna's lameness 'weighted her life with a cross hard to bear',[124] but some crosses threatened to be even heavier. Anna was about to enter the darkest phase of her life from which she would not fully emerge until some six years later. Even then her resurgence would be more spiritual than physical. Aged only nineteen Anna was to become an invalid beset by physical impediments and racked by spiritual doubts.

FIVE

The Irresistible Charm
of Worldly Things
1839–45

*I may as well mention here what I suffered at this time from another
cause.* (*Black Beauty*, Chapter 46)

By the time Anna turned nineteen in March 1839 her lameness
had become only one in a tangle of symptoms that included
chest pains, weakness and pain in her back, inability to concentrate,
extreme fatigue, and periods of depression. On a trip away from
home she had fallen 'into the hands of a doctor who bled her
severely' for her lameness, but the remedy, Bayly writes, 'proved
worse than the disease', and Mary blamed this 'draining-away of
life' for the additional afflictions which now marked Anna's
health.[1] 'That one so gifted by nature, so exquisitely trained for the
good and the beautiful, so artistic, so intellectual, so charming in
every way, should for the larger portion of her life have been
handicapped by bodily frailty,' Bayly writes, 'is a fact we can only
record in silence.'[2]

Anna's invalidism resembled that of other Victorian women
such as Elizabeth Barrett, Christina Rossetti, and Florence
Nightingale, but was in its own way more permanently
debilitating. 'Many infallible cures were tried', Bayly writes, 'and
proved most fallible. Much was spent on physicians, but the poor
patient was nothing the better.'[3] No diagnosis of Anna's case
seems to have been made beyond 'invalid', but the many doctors
she consulted probably ran through their minds such conditions
as hypochondria, suffering from 'nerves' (then believed literally to
have stretched), hysteria (which could cause neuralgia, paraplegia,
and symptoms affecting head and spine), and what would later be
termed neurasthenia. Neurasthenia presented symptoms similar to
those of myalgic encephalopathy (ME) and Anna's own: chronic

fatigue, poor concentration, tenderness in the lymph nodes, muscle or joint pain, and headaches. ME and neurasthenia, however, are not usually permanent, while Anna's 'many disablements', as Bayly reports, remained with her for life: 'fluctuating while youth was strong, with intervals of "better" as well as "worse," but as time went on, gradually multiplying and increasing till, one after another, her loved employments had to be laid aside.'[4]

The disease that most closely fits Anna's symptoms is one that was unknown in her own lifetime and is today still difficult to diagnose as its symptoms mimic those of so many other conditions. Anna may have suffered from Lupus, in particular from Systemic Lupus Erythematosis (SLE), a severe form of the disease.[5] Ninety per cent of SLE sufferers are women and the disease, although insidious in its onset, often manifests in adolescence; for Anna near the time of her fall (or possibly even as early as her dislocated elbow). SLE is a chronic auto-immune disease in which the body attacks its own organs and sufferers typically experience 'flares' of debilitating symptoms between periods of better health (which vary in length from days to years). Anna's lameness and other ailments follow this flare pattern. Flares can be triggered by stress, overwork, sunlight, injury, or by no obvious cause. Each case of SLE is unique as the disease affects people differently depending upon which (of almost any) bodily organs are affected. Typical symptoms include prolonged and extreme fatigue, muscle pain or weakness, joint pain and swelling, headaches, foggy concentration, back and chest pain. Most of these Anna experienced. Two paintings of Anna,[6] one of her in her early teens and one probably in her early forties, both show her with rosy cheeks. This might have been artistic licence, or it may indicate the classic – but by no means universal – Lupus 'butterfly' rash across the sufferer's cheeks. SLE is an isolating disease because the level of exhaustion, even between flares, often makes everyday things – walking to the post office, going out with friends, even reading a book – difficult, if not impossible. Periods of associated depression, moreover, are not uncommon.

Anna's afflictions during her remaining six years in Brighton were not merely physical but religious and emotional. Spiritual dissatisfactions filigreed her mind, and she fell into what she referred to as 'the darkness'. Perhaps in part through trying to reconcile a belief in a just God with the injustice of her physical condition, Anna experienced an 'eclipse of faith',[7] and her soul's cry was, as Bayly records, like 'Job's, "Oh that I knew where I might find Him!"'[8]

The longings of Anna's heart were at odds with the faith that had until now, despite her quest for a new spiritual home, seemed fairly stable. She wrote in her journal of the irresistible charm of worldly things[9] and surely longed for love, freedom, excitement, and the pleasures and entertainments she saw passing her by. Yet Anna also longed for faith and spiritual calm. Her spiritual crisis was not a rebellion away from religion and towards the 'world', but rather, because her faith was so much a part of who she was, it was a distressing ongoing struggle to follow God's will and keep her own desires in check.

Anna was very severe on herself for perceived sins and lapses into worldliness and she prayed for enlightenment. 'Lord, do break my bondage', she wrote, 'for I have not strength to do it myself. I have not strength to give myself up to Christ in the sense of being willing that His perfect Will should be fulfilled in me, lest it should mean an entire crucifixion of self.'[10] This destruction of 'self' was to become one of the prime tasks of her life, but at a time when her adult self was newly emerging, having to suppress her desires cost her those agonies that only the young feel so deeply.

Decades later Mary would write of Anna's invalidism:

and so the years passed on, neither of us yielding to despair – [Anna] always doing the most she could do and doing it cheerfully . . . what she suffered never made gloom or a cloud in the house. She never brooded over her loss of power or the loss of the changes in amusements which others enjoy . . . there never came the slightest cloud between us.[11]

In later years this idealization proved more accurate, but, during Anna's early twenties, brooding, depression, and strains in the mother–daughter relationship certainly did arise. These were years of adjustment and anxiety and, like a constant ache that masks deeper pain, awareness that Anna's condition was not improving lay between them. Anna had her own difficult forest to hack her way through but her family, who never gave up hope of a cure, also had to adjust to Anna's new situation, as Mary later admitted:

> I conclude *now*, that the blessed Lord saw that he could make a more exquisite character out of that noble independent courageous capable creature by imprisoning it in the strictest limitations than by giving it the play of a full development – but Oh how often did my heart yearn over those apparently wasted faculties. How often did my heart bleed to see the cramp of these crippling fetters sometimes upon one faculty, sometimes upon another leaving her powerless to execute what she could see so clearly & do so well.[12]

Anna must have experimented with the cures on her own doorstep. Besides its salutary coastal air, Brighton offered sea and spa waters for both bathing in and drinking. She may have been carried out over the waves to a bathing-machine by what A.B. Granville, in his 1841 *Spas of England and Principal Sea-Bathing Places*, calls one of the 'lusty neptunes' employed for the purpose'.[13] There, dressed in a long flannel gown and cap, she would have been plunged into the sea by a female 'dipper'. She may have visited one of the bath-houses or the chalybeate spring or taken the waters at the Royal German Spa which offered mineral waters that imitated those of the famous German spas such as Carlsbad and Marienbad.

The 'cure' Anna most commonly took was a change of air and scenery, and visits away also provided her with an opportunity to consult a wider range of physicians. In February 1840 she was in Croydon for over a month staying at Broad Green Lodge with Mary's cousin, Emma Crowley. Croydon offered new company and, like Buxton, offered that which increasingly gave Anna her only physical sense of liberty and power: horses. 'I hope thou rides on thy pony every day', Mary encouraged her.[14] In Brighton it was impractical and unnecessary for the family to keep a horse, but horses were, implicitly, one of the cures attempted for Anna's condition and in the long run by offering her happiness, companionship, freedom, and literary purpose they gave her far more than any other remedy she would try.

'Pray let me know always more particularly about thy health than anything else,' Mary told Anna: 'if E Japlines medicine does not produce the desired effect I should after a short trial think of A Todhunter's[15] Doctor as time is wearing away – I think thou shouldst go on with Hoopers pills because Edward['s] prescription does not affect "thy things?"'[16] She soon wrote again asking Anna, 'How does painting affect thee?'[17] and gave further medical instructions:

My dearest child I have just received a reply to my letter from A Todhunter. She very kindly went immediately on the receipt of it to Dr B— and read to him the minute description I gave to him of thy case, both as it affected thy mind & body. He would not give a decided opinion without seeing thee but Anne says he thought the homeopathic system the only one likely effectually to reach thy case and he saw no reason why it should not – Father & I have concluded that it would be best to see him once and hear what he says, he will not undertake the case unless he is well satisfied that he can cure. Anne mentions that she will go with thee on Saturday Monday or Tuesday morning whichever may be most convenient to thee . . . Thou hadst better go up by an Omnibus and then ask the driver to put thee into a coach or Cab to take thee to Sackville Street where the Dr lives – thou wilt be sure not to get *run over*.[18]

That Anna's ailments were spiritual as well as physical is made clear from a letter that missionary *manqué* Philip sent to her at Croydon. Philip was now living in Lewes, a market town eight miles from Brighton, where he was a clerk in the London and County Bank. He was taking Greek lessons and studying in the evenings towards his new goal of becoming a missionary, and on Saturday evenings regularly walked to Brighton to spend Sundays with Anna and his parents. On 6 February he told Mary that he was reading Josephus's account of Hades and 'The bosom of Abraham' which claimed that: 'At the Resurrection all are clothed with their own bodies rendered incorruptable – with this addition to the lot of the wicked "that all the diseases &c" which their bodies had cleave to the immortal one immortally – but the bodies of the Righteous are rendered pure.'[19] This statement casts light on what Anna might have imagined or feared for her own afterlife: if righteous enough a cured body, if not eternal suffering.

Philip wrote to Anna in more directly ministering tones:

It is more and more apparent to me, that God loves your soul, and had his eye particularly directed towards you, to aid, and preserve you, and gradually to lead you to place your life and delight in him alone, and in the unconditional and voluntary submission to the whole of his divine will. To this end, are all your sufferings and troubles, and from this arises, chiefly, all your vexations, and the *disrelish* and *indifference you feel towards divine things* because the Life of Self sees its end approaching, and still does not like that its fate is so fully decided, and that the sentence will be executed, without mercy. I conjecture also, that there are sometimes seasons, in which a little hope and encouragement is given to this Life of Self, which makes it feel still more severely, when the hand of Divine love again nails it to the cross, and leads it whither it would not.[20]

He urged Anna to 'be *submissive* and wait', as her suffering was part of God's plan. 'Do not regard yourself too much', he warned. 'The saviour had incomparably more to endure in order to redeem us, and still he heals our burdens.'[21]

These sentiments may well have provoked in Anna gall and guilt in equal measure, but Philip was not merely being pompous. In the God-loving Sewell family in God-fearing Victorian England the state of Anna's soul was of even more concern than the distressing state of her body. Not only, as Mary believed, is there 'no other "exceeding joy" left for' people 'who will shut God out',[22] but spiritual doubts might herald the eternal damnation of one's soul. Thus Anna's family gave her spiritual encouragement in any terms they saw fit.

While she was in Croydon Isaac was recommended for a new banking position and Anna, Philip, and Mary agonized over the possibility that Anna and her parents might have to move, probably to somewhere in or near London and away from Philip. '[H]ow curious it is', Mary noted to Anna, 'that our times of perplexity always almost occur when we are separate. I conclude we should not be sufficiently *exercised by it* together.'[23] She warned Anna not to discuss the matter with anyone at Croydon and reported that Philip's '*will* was very much opposed to' the move.[24] She told Anna 'that there were two sides to the question, and that self denial and sacrifice lay on the side of wife and children',[25] but also expressed her vexation over Isaac's attitude:

> Philip was surprised to find how much [Father's] mind inclined to the change and how entirely it escaped his observation that we should have anything to give up it is absolutely astonishing to me how he overlooked our side of the question. So thou knows if we have to leave we shall get no praise for our self denial . . . but thou knows we may not have to go, this may only be a shaking to alarm us.[26]

After much agitation and prayer a decision was made to leave the matter in the hands of God in the form of the directors of the London and County Bank, who decided to keep Isaac in Brighton.

Although some family resentment festered against Isaac in regard to his position as *paterfamilias* and thus decider of residential fates, Mary also reassured Anna that all at heart was well:

> Thou asked in one letter if father was nice and pleasant, nobody can be more so and no good Darby and Joan can jog on more amicably than we do. He is quite in his high places now as is likely, the respect held [for] him in the meeting and the proposal of his name for this situation would affect a man less susceptible of inflation.[27]

Comparatively little is known about Isaac beyond the fact that he was tall, very kind, and a respected Quaker. A writer of a 'sketch' about Philip Sewell described Isaac as 'a shrewd man of business, but a very loveable nature with a keen sense of humour'.[28] Bayly's daughter, Elisabeth Boyd Bayly, recalled: 'All who knew him, however slightly, will remember his overflowing kindliness, and a peculiar courtesy of manner, alike to rich and poor.'[29]

Mary's letters to Anna in this period were loving, concerned about Anna's health, chatty about family matters, and deep about religion but they also often contained motherly advice or criticism that could be unflinchingly candid. In one of her letters to Croydon, Mary informed Anna:

> I have been scrutinising thy writing to see what is the cause of its looking so very poor and I think it is the very ugly angular turns back thou terminates so many of thy words and the very small Capital letters – I . . . give thee praise for thy increased neatness in writing but I [do not] like the character of the writing it looks pinched and mean.[30]

She also often admonished Anna for her erratic spelling: 'pray do not make mistakes in the spelling – "present" thou always spells wrong and "underneath" and "Arnott" should be spelled with a Capital letter'.[31] Philip, too, felt a younger brother's freedom to chastise: 'when thou writes the words "Holy Ghost – do not please spell it "*Holy Gohst*" as in my letter of today'.[32]

Bayly notes of Mary that it 'is rather striking that one so full of intense sympathy with the erring and fallen could be so merciless, not only on cruelty and oppression, but on easy, slippery faults – laziness, bad work, wastefulness, and every sort of giddy way that tends to break the hedge of modesty and reverence'.[33] A friend later recalled that Mary 'was very conscious of her own tendency to speak sometimes more strongly than she intended, whether in criticism or rebuke, and had a kind of despairing admiration for those who could keep the iron hand in a velvet glove'.[34] Anna certainly experienced some non-velvet treatment that at this stage of life she may not have appreciated.

Mary's most searing extant maternal remarks are enclosed in a prompt to Anna not to outstay her welcome in Croydon:

> I should be sorry that as thou art going to see [Dr B—], that thou shouldst leave Croydon just yet and yet thou must now mention it . . . 'Thou seems my dear child to be staying very quickly on at our kind relations, as if thou have hadst no desire to change thy home, but thou knowest there is such a thing as wearing out your welcome after a months visit, especially if you are an invalid who usually gives more trouble and affords less pleasure than other visitors – therefore although thou hast not at present derived the

benefit that we had hoped from change of air &c yet father and I both think thou must not longer trespass upon the kindness and hospitality of our friends, but proceed to pay the third visit thou mentions at P Friths and then return to thy own dear home where thou will be welcome always in sickness in health in low spirits or high.'[35]

However used to plain speaking Anna was, Mary's wince-inducing comments about the pleasureless imposition of invalid guests cannot have failed to sting and can have done little to lift her mood at a time when the fluxes of her life seemed weighted towards pain. Strangely this paragraph may have been meant to be read aloud by Anna to her relatives as Mary uses quotation marks and prefaces it with the words, 'I will try to write a sentence that may be read' – possibly as a ploy to induce Anna's hosts to insist 'Oh no, you are no trouble, please stay longer.' Equally mysteriously, however, on the back of the letter there is a postscript probably in Mary's hand stating, 'Put this letter immediately in thy pocket and burn this half sheet the first opportunity.'[36]

Anna did not burn the letter, instead she jotted down on it a prescription for treating her feet:

1 of kesin
4 of diaculum
to make as adhesive plaister for bandaging sore legs after strapping the wound round with strips of plaister bandage the leg from the toe up to the knee with calico bandages do this every day.[37]

She did obey Mary in moving on from Croydon to the home of P. Frith, possibly another of Mary's many cousins, who lived at Thornton Heath near Croydon.

Despite their sometimes preacherly advice – 'It is a good plan to be continually obstinately determined to frustrate Satan'[38] – Philip's letters to Anna were also newsy and had brotherly touches. He notes in one: 'If this appears to be most illegible & badly written please to remember that I am sitting in my bed room & have been up since 10 minutes to six & am now gradually freezing.'[39] In signing off another he noted, 'I need not go over all that rigmarole abt unaltered affection &c that thy often do.'[40] He also included titbits that would interest her, such as this from a letter in April 1840:

> I went to see an old man the other night 84 years old who had served in Nelsons fleet a long while & he told me that he looked thro a telescope at the moon once '& it was just like the Earth there was a river and trees growing on each side & some cottages near the banks of it, & some large stones he should suppose abt 8 or 10 ton weight each'![41]

From Thornton Heath Anna travelled on to Buxton, at a time when some distressing family event had occurred, possibly concerning her Uncle Richard, and Anna was very concerned about the impact of this on Mary. 'I want thee to watch over her as much as thou canst at Lewes', Anna directed Philip on 18 April 1840:

> if she is not taking something for her cough thou must get her something because she is so very backward to take care of her self & dear father though very kind has not perception enough to be a good care taker of others. I am afraid that after all this distress and anxiety with a cold and cough which is always so long in leaving her that she will be completely knocked up as she was a short time since . . . I am very sorry that the Ellises are come to trouble her do not let her follow her kind feelings towards poor EE to her own inconvenience & trouble because any other person in the house at such a time as this must be a trial I think thou must go over some evening this week & see how she is & how things go on & comfort & strengthen her as much as thou canst. Now dear I do depend upon thee to stand a little in my place & make her consider herself as well as others, do not think that I am in a stew & a fright about her because I am not only I know how a little upsets her & especially in the Spring when she is never strong. Do not tell her thou hast had this or else she will think that I am anxious & she will not write to me freely about herself lest it should make me more so but please dear Philip do write to me by return of post & tell me all about things & how mother is in health & spirits. I sadly want to be at home but must depend upon thee. What a dreadful state

poor Uncle is in what will become of him. May we all be the better & holier for this affliction & learn the lesson that this is not our rest.[42]

'EE' was undoubtedly Elizabeth Ellis, one of Sarah Stickney Ellis's stepdaughters, who was, like Anna, an invalid and had stayed with Mary more than once during the past two months, something Mary confessed to Anna was a 'trial'.[43] Anna may well have felt chagrin at Elizabeth's time-consuming presence in her own absence. The mal-timed visits of invalid daughters, however, were not a one-way affair, for six years later on 10 May 1846 Sarah wrote: 'Anna Sewell is coming to spend to-morrow with me, and from seven in the morning till twelve at night I have never ceased working.'[44]

On 22 April 1840 Philip wrote to Anna at Buxton, thanking her for 'thy advice abt sloth. I prayed against it at Sacrament on G Friday & hope that the prayer of faith was given me.'[45] 'I am glad thou art reading D'aubegné,' he told her, 'I like it very much.'[46] This was Jean Henri Merle D'Aubigné's recently translated *History of the Great Reformation of the Sixteenth Century in Germany, Switzerland, &c*. Its title might indicate a rather dry read, but Quaker diarist William Lucas described the first two volumes as 'written in a flashy, almost dramatic style, startling and interesting, but not in the calm, rational manner that becomes history'.[47]

Philip also passed on to Anna his employer Mr Drakes's remarks about her: 'Mr D is now interrupting me & saying thou art "none of your stuck up ones" nothing finikin abt her "& possessed of very good sense" only she has bad health poor thing. She is one of the right sort Boxer for Ever!!!"'[48] '[T]hanks to Mr D for his fine speaches of me only do not tell him so', Anna replied on 30 April.[49]

Anna was, as Mr Drakes professed, a young woman without pretensions. She was also unswayed by the intellectual or spiritual whims of others and examined her own beliefs with exacting care. This precision of thought together with her sense of probity and fierce desire for truth undoubtedly caused some of her spiritual difficulties at this time. Slovenly thinking was something she fought against in herself and on occasion chastised others for. On 22 April Philip had informed her, 'Mr Nicolayson of Jerusalem has discovered the old Temples Foundations – it is believed.'[50]

Well-versed in current events herself, Anna was having none of Philip's imprecision. In mock shock that 'my staid matter of fact brother too!!' could be so inexact, she rebuked him:

> I am quite amused at finding that thou like some others here have quite decided that the foundations found by Mr Nicolayson must be those of the old Temple now the Record does not say they are & only suggests that they are some of the foundations of Zion it is a delightful idea that a Christian church should be built on the very stones of the ancient Temple but I think we must not give it out as thou doest . . . that the foundations of the Temple are discovered . . . however it is said that they shall build the old wastes.[51]

Anna's tenacious mind was nothing lacking, but her health at Buxton was still poor although only a fleeting postscript, 'I am rather stronger the last day or two', acknowledges this.[52] She was leading a desultory life at Dudwick Cottage, even though spring was transforming the countryside and the cuckoos were singing: 'I do not know what to write about', she told Philip, 'as there is nothing going on here & I have no Sunday School as thou hast to tell about and as for my self I am so very barren of all that is good or interesting that I can not look for any thing from that Quarter.'[53] She did, however, want to know about her beloved plants: 'Wilt thou tell me when thou writes next (for I think thy thoughts are more disengaged than mothers) how my little accacias are looking & how the plants in general do whether the Arum is in flower & if the Baseliana is brought upstairs yet &c &c.'[54]

'[B]e sure to tell me how mother is when thou writes', she directed Philip, 'I have not heard from her for some time but I suppose she is very busy I rather look for a letter today they have not sent me last weeks Atlas. Grandfather & Aunt Ellen & I want to see it very much & this weeks too but I suppose they cannot be sent after they are a week old can they?'[55] The requested 'Atlas' was probably *The Atlas*, 'a newspaper and journal of literature' designed for 'India, China and the colonies'. Anna may have been physically static for long periods but her mind roved the world and she was eager for news and stimulating material. Before she even finished writing her letter that wish was gratified, as she told Philip: 'The Post is in & no letter for me tell Mother I am very much disappointed but one Atlas is come & I am glad of that.'[56]

She had also just read John Bunyan's *A True Relation of the Holy War Made by King Shaddai upon Diabolus for the Regaining of the Metropolis of the World or, the Losing and Taking Again of the Town of Mansoul* (1682), a spiritual allegory after the manner of his *Pilgrim's Progress*. 'I am afraid that I have a great many of the Diabolonians lurking within & around my walls still,' she told Philip, 'especially one Carnal security & one Love the Flesh who are very great enimies to Mansoul.'[57] She clearly felt that she was giving into the charms of worldly things at the expense of the spiritual.

Anna's denominational search also continued. 'I should like to have my Moravian papers sent I dare say they will come for 2*d*', she told Philip.[58] The Moravian Brethren, who she may now have been considering as her Quaker replacement, had links with the Lutheran church and followed a plain and unworldly form of Christianity, using hymns mainly of German origin, and rejecting doctrinal formulae.

During her Brighton years Anna's remedies for body and soul involved trying to keep to the path of legitimate medicine and authentic religion without being taken in by quackery or false preachers, but in Brighton the straight and narrow was sometimes hard to find. 'We came into a world of very varied interest at Brighton', Mary wrote, 'and I was not as quick as I might have been, to see that all is not gold that glitters. I am afraid I wasted a good deal of my time on people and theories that gave me nothing worth having in return.'[59] An 1851 guidebook states that the 'supply of "pet parsons" in Brighton has always been large',[60] and Anna and Mary with their religiously questing minds were likely targets for unscrupulous or misguided fishers of men, or what was so much more pervasive, of women. Mary was more receptive than Anna to voguish spiritual offerings, as she admitted: 'I am so ready to believe there must be something to learn from those who profess to teach. I have been rather given to listen to "Lo heres" and "Lo theres" in my time, and pay my threepence, or whatever it might be. And *I* have been bitterly disappointed, many times.'[61] For a while they attended the services of a man who, in Bayly's words, 'professed to have received direct teaching from Heaven, and to have fresh light to impart, especially concerning the work of the Holy Spirit'.[62] Mary seems to have been susceptible to the charms of earnestly spiritual men, but even clearer-eyed Anna was swept along this time and both had very high hopes of this preacher. Discovering him to be a false idol they were, as Bayly recounts, 'proportionately disappointed when the disenchantment came'.[63]

This artful prophet may have been the Reverend Henry James Prince, an Anglican minister who founded the messianic, millenarian Agapemonite sect. He came to Brighton in 1843 and set himself up as minister of the proprietory Adullum Chapel in Windsor Street. A magnetic and persuasive preacher, he held particular charm for women and wrote a series of popular books and pamphlets. In *The Great Declaration* he claimed that he had been chosen above all others by God as the perfect man in whom sin could not exist and that his own immortality might be shared by those who believed in him. He also maintained that 'spiritual marriages' with 'soul mates' were possible without marriage, thus the pleasures of the flesh could be indulged in without either the bonds of marriage or any trace of sin. Prince amassed around £30,000 from Brighton followers before leaving to set up his *Agapomene* or Abode of Love in Spaxton, Somersetshire where he took many 'spiritual wives' and caused numerous scandals.[64] It is improbable that Anna was ever a 'bride' of Prince, but his magnetic qualities or those of any similarly magnetic preacher might well have caused some degree of para-spiritual infatuation that left her distraught when the hero fell. This 'false teaching', at Brighton, Bayly writes, did not delude Anna but it 'dimmed and unsettled the old bright faith'.[65]

In October 1840 Mary and Anna were both experiencing a doldrums of faith. Mary was in Dover giving solace to 'our dear cousins', John and an ill Mary,[66] whose baby had just died, probably at birth. She told Anna that spiritually she had offered the bereaved parents guidance and practically she had done what the parents could not:

Yesterday I took the baby in a Fly to be buried . . . I took the servant with me, and walked as chief and only mourner over the little one . . . In the evening I went to the Wesleyan chapel and did not pick up a crumb – I can assure thee I am not at all overdone –

thou knowest enough of thy queer mother to be aware that I [will] be all *alive*, where there is *death* or *danger* but though alive in the *flesh*, I am still dead in the spirit – and am only amazed at my proficiency in playing the hypocrite.[67]

'The violence of their grief I am glad to say is very much abated', she told Anna a few days later, while confessing her guilt at not opportunistically evangelizing:

I do not think the arrow has gone deep enough to do much good. They will presently be just as heretofore & I feel I do not make the most of it. I never was in a position that seemed to chide me more for not taking advantage of it but I am powerless . . . I get wickeder & wickeder and yet positively they think I am good, I'm quite ashamed.[68]

Anna's own struggles with faith continued, and her health or spirits had also again plunged, Mary asking her, 'father tells me my darling is not quite so well. What is the matter? Thou didst not mention it – pray tell me in thy next – let me also say pray take care of thyself.'[69] In her second Dover letter Mary reiterated her concern, 'I had a very nice letter from dear Philip yesterday but the part did not please me in which he did not think thee nearly so well. Thou must let me know exactly how this is and what in particular is the matter.'[70]

Despite her condition, Anna was involved in training the servants who surely provided welcome company when her health and Mary's activities meant she might for hours have no other. She undoubtedly taught them to cook her own specialities: plum puddings, sausage rolls, and apple pies,[71] but more integral was moulding their moral and religious natures. In December 1843 she would report to Philip, 'Our Sarah is quite awakened to see that she is a great sinner but she can not yet believe.'[72] In 1845 she told him of another servant: 'Mary took the sacrament this morning Mother thinks she is quite fit to do so how pleasant it is to have Christian servants.'[73]

During her early twenties Anna paid more than one visit to Royal Leamington Spa.[74] She was certainly there early in 1841, at a time when Leamington was one of the most prestigious inland spas in the country, frequented by the cream of fashionable society.[75] Her treat-

ment may have involved taking Leamington salts or having
prescriptions made up at one of the many chemists who flourished
on the new prescribing system of medicine.[76] She perhaps consulted
Dr Jephson, a prominent physician, who like many doctors at the
time favoured a one-remedy-cures-all-ills approach, his particular
physic being 'preparations of iron, with or without sulphuric acid'.[77]
She possibly bathed or took the waters at the Royal Pumproom
which touted itself as 'excelling all the baths in England, and
rivalling the thermæ of the ancients'.[78] It may have been safer not to,
however, for its water, drawn from a river that received the town's
effluent, had in Granville's observation, 'an exceedingly nauseous
taste and a most objectionable look besides, being of a dark
yellowish green hue, with many floating particles in it'.[79] Bathing
cures were offered at establishments such as Mr Goold's which
boasted white marble-tiled baths and 'besides every other
convenience . . . that luxurious appendage to a lady's toilet, a *cheval
glass*'.[80] Anna's health, however, seems to have worsened rather than
improved for her stay was prolonged.

'[H]ow much I sympathize with thee in thy further detention', her
cousin Lucy wrote on 2 April 1841. 'I have just had a short note
from thy dear mother in which she says, "we do not indeed know
what a day may bring forth."'[81] These were painful months for
Anna, and the family were clearly very worried about her condition
and about other unnamed family tribulations in Norfolk. Lucy
urged upon Anna spiritual discipline, confidence in God's love, and
advised her to be 'anxious for nothing but in every thing by prayer
& supplication with thanksgiving let your requests be made known
unto God'.[82] Her words of spiritual comfort must have offered Anna
some emotional salve for she marked the letter, 'To be kept.'[83]

'I am very thankful that thou art arrived safe at the end of thy
journey,' Mary wrote to Anna on a later Leamington visit either in
late 1842 or early 1843:

> no doubt very tired but that thou left out but so far all is well and
> I hope in thy next letter it will be still better . . . when the coach
> wheeled off & I could see thee no more I bolted my heart down
> my throat & followed thy loving advise and went and ordered
> soap & butter . . . Pray write me directly the doctors opinion

about thee. Thou left after all my trouble the statement of thy maladies at home.[84]

Anna's companion on this visit seems to have been fellow family invalid Aunt Wright who, in late 1841, had herself been confined for many weeks to a 'Hydrostatic bed' although she always asked after Anna:

I hope dr Anna is better I was grieved to hear her foot was again a check to her activity – how remarkably that dr girl is laid by – that one cannot but mourn for her whilst faith whispers it must end well for her dr Spirit; Her hopes . . . & submission speak a lively lesson to us – she is a sweet dear creature.[85]

Anne Wright would have been an ideal companion for Anna as she understood the experience of invalidism, was strong in her own faith, a keen reader, and passionate about the natural world.

Anna's second Leamington visit coincided with Philip's moving to Yorkshire. The loss of his companionship, even if it had only been at the weekends, must have further depressed her spirits. After vacillating over whether a missionary or banking life was his true calling, Philip had decided for the ministry and had been accepted at Cambridge for the necessary training, but before he could take up his place he suffered a breakdown in his health. His dreams of missionary life were dashed and even his banking career was drawn-up short because his doctor advised him to pursue an outdoor career. He decided to train as a civil engineer and in 1842 or 1843 had taken an engineering position with a railway company in Yorkshire and was living at the home of Joseph Thornton at Kettlethorpe Hall near Wakefield.

Anna wanted to know all about Philip's new life, which was, Mary reported, truly an armour-buckling experience:

The moral character of things . . . is unqualified evil masters and men all alike no recognition of God in any way, but swearing & every evil work . . . [Philip] seems to have set his face as a flint with determination through the grace of God to walk uprightly and reprove faithfully and it is evident from two or three little things that he has already acquired a *little* influence . . . he feels no doubt whatever as to the propriety of his choice though [he] is indeed in a moral wilderness . . . I have not so many particulars as thou wished for, next time I hope I shall have more.[86]

After her return from Leamington, Anna wrote frequently to Philip, always keen to know when he might visit home again. In early December 1843 she reported some good news to him, perhaps a resurgence in her faith or health, for on 8 December he replied, 'Many & great thanks to thee for thy nice letters & for the glad tidings which they bring – One would think even the stones ought to cry out at the great mercies which you seem to have showering down about & upon you.'[87] He reported on his decision to formally resign from the Quakers, which would become official on 16 February 1844:[88] 'I have sent by this post to Father my resignation to Friends – do thou look at it please & see where thou thinks it wanting & then when I return we can talk.'[89]

During her Brighton years Anna did have periods when she could walk and indulge in social activities typical of her age and station in life, and she clearly sought stimulation. In 1844 she wrote in her journal of 'pleasant walks with her friends' and visits to art galleries in London.[90] She probably attended the Royal Academy exhibition which that year included paintings by one of her favourite artists: Edwin Landseer, the painter, engraver, and sculptor famous for his animal studies.

It was not her intellectual or artistic life, however, but her emotional and spiritual one that needed feeding. Of history classes she attended she confessed: 'They are very interesting, but they do not satisfy the soul. I am very miserable.'[91] She had clearly experienced depressive malaise in addition to her other ailments over the past few years, and this was possibly exacerbated or provoked by that which induces a misery almost unmatched by any other – unrequited love.

There is no firm evidence of any potential suitor, but, given Anna's age, the comparatively social nature of her life at this time, and the probability that her friends were involved in romances or marrying, it is not implausible to suggest that she may have set her heart upon some unreciprocant or a person unsuitable.

Two possible love-interests emerge. One is Henry S. King who remained a family friend for many years. Three years Anna's senior and described in later life as 'a man of no ordinary force of character', Henry was hard-working, enthusiastic, and urbane, a thorough businessman, an excellent conversationalist, and, like Anna, had an iron will and strong sense of duty covering a tender and loving heart.[92] Later to become a respected publisher, banker, and East India agent, and play an important role in the establishment of Mary's writing career, when Anna met him he was a self-made man running a bookselling business in Brighton.[93] A brother's close friend in whom one's mother delighted was undoubtedly a suitable marriage prospect and frequent caller, and Anna may well have developed feelings for Henry.

Anna's other feasible love interest is her stepcousin, Robert Crewdson, one year older than she, who on her Manchester visit had read Boswell's *Life of Johnson* aloud to the young company. From Manchester Anna had reported to Philip that Robert had returned home early one day when all but Anna had gone to Meeting, '& enlightened me on the subject of the corn laws & reciprocity system as conected with shipping interests. I never saw any body with so much information especialy on history as Rbt & he thinks about everything.'[94] A conversation about trade and economy might not seem the stuff of ardour, but Anna's tastes were surely towards intelligent and earnest men. She was also a passionate newshound and anything that improved her knowledge of current affairs appealed. Her most telling phrase is 'he thinks about everything', making him a man after her own heart, but whether that heart was romantically inclined towards this cogitative young man can only be speculation.

Anna's heart had been broken, if not romantically then spiritually, but in 1845 she found a love that would not fail her. 'At the beginning of this month we went on Sunday morning to Clarence Chapel', she recorded in her journal on 7 January:

Mr Warren preached from the text, 'Christ has redeemed us from the curse of the law, being made a curse for us.' It was a powerful sermon, and the Lord mercifully used it as the conveyance of His good Spirit, to bring again life and light to my dark soul. As I listened, I truly felt Christ precious. I believed, and was justified from all things. I was made to sing as in years long past. This is not, I trust, a transient revival. I do now trust in none but Jesus.[95]

Although she would experience phases of spiritual relapse, Anna's 1845 resurgence of faith did prove to be more than transient and brought with it greater calm and happiness, both about the here-and-now and the hereafter. 'I heard today of the happy death of another of our Sunday School girls', Anna told Philip. 'She had left the School & had shewn for some time by her fruits that she was a branch of the true vine – is not it very encouraging? I more & more value Sunday schools.'[96]

On her twenty-fifth birthday Anna wrote in her journal: 'This is my birthday. Oh, what a happy one compared to any I have had so long! I feel as if I had exchanged a rough, stormy sea for a calm, smooth river.'[97] The settling of her passions came to her as an enormous relief, but obedient faith required constant endeavour, as she confirmed the same day:

Last Sunday was the first time I took my class in the afternoon. I did not get on very well, for in the morning I had given way to sin, and therefore did not get near to Christ, for I sinned wilfully, knowingly resisting the voice of the Spirit in my heart, and so the sting was left behind. The darkness returned for two or three days, then I was able to lay my sin at the feet of my Saviour, and leave it there. To-day (Sunday) I had a very pleasant time with my children, and taught them from Daniel, third chapter.[98]

By the time Anna regained her faith and spirits Brighton had become a much busier place. In 1841 the London–Brighton railway line had opened making travel not only much faster (around two hours versus a coach trip of four or five), but cheaper. On 21 September 1841 the bells of St Nicholas pealed out and townsfolk watched through thick fog as the first train to London left at 6.45 a.m. Perhaps Anna was among the throng that gathered around the railway station and along the line in the beautifully clear afternoon cheering as the first train from London steamed in, auguring great things for the town.[99] Brighton teemed ever more with visitors and residents, the population increasing from 46,661 in 1841 to 65,573 ten years later,[100] and even churches were becoming overcrowded.

This railway-forged burgeoning was marvellous for travellers and Brighton businesses but not so delightful for those who relished a degree of peace and quiet. Brighton was a place which, in Granville's terms, suited those 'on whom a living panorama of artificial life, rather than the aspect of nature, makes a favourable impression'.[101] Mary had always lamented the lack of rural vistas, feeling, 'It was all dead in Brighton, houses and stones,'[102] and Isaac understood her countryside yearnings, taking her by train out of Brighton sometimes 'to feast her longing eyes with the sight of a wood'.[103] It was probably Mary's distaste for living in crowded towns, perhaps recalling the painful period of Anna's infancy in London, that led the family in 1845 to move to Lancing, nine miles west of Brighton along the Sussex coast. The quieter, more rural conditions of Lancing may also have been thought preferable for Anna's health, and that commonest of motives for Victorian home moves – financial pressures – may also have added impetus. Even in 1841, Granville reported, the 'cost of living, in every article, is about 33 per cent more [in Brighton] than in London'.[104] Queen Victoria in 1845 also decided she had had enough of Brighton visits because 'the people are very indiscreet and troublesome here really, which makes this place quite a prison'.[105]

At twenty-five Anna had emerged from her own sense of imprisonment and had survived one of the hardest phases of her life. Resurgent spiritually if not physically she was now about to embark on a period which would bring her new homes, new hopes, and new vistas.

SIX

Finding Pearls

1845–9

I was good-tempered and gentle. (*Black Beauty*, Chapter 28)

Anna may have missed Brighton's social vibrancy when the Sewells moved to Lancing sometime before the end of May 1845. Yet, at just nine miles away, the town of her youth was still accessible and remained a hub of interest, although regular charity work, chapel attendance, and teaching in Brighton ceased.[1] Situated west of Brighton on the Sussex coast between Shoreham and Worthing and bounded on the east by the River Adur, Lancing in 1845 had a population of 781.[2] When Anna moved there it was an area of farms and market gardens, scattered with predominantly flint-built houses and cottages.

The Sewells moved into Miller House,[3] later known as Fir Cottage and Fir-Croft. As 'Fircroft' it operated as a guest house with a riding stables in the 1930s, and was demolished in the 1950s. The cottage had been built for Thomas Miller around 1801, and was in the hands of his widow's executors when the Sewells became tenants. It was on the western edge of North Lancing, sometimes known as Upper Lancing (or the 'rooks'), which merged into the Sussex Downs to the north, and was set a mile above seafronted South or Lower Lancing (or the 'seagulls') below. The house stood on its own amidst open fields, quite far back from what is now Manor Road, then a main route from Arundel to Brighton.[4] Miller House had a little land with it, and as in her Palatine Cottage days, Anna once again helped tend a few animals, and surely recommenced bee-keeping.

For what seems to have been the first time in her twenty-five years, the Sewells also owned their own horse, so Anna's equine contact increased considerably. Twice a day she drove their pony-chaise into Shoreham where she dropped off or collected Isaac from the railway station for his commute to the Brighton bank.[5] She probably followed the route east along the (Old) Shoreham Road past the Sussex Pad Inn, a reputed haunt of smugglers, across the toll bridge over the Adur and on into Shoreham, a market town of seafaring and shipbuilding and the chief port for the Brighton area.

On 24 November 1845 the Shoreham-to-Worthing section of railway line opened including a station at Lancing so Anna's role as her father's driver may only have lasted a few months, but she continued to drive Mary and herself wherever they needed to go. She also rode recreationally, perhaps following the woodland path that led up to the North Lancing windmill then went west along an old Neolithic track past the chalk pit from which Lancing residents freely dug chalk for building or manuring.[6] Further along was a group of beech trees on a hill summit known as the Lancing Ring, further still the site of a Romano-Celtic temple,[7] and beyond were the open rolling Downlands. One contemporary guidebook also advised that the ride between Upper Lancing and Lower Lancing was 'rural in a high degree',[8] and Anna must many times have ridden this bucolic path down to the seafront with its shingle beach and never-ending sea, and gazed out east to the white Sussex cliffs in the distance.

Anna's regular Lancing activities were sewing, reading, and household tasks, riding and driving, tending to plants and animals, letter-writing, painting and drawing, and observing nature in all its forms. There were also visits away or guests staying: nearby friends the Benwells, various of Anna's many cousins, as well as aunts, uncles, and friends. What charitable roles Anna and Mary at this time fulfilled is not clear, but there is likely to have been poor visiting. Anna may have taught at either of the two day-schools or one evening school which five girls and twenty-two boys are reported as attending in 1846–7.[9] These schools were probably run by Lancing parish church, a near neighbour, which Anna and Mary likely attended, although a Wesleyan chapel in South Lancing was also available.[10]

During her Lancing years Anna achieved a new contentment in her life and inured herself to the lameness and vari-symptomed invalidism that still plagued her. On 27 May 1845, soon after the move to Lancing, she wrote in her journal:

Mother went to Brighton, and I stayed to attend to the planting of seeds in the garden; my feet were very weak, and I prayed that they might be strengthened sufficiently for me to attend to what was necessary. The Lord most graciously heard me, and gave me more strength than I have had for some time, so that I am able to see after the garden properly.[11]

Spiritual skirmishes still took place in her mind as she struggled to live up to what she saw as God's expectations of her. 'I am very much concerned,' she wrote,

in reading the lives of holy people, to find how unlike them I am in my hatred of sin and love of holiness. But I must look to Christ too. O Lord, make me of one mind with Thee. Open Thou my eyes, that I may see things as Thou seest them, and as they really are. My mother very truly says, we cannot love holiness as an abstract thing, but that it must come in proportion as we love Christ.[12]

On a later date she heartbreakingly reveals how she is trying to reconcile her feet with her faith:

I have felt it very sweet to receive this improvement in my feet (which continues) from the Hand of Jesus. I would not be without this dispensation, and pray Thee, Lord, to do with me what Thou seest best. I thank Thee, for my lameness. I am sure it is sent in love, though it be a trial. I should without it have too much pleasure in the flesh, and have forgotten Thee.[13]

While Anna's life was often static, Philip's was dynamic. He spent some time in the south of France, where with a group of fellow engineers he examined the logistics of draining salt marshes. The French he had eagerly learned in his Stoke Newington boyhood proved a lifesaver when, as his party were arranging boats to cross the Rhône, he overheard and thus foiled the boatmen's plans to rob, and if necessary murder, them in the middle of the river.[14] By January 1846 he was in London where he stayed – with some interruptions – for most of 1846 and on into 1847.[15] He was now close enough to travel to Lancing to see Anna and his parents reasonably often.

Anna was always eager to see Philip, urging him on 8 January 1846, 'Canst not thou come & spend thy birthday here just try to make a little business in Brighton for that day.'[16] Their Aunt Maria Wright, who had been ill, was staying with them and Anna reported that Maria and Mary were planning a trip to Bath. For her part, she told him: 'Thou knows how busy hens with one chicken are said to be – well I am as busy as the essence of 40 hens so situated.'[17] One doleful event that was keeping her busy she mentioned quite forthrightly: 'Aunt M is better again the Pig dies tomorrow.' Anna was not squeamish and would have regarded the killing of their pig as a necessity, although she undoubtedly preferred its death to be swift and merciful rather than the 'eight or ten minutes dying, at least' that Arabella Donn recommends in Thomas Hardy's *Jude the Obscure.*[18] Ever practical, she told Philip, 'I have been searching in Shoreham for a Pork tub but there is no such being as a Cooper there & tomorrow I must go to Tarring & order one.'[19]

Philip was unable to travel to Brighton for his birthday so Anna wrote to wish him 'a great many blessings for this 25th year that thou art entering upon'.[20] She was helping her mother and aunt pack for their trip which was no longer to Bath but to Buxton where Anna's grandfather had suffered sudden illness. 'Mother intended to write to thee', she told Philip, 'but has not time. But she wishes me to tell thee that she sends thee all the good wishes that thou couldst possibly have for thy self. I hope she will have the opportunity of telling thee so herself tomorrow but perhaps thou mayst be out.'[21] She advised Philip that Mary would bring a birthday parcel for him 'containing both our offerings . . . There are several defects in what I have sent thee for which I am very sorry but I hope thou wilt excuse it as I am not used to the work.'[22] She continued:

I am very glad that Mother has the excuse of going to take care of Aunt M to take her to Buxton for I am sure she would have been wretched with anxiety if she had been staying here & if this attack should return & end fatally I shall be very thankful that she went I can not say but that I much fear what the termination may be but we must hope for the best.[23]

Anna's grandfather recovered, but her own health needed boosting. In the summer of 1846 with Mary, Philip, and her Aunt

Ellen, Anna travelled to Germany to attend a spa. This was almost certainly Marienbad (Mariánské Lázně),[24] a still popular spa town situated in a valley of the Bohemian mountains, 120 miles west of Prague and 8 miles east of today's German border in what is now the Czech Republic. Attending spas offered Anna a change of air and scenery, new social experiences, a holiday atmosphere, hope for improved health, a chance to indulge in some self-cossetting, and sometimes provided (or coincided with) temporary improvement of her ailments. Although Anna did not partake of the traditional 'Grand Tour' of Europe, her invalidism paradoxically enabled her to see places and go further than she might otherwise have done. German spas were highly regarded, partially as a result of A.B. Granville's influential 1837 account, *The Spas of Germany*. European cures and periods of continental residence could also be cheaper than their British equivalents.

Anna's party probably travelled by steamer from Shoreham to Dieppe or from Ramsgate to Ostend, then on to Germany by a combination of train and diligence (as public coaches were known on the Continent). Founded in 1808, Marienbad was comparatively new and although it was one of the quieter spas, it already had a strong reputation for effective mineral waters. The family would have stayed in one of the sixty or so lodging-houses at the top of the town which nestled in a horseshoe curve near the summit of the densely forested hills. They assuredly visited the pump room and assembly room, looked through the colonnade of shops, and walked in the pleasure gardens at the base of the valley. There Anna would have visited the springs which were inside buildings shaped like temples and other elegant structures. She may have taken the popular Kreutzbrunnen waters which when warmed tasted like veal broth, bathed at the Ambrosiusbrunnen with its 'Gothic canopy', or tried the potentially lethal gas baths:

> where, by a peculiar apparatus, a stream of gas can be applied to any part of the body affected with disease. When the whole person is subjected to the gas, the patient enters a sort of box, provided with a lid, through which his head projects: the gas is admitted from below in pipes, and care is taken to prevent his breathing it, which would be injurious, or fatal.[25]

Spa visits encouraged excursions and they may well have hired a carriage to visit local sights such as the convent of Töpl or Prince Metternich's chateau.[26]

This 'pleasure-trip',[27] as Bayly terms it, benefited Anna who on leaving Marienbad appears to have been walking reasonably well and to be stronger generally. The party's journey home in the heat of a European summer was, however, abruptly halted when Ellen fell seriously ill after they reached Brussels on 22 August. They were staying at Hotel de Suede, a principal yet moderately priced hotel in the old town,[28] which Philip told Isaac was 'very quiet & comfortable and as Aunt E could not be moved it is a great blessing it is so'.[29] Mary anxiously nursed her youngest sister, Anna helping where she could, but Anna's health, although improved, was not strong and Mary feared any regression. She therefore encouraged the excursions Anna took with Philip to Antwerp and Malines.[30] They perhaps also took the eight-hour carriage excursion to the battlefield at Waterloo, which included three hours to rest the horses and view the site.[31]

In the week or so that she was there Anna had time to explore Brussels, the city Charlotte Brontë in 1853 would fictionalize as *Villette* and whose streets just a few years earlier, at Anna's very age, she had paced with unrequited love for a married man in her heart. The secrets of Anna's own heart as she wandered in the sunshine are unknown, but she must have appreciated the picturesque buildings and admired the Gothic splendours of the Grande Place. Visiting art galleries and museums, she perhaps stopped off in a shaded café or treated herself to some of the famous Brussels lace.

'Mother is so occupied with nursing Aunt Ellen that she has no time to write except to Buxton', Philip told Isaac on 29 August:

> however Aunt E is . . . beginning to mend tho' she is yet so weak that she cannot walk about the room – John[32] & Anna will be in England on Second day in all probability . . . Anna will I should think hardly be home before 3rd day it will depend so much upon how the boat gets into Ramsgate whether late or early – if I accompany them across I shall . . . send Anna on by the best train I can so that perhaps if they leave tomorrow & get to Ramsgate in good time she may come down by the last train and spend the night of Monday at Mrs Benwells . . . Mother is afraid to keep

Anna here any longer lest the heat and noise and confinement consequent on only having a town to walk in should do her harm and take away from the good she has recd.[33]

Anna must have made the journey as planned taking the roughly twelve-hour steamer crossing from Ostend to Ramsgate, very feasibly plagued by the seasickness that beset so many channel-crossers. Back in Lancing she and Isaac, like the Buxton relatives, anxiously awaited the latest news of Ellen. Philip had remained in Brussels, scouring the town for 'physic jellies and nurses', and reported to Isaac on 4 September that Ellen was still very weak.[34] Mary added a postscript which showed that even with her sister near death, she worried about Anna's health:

My dear Isaac I was so truly glad to have thy letter this morning & hear that our dear Anna had arrived safely at home I hope she will ride and drive and walk about and keep up the bodily strength she had gained. I dare say E Hunton[35] would come & stay a little while with her if she wishes it.[36]

'I know there is nothing like a letter from my own hand', Mary a few days later told Anna. 'I hope you will be fortunate in your cow hunting expedition.'[37] She told Anna that she planned to call in the Belgian King's physician who was Scottish, to give a second opinion on Ellen, but discovered that he was 'not allowed to leave the Palace' so they would consult a Belgian physician instead. '[P]ray my dearest take care of thyself', she told Anna, 'as I do of myself and am quite well'.[38]

Ellen's condition deteriorated and Anna's Aunt Elizabeth travelled to Brussels. She and Mary prepared the family for the worst, but on 21 September were able to report to their sister Maria that the danger had past. Ellen had taken 'two or three spoonsful of Veal broth' and 'half a cup of tea and a little mite of biscuit', Elizabeth reported.[39] She also praised Philip's steadfastness: 'he is very well & so clever in providing & procuring all that is needed – Mary's praise of him this morning was that he was just the thing for he was a man & a woman too!'[40] Mary made sure those at Buxton were updating Anna, directing 'I have not written at all to my own dear child so you will *continue* to feed her with the reports bitter and sweet that come to you.'[41] Eventually Mary, Elizabeth, Ellen, and Philip made their way home. Anna meanwhile had been running the household and had probably found herself a cow.

At New Year 1847 Joseph Stickney Sewell visited Anna and her parents in Lancing. The son of Dorothy and Abraham Sewell, he was a mutual nephew of Isaac and of Sarah Stickney Ellis and was just three months younger than Anna. He had also experienced a teenage crisis over Quakerism but had remained in the fold and, like Philip, had become enthralled by the idea of becoming a missionary. Anna must have had many interesting conversations with her cousin and would certainly have kept track of his future activities. He was about to become superintendent of the Quaker school at Rawdon. Two of his children were to die there as, in 1860, would his wife, leaving him with four daughters, one of whom, another Anna Sewell, was blind. In the same year he became a Quaker minister and in 1862 moved to Hitchin to become a banker before a missionary opportunity arose in 1867 which he embraced fully.[42]

In January 1848 Anna was visiting Buxton, surely riding as much as she could and enjoying time with her grandparents and aunts. With Anna away, Isaac at work, and no consuming charity role to fulfil, Mary dissolved into loneliness. On a very snowy 21 January 1848 she wrote to Philip, who was now living in Gargrave near Skipton, Yorkshire, and working on construction of the Settle and Carlisle railway.[43] Their house had been sold but the new owner was letting them stay on as tenants, she told him, but she missed Anna:

> as to being alone it is a serious business, and except for a time not undesirable. A woman, with all her thoughts feelings and sympathies, to be shut up alone without objects to expend them upon, is a pitiable object and she can hardly avoid running into some eccentricity as an outlet for the imprisoned stream – If she have not a husband and children or friends in close companionship, she must have cats, dogs, birds, or a hobby of some kind however ridiculous, to preserve her from nervous irritability or moping melancholy, or from the whole current of thought and action centering around selfish, enjoyments. Men can follow pursuits for *themselves* women must have others in view to

give energy and interest to their pursuits . . . do not at all suppose
I am experiencing the misery of solitude, I have plenty to do,
many to write to and father home at night and time to read which
is a great pleasure and it is only when I look at dear Nanny's
empty seat in the dark home that I feel half inclined to cry.[44]

Her comments reveal her own view of women's social role and
cast light on what she saw as important for Anna, whose life held
far more solitude than her own: pets, hobbies, and as much activity
as possible. She missed her daughter, but also recognized that it was
beneficial for Anna to visit elsewhere both for social and health
reasons. It might be tempting to see Mary's need for Anna as
bordering on the damaging but that would be to underestimate the
narrow focus of women's lives at the time and to deny, despite their
almost fiercely independent natures, the strength of what was a
mutually strong relationship. The loneliness Mary expresses here
was not uncommon among middle-class women; certainly Sarah
Stickney Ellis always tried to persuade people – including Anna,
Mary, and Isaac – to come and live with her when her missionary
husband was away in Madagascar.

Philip had recently become engaged to Sarah Woods, a Quaker
from Tottenham, north of Stoke Newington, who Mary would always
regard as in every way '*very* lovely'.[45] The engagement brought
happiness and excitement to the Sewells, but one heart was broken.
Anna's Manchester stepcousin, Elizabeth Crewdson, had fallen in love
with Philip and may have had reason to hope for a match. Elizabeth
wrote to Mary confessing the state of her heart, Mary telling Philip:
'so exquisitely beautiful are her feelings and conduct that for the glory
and beauty of womankind they ought to be known if that were
possible – but of course they are sacred with me except the message
she expressly sends to thee'.[46] This message was: 'I have no feeling of
unkindness, but that of unmixed kindness towards him . . . nothing
can quench my affection for him, or lower my opinion of his
character, I can thankfully rejoice that his lonely path is likely to be
cheered by one so entirely worthy of his love and of whom I think
with fond affection.'[47] 'The thought that thou art all alone has
sanctioned in my own mind the freedom with which I have written,'
Elizabeth told Mary, 'I wish my precious Anna was thy companion.'[48]

Anna, instead, was soon to be Elizabeth's companion in Manchester, as Mary informed Philip: 'I have volunteered for our dear Anna to go there after her stay in Norfolk is completed, dear E jumps at the prospect.'[49] Anna would have enjoyed being back in Manchester. She surely soothed Elizabeth's sore heart and perhaps discussed the state of her own.

By April Anna was back in Lancing appreciating spring's dawn across the countryside and hoping that if Philip had wood sorrel in Gargrave she could send him 'a little conveyance for some'.[50] She was no doubt at this time thinking about Philip's impending marriage. Mary certainly was, asking Philip what he thought of his prospective in-laws and planning wedding present strategy:

I am very glad the Thorntons affairs are at last settled do they ever mention a present to thee now because if they do, it might be well for thee to know that uncle John intends to give thee a tea & Coffee Pot

They did at one time make a Parade of spending £50 now thou art going to be a Housekeeper they could not do better than give thee a Piano, which is a very suitable thing to give if their intentions come up to such an amount.[51]

Now twenty-eight, Anna was developing the calm exterior and sweet nature that was to typify her middle and later years. She seems to have found a core happiness and placidity, or at least managed to show that veneer to people around her, even those as close as Mary, for on 25 April Mary revealed to Philip:

I find Anna about as well as she has been for a long time, in very good spirits and finding many pleasures in nature and art but especially the former. The beautiful system of compensation is remarkably borne out in her case, she finds so many pearls where others would only see stones and is far happier than the generality of person you meet.[52]

Although Anna was happier in herself during her late twenties and thirties, '[t]hese years were', Bayly writes, 'much occupied in a weary search after improvement in her health.'[53] She tried most treatments on offer: pills and potions, exercise and rest, change of scenery and air, being bled by leech or 'cup', homeopathy, and possibly mesmerism which Sarah Stickney Ellis among many others practised, although Philip thought little of it.[54] Her most consistent treatments were driving and riding horses, spa cures such as those at Leamington and Marienbad, and the newly popular hydropathic or water cures which were more intense than spa treatments but still relied on water as a cure-all. Usually Mary would travel with Anna to the spa or water cure centre and leave her there to take the full treatment.[55]

At one water establishment Anna met someone who was conceivably already an idol to her: Alfred Tennyson, whose *Poems* of 1842 had heralded him as one of the star poets of the day. Anna's niece Margaret Sewell recounts that Anna and Tennyson met when they stayed in the same hotel: 'She must have seen a good deal of the poet; she used to tell of walks and talks with him, and he gave her a signed portrait of himself . . . She learned a great deal of his poetry by heart with much pleasure.'[56]

These few brief lines are all that is known of Anna's relationship with Tennyson. His own biographers and letters offer no more, but speculation is irresistible. Anna, now in her late twenties, had led a life of almost Lady of Shalott-like seclusion, with her mind doubtless having echoed in darker times the refrain of Tennyson's waiting Mariana 'I am aweary, aweary, / I would that I were dead!'[57] To meet the famous writer of such sad mellifluous poetry must have been to her like the 'half sick of shadows' Lady of Shalott being dazzled by the handsome knight Sir Lancelot. For not only was Tennyson, then in his late thirties, a famous poet, but he was also stunningly attractive to women; his poetry and his looks combining to create a compelling presence.

Margaret Sewell recalls that Anna probably met Tennyson at Matlock, but Tennyson seems not to have been treated there. Suffering from 'hypochondria' or nervous illness, he was in the 1840s treated at Prestbury, Malvern, and Umberslade Hall near Birmingham. Margaret states that the meeting was after Anna's German spa visit, making Tennyson's 1843–4 stay in Prestbury too early. The most probable mis-remembering for Matlock is Malvern and the chances are increased by Tennyson having visited there twice, first briefly at the end of 1847, and then again for one to three months from July 1848. The Malvern water cure was highly regarded and much publicized, making it likely that the Sewells would have wanted Anna to try it. A meeting in Malvern in 1848 seems the most likely, although if they did meet at Umberslade Hall in May or June 1847, the regimen would have been very similar.[58]

Based on the water cures developed by Vincenz Priessnitz in Gräfenburg, Dr James Manby Gully had established the Malvern water cure in 1843. His hugely successful 1846 book, *The Water Cure in Chronic Disease*, sets out its principles. Chief among these was a reaction against the use of drugs in treating illness, a practice which had expanded rapidly in the 1830s and 1840s and which Anna had certainly tried. Gully argued that it was the body itself which cured ailments, not external remedies. He directed patients to exercise in Malvern's fresh, bracing air, drink its pure water, undergo hydropathic treatments to tone the body to optimum condition, retire and rise early, and refrain from all drugs, alcohol, rich food, and tobacco. There was no shirking on one of Gully's regimens and every day Anna and Tennyson would have been prescribed a strenuous routine of mainly cold-water treatments. These included cold compresses, being tightly wrapped in wet sheets, being blasted or douched with cold water, taking sitz baths, foot baths, or plunge baths, and plenty of water drinking. These were all designed to get the circulation working properly which Gully saw as the root of most problems.[59]

Although Tennyson wrote that the water cure 'renders letter-writing or anything, except washing and walking, more difficult than those who have not past [sic] through the same ordeal would easily believe',[60] Anna and Tennyson had some energy left over to talk. They doubtless conversed about what they had read, their views of the treatment, their surroundings, and possibly Anna talked to him about his poetry. They perhaps felt an empathy through both having had to adjust to life-changing losses, Anna to her lameness and loss of health, Tennyson to the death of his great friend, Arthur Henry Hallam. Jane Carlyle commented that Tennyson was embarrassed 'with women alone – for he entertains at one and the same moment a feeling of almost adoration for them and an ineffable contempt!'[61] Yet his biographer, Robert Bernard Martin, notes that he 'liked to be with women who fenced conversationally'.[62] However awed, charmed, or quite possibly in love with Tennyson Anna might have been, she was certainly a 'fencer', if a gentle one, when drawn and he would have received little simpering acquiescence or conversational coyness from her. They met at a time, too, when Tennyson's 1836 engagement to Emily Sellwood had been for many years in abeyance. His financial situation had also improved after a disastrous setback and Gully had now reassured him that he did not have the epilepsy he feared he might pass on to any future children, so barriers to marriage were being removed.[63] The now untraceable portrait he gave Anna, which was more likely at that period to have been a drawing or engraving than a photograph, indicates some measure of affection for Anna on Tennyson's side.

For her part, Anna cannot have been anything other than thrilled by meeting Tennyson, but again the secrets of her heart remain just that and there is no evidence of correspondence between them. Meeting the poet at the very least must have burnished her love for his work. Both she and Mary were passionate about poetry and they often read and recited poems together, especially the Romantic poets Keats, Coleridge, and Byron but also Tennyson. They preferred Tennyson's shorter poems and lyrics, to his later many-volumed Arthurian epic, *Idylls of the King*.[64] In later years her niece Margaret tellingly remembers Anna 'repeating poem after poem of Tennyson's. We used irreverently to consider her delivery exaggerated, but English youth is chary of emotion.'[65] When in 1850 Tennyson finally married Emily Sellwood, became poet laureate, and published that Victorian masterwork of grief, religious doubt, and spiritual renewal, *In Memoriam*, Anna must have felt mixed emotions. Especially so as in 1851 the Tennysons settled within eight miles of where Anna was then living – although as it transpired, only for a fortnight.[66] Like so many Victorians, she dipped into *In Memoriam* many times, and even annotated her own copy.[67] To the grieving or spiritually doubtful there was fellow-feeling as well as comfort to be found in Tennyson's elegy on the loss of his friend, but for Anna its keenest message may well have rested in some of its most famous lines:

'Tis better to have loved and lost
Than never to have loved at all.[68]

In December 1848 Anna and her parents were hoping that Philip would join them to celebrate his last Christmas as a single man, but he could not make it until mid-January. 'Nanny feels it as a sore disappointment', Mary told him, 'and she has just now a bad cold.'[69] Christmas day was a quiet one, 'a poor little meagre party only the old trio,' Mary wrote, 'we shall eat our Turkey alone without any of the best sauces . . . we have engaged Charles Dickens to amuse us'.[70] They probably read aloud Dickens's Christmas 'fancy' for that year, *The Haunted Man and the Ghost's Bargain*, which he had completed while staying in Brighton the month before.

Anna's Uncle Richard visited Lancing just before Christmas. He had recently married and, implicitly as a result, had fallen on hard times. 'I should think that by this time thou hast kept house long enough to know that when all the expenses of board, firing & washing are paid for two people', Mary advised Philip, 'there is not much left out of a pound, to speculate with, or to buy clothing, or meet illness or any accidental expense so my dear Philip instead of thy poor Uncle being suspected or blamed or looked coldly upon – he is "very much" to be felt for, & I think very much to be approved and admired and sympathised with.'[71]

The ramification of Isaac's now offering financial aid to his brother-in-law Richard was that he himself had to borrow from his children. Philip had offered to lend the money but Mary would not hear of it, telling him:

I borrow it of Anna because father is very short at the close of the year – Anna is always with us and all that we have is hers. She will have her money as soon as she wants it . . . but the case is totally different with thee. Thou hast very many expenses upon thee and thou hast beside to furnish a house marry a wife and that is quite enough for one year.[72]

Anna's money probably came from dividends as she owned shares, including some in the London and County Bank, at the time of her death. Middle-class women did not generally work for payment, apart from governessing if necessary. Anna's uncle's new wife, however, seems to have had a working past and had married 'up'. This was the first time the Sewells had met her. 'I entirely believe [Richard's] testimony of her that she is the pattern of a virtuous and industrious wife', Mary told Philip, '& that she has done him good and not evil ever since they were married . . . Anna and I both like her & could do much better with her than with many who take a higher standing – She has not a cultivated mind but she is by no means stupid and though not strictly a lady she is [not] awkward . . . They seem very much attached to each other and his conduct to her is beautiful.'[73]

After Christmas, Anna's Aunt Maria came to stay and joined in the family's excitement about Philip's impending wedding, Mary telling him on 3 January 1849:

Aunt Maria adds I hope he will not fail to bring Sarah a ring as it is a universal practice now for engaged ladies to wear the betrothing ring – not the gold circlet but a fancy ring on the same finger – I find Maria & Sarah had some talk about it together and she said she should so like thee to give her one – she had a ring of her own, but she did not like to put that on for herself, as it should be especially the gift of the elect husband himself so thou wilt know what to do.[74]

Anna and Mary in early January spent a few days in London visiting their doctor as well as paying social calls with Maria and bride-to-be Sarah. Around the time of his birthday on 14 January Philip arrived in Lancing, Sarah and Maria also staying. It was a very happy household and Anna, Philip, and Sarah sang together in the evenings making them for Mary the 'very brightest in her whole life'.[75]

Philip and Sarah married sometime later that year, settling in Gargrave where Philip was still working and there on 5 May 1850 Anna's first niece, Mary Grace, was born. A friend of Mary's recalled that after Philip's marriage Mary and Anna became 'more than ever all the world to each other as companions. Mr. Sewell was away all day, and though he sympathised in all their works of kindness, I do not think he cared much for the books they read.'[76]

Isaac did not, however, try to impose his own tastes, and was in Mary's view always a 'very unselfish' man.[77]

Isaac was reconsidering his career and in March 1849, having entered into business as a brewer, he resigned from the bank.[78] Why he made this decision is not clear. Banking had been hit hard in 1847 and 1848 with many banks being forced to close,[79] and economic and political panic across Europe had fermented into the explosive year of 1848 when famine and rebellion rocked Ireland and revolutions erupted across Europe. Although escaping its own bloodbaths, in England the working classes were full of unrest and desperation, the middle classes full of fear and unease, and the economy full of manufacturing and business failures. Cholera, typhus, and influenza swept the country and while the situation was worse for most, for the poor it was dire. These were the real 'hungry forties', as the Sewells, always involved in charitable endeavours for the poor, well knew. It was probably hopes of improving their own economic situation, however, that encouraged the move Anna and her parents now made to Haywards Heath, a new commuter town on the London–Brighton railway line.

SEVEN
Enforced Idleness
1849–58

[I]f there was one thing that I missed, it must not be thought I was discontented; all who had to do with me were good, and I had a light airy stable and the best of food. What more could I want? Why, liberty! (Black Beauty, Chapter 6)

Situated on the rail link thirty-eight miles from London and twelve from Brighton, but precluding the need to live in either, Haywards Heath was probably chosen by the Sewells as a convenient yet quiet home. It met Mary's desire to avoid busy town life yet also satisfied Isaac's business needs which now became various. Taking its name from its heath and, legend has it, from Jack Hayward, a highwayman who was hanged in chains upon it, Haywards Heath had few inhabitants before the coming of the railway in 1841. Arriving just eight years later, Anna was among the first flush of residents who caused the area to grow into what in 1877 would be termed the 'Metropolis of Mid Sussex'.[1]

Isaac's move out of banking must have been a financially beneficial one judging from the 'mansion'[2] into which the Sewells moved. Petlands, set back from the north-east corner of Hazelgrove and New England Roads and also known as Petland House, was a charming, white, Gothic-style house built in 1830[3] and set amid open farmland with its own extensive grounds.[4] It had land enough for the Sewells to keep a few animals: cows and pigs, a pony, and probably again Anna's bees. Petlands was demolished in 1955 to make way for new housing,[5] but in April 1996 a blue plaque commemorating Anna's years there was unveiled at Heyworth County Primary School which occupies some of Petlands' former land and which, in her honour, uses a black horse and horseshoe logo.[6]

The house was in a peaceful, rural location with many woods nearby through which Anna undoubtedly rode. At the other end of New England Road from their own, William Allen, a Quaker philanthropist, abolitionist, scientist and reformer, had with the assistance of John Smith, MP in 1825 established an experimental allotment community known as the 'American Colony' or simply 'America'.[7] Aiming to reduce the amount of poor relief being paid out and avoid the practice of paying the poor to emigrate, Allen provided impoverished agricultural families with cottages, plots of land, and a moral code. Although Allen had died six years before Anna's arrival in the area, the colony was still thriving.[8] Its ethos of helping the poor help themselves was something Anna, like her parents, would have supported.

Comparatively little is known of Anna's life from the age of twenty-nine to age thirty-eight but it surely continued in a similar vein with lots of sewing, painting, reading, riding, domestic activities, and visits away. Ongoing oscillations in her health meant there were periods when all her usual activities had to be put by, but Anna endured these flares with what Mary termed her always 'cheerful, patient courage'.[9]

Spiritual matters remained important. Haywards Heath did not then have a village church. Some Sunday afternoon services were held in the loft of a carpenter's workshop, but as entry to the loft was via 'ladder-like steps' it may not have proved user-friendly for Anna.[10] Instead, she probably drove Mary in their trap or chaise – the one-horse, two-wheeled vehicle that was the commonest in the land, the most affordable for the middle classes, and thought the most suitable for women drivers – to services in nearby Cuckfield or Lindfield. Cuckfield also offered Baptist and Congregational chapels for Anna and Mary to sample.

Although she led a quiet and restricted life, Anna was no recluse deliberately shrouding herself from the outside world. She was reserved in manner but neither shy nor inhibited. It was circumstances rather than nature that held her back and generally the physical rather than the emotional that impeded her social life. When able to she joined with zest in the activities available to her, however seemingly docile to modern or secular minds. She made the most of what life offered her, but naturally must have gone through phases of great difficulty when the world seemed a bleak and unjust place. Perhaps in some measure to compensate for the physical control she had lost, she tried to exert dominion in other areas of her life to a sometimes excessive degree. Living up to her own high standards of spirituality, probity, and truth was an almost impossible task, but for Anna controlling herself, seeing things clearly, and accepting her situation with equanimity and true faith was her determined mission.

Isaac meanwhile seemed to be on his own mission to try as many business opportunities as possible. Haywards Heath's position on the rail line attracted not only commuters but also those interested in the freighting possibilities of the railway. Goods yards for grain, stock, coal, and timber were quickly established,[11] and it may have been this aspect of the town that attracted Isaac. The 1851 census lists him as a maltster, brewer, and coal merchant. Not all – if indeed any – of his business was undertaken in Haywards Heath. He became, if not now then soon, the owner of coal works in the Forest of Dean and *Folthorp's Brighton Guide* for 1852 lists him as a maltster with premises in Warwick Street, Brighton.[12] Malting involved transforming barley into malt suitable for brewing through a process of soaking, germinating, and kiln-drying. Barley grew well on the South Downs and perhaps Isaac got his supply from farms around Haywards Heath. Maltsters often had premises near their own brewery,[13] and there is some indication that Isaac may have had a brewing business in St James's Street, Brighton[14] or been involved with Griffith and Co. which did.[15]

Isaac's becoming a brewer might sound surprising given his loyal Quakerism, Anna and Mary's impending involvement in the temperance movement, and Anna's attacks on alcohol in *Black Beauty*. Brewing, however, had long been a respected Quaker occupation – indeed, Anna's great-grandfather Richard Wright had also been a maltster[16] – and Anna and Mary's temperance activities still lay in the future.[17] Isaac's brewing years did, nevertheless, materialize just before the rising temperance movement made brewing for many Quakers untenable both economically and morally.

Diarist William Lucas and his brother, the artist Samuel Lucas, to whom Anna was distantly related by marriage, were Quaker brewers and maltsters in Hitchin. As early as 1839 William had been advised to give up his business under the pressure of campaigns for Teetotalism – total abstinence from alcohol – rather than temperance which initially focused on spirits.[18] He felt growing qualms about owning public house property but also felt he had to provide for his family. 'Total abstinence is certainly irrational, unchristian and inexpedient,' he wrote, 'temperance is quite another thing.'[19] Yet by 1843 he was hoping that his sons would go into a 'less objectionable trade'.[20]

Although a majority of Quakers became teetotal over the course of the nineteenth century, increasingly pressured to do so from the 1850s onwards, it was never mandatory or all-encompassing.[21] In later Haywards Heath years Isaac probably came under family pressure to give up brewing, but it was not until 1874 that the Friends Yearly Meeting officially and 'in kindly and moderate terms' urged those 'who were engaged in the manufacture of intoxicating drinks . . . to change their trade if possible'.[22]

No longer being a Friend had opened up Anna's options for marriage and motherhood. Remaining a Quaker would have meant that until 1860 she could only have married another Quaker or face expulsion,[23] and Quaker women outnumbered Quaker men even more than in the female-weighted imbalance in the population at large.[24] Although many Victorian women married in their early twenties, there were also plenty who married in their late thirties and who still went on to have children. Her Aunt Anna had married at thirty-five, taking on six stepchildren and going on to have four herself in the ensuing seven years. Elizabeth Barrett, who had warned Robert Browning that marrying her at forty was tantamount to spilling his 'water gourds into the sand',[25] went on to have one son at forty-two in between three miscarriages. At twenty-nine there may well still have been hope in Anna's heart.

Anna, however, like her three unmarried Buxton aunts and in time like all of her own nieces, was destined to be one of the so-called 'odd women' of the period. Caring for a husband and children was seen as the ordained and truly Christian life-role for middle-class women and remaining an 'old maid' was seen as a lesser state of being. Yet Anna was far from alone in remaining single. The 1851 census showed that there were 6 per cent more women than men in the twenty-to-forty age group but that 30 per cent of English women in that band were not married[26] The matter of 'redundant' women became the subject of contemporary essays and articles. Writers like William Rathbone Greg decried 'this vast amount of super-normal celibacy' among middle- and upper-class women,[27] while others like Ann Richelieu Lamb staunchly argued against the legal erasure of women's rights upon marriage and maintained that women should not feel obliged to marry. 'For it is unquestionable', Lamb wrote, 'that nowhere can we meet with more kind-hearted, happier, and more *intelligently* contented women, than among those who from different motives have *chosen* to remain single, instead of encountering the arduous task, the unceasing toil and anxiety, which attend the votaries of Hymen.'[28] The perils of marrying were recognized by many women who wished to 'do' such as Florence Nightingale. Frustrated that women had 'passion, intellect, moral activity – these three – and a place in society where no one of the three can be exercised',[29] Nightingale wrote in *Cassandra*: 'So much for the satisfaction of the intellect. Yet for a married woman in society, it is even worse. A married woman was heard to wish that she could break a limb that she might have a little time to herself. Many take advantage of the fear of "infection" to do the same.'[30]

Anna rarely lacked time alone, but not marrying may have been through choice or circumstance. No mention is made in the material that survives of the absence of suitor, spouse, or children in her life, whereas her loss of activities and energies is reiterated, perhaps implying that someone in her physical condition could not expect to marry. Ideals of feminine attractiveness must have made her doubly aware of her lameness. *Female Beauty*, for example, warned men who sought unblemished female specimens: 'the wide, flowing petticoats which women wear are generally sufficient to conceal any slight deformity in the shape of the limbs; the existence of such defects can then be surmised only from their style of walking, which requires great attention'.[31]

Whether any romantic prospects arose for Anna is unknown. She probably did have feelings for Henry King, Robert Crewdson, Tennyson, and possibly attractive preachers of one kind or another but how deep these ran only she ever knew. By the end of 1850 the three likeliest candidates were all married: her stepcousin Robert in 1846, and both Tennyson and Henry King in 1850. The likeliest explanation is that with her restricted life Anna simply did not have the opportunity to meet the right man or if she did she was not the woman for him. If there were suitors she may have turned them down because she felt it was not right to burden them with an invalid wife or more probably, as in Christina Rossetti's case, because of religious differences. There is always the possibility that she was attracted to women rather than men although there is no evidence to suggest this, or that she chose not to marry in order to retain some freedom or at least a known environment. For a woman with such strong religious faith as Anna, no mortal man may have lived up to her ideals, and it is likely that the passionate side of her nature during these years started to move away from thoughts of men and become more bound up in her love for Christ. On her thirtieth birthday she may have felt much like Florence Nightingale who wrote on her own only six weeks later: 'Today I am 30 – the age Christ began his mission. Now no more childish things. No more love. No more marriage. Now, Lord, let me think only of Thy Will, what thou willest me to do. Oh Lord, thy Will, Thy Will.'[32]

One year later, Sunday, 30 March 1851, was both Anna's thirty-first birthday and census day. She is not listed with her parents, their 24-year-old housemaid Jane Potter and 23-year-old cook Jane Bonniface at Petlands. Instead she was celebrating at Buxton with her grandfather (aged eighty) who is listed as a farmer of 200 acres, her grandmother (seventy-three), and her aunts Elizabeth (fifty-two) and Ellen (thirty-seven). Two house servants made up the remainder of the Dudwick Cottage household. Philip, Sarah (both twenty-nine) and one-year-old Mary Grace were also at Buxton, as was Anna's Aunt Maria (forty-nine), all staying with her Uncle Wright (listed as a magistrate, fifty-six) and Aunt Wright (fifty-eight) just over the lane in Dudwick House which had a footman, cook, housemaid, and scullier in addition to a nursemaid probably employed by Philip. It was a wonderful opportunity for Anna and Philip to be back in Buxton together. As in the days of their childhood summer holidays they surely rode out to some of their favourite haunts.

All the Wrights were involved in local charitable concerns, especially those involving education and the Buxton workhouse. Anna's Uncle Wright had in 1833 built and still supported the local village school which is still in use today. In 1850 he began helping ex-prisoners, some of whom he accepted on licence to work on his farm properties.[33] In 1853 he was instrumental in founding a reformatory, 'for the maintenance and religious and industrial training of forty lads under the age of twenty'.[34] The Buxton Reformatory would become the focus of Wright and Sewell charitable and educational passion for generations.

Anna's Aunt Wright had also become an author. In 1849 she produced *The Passover Feasts and Old Testament Sacrifices Explained*, which was intended for children of all classes, for use in schools, and to transmit a religious message. She followed this up with her detailed and highly praised *The Observing Eye; or Letters to Children on the Three Lowest Divisions of Animal Life* (1850). Queen Victoria gave a copy of this to her children, 'direct[ing] that her thanks should be presented to the author'.[35] Over the succeeding years Anne Wright would continue her scientific writing for children, which adults also read, producing the well-reviewed geological guide *The Globe Prepared For Man* (1853), *Listen and Learn: A Short Narrative of a Three Day's Ramble* (1856), *What Is a Bird?* (1857), which discouraged the popular boys' hobby of bird-nesting, and *Our World: its Rocks and Fossils. A Simple Introduction to Geology* (1859).[36]

Around this time – possibly the Buxton stop was en route – Philip and family moved south, taking a house in Kings Road, Brighton.[37] Philip was engaged on a project to deepen Shoreham harbour, creating a 'floating canal' and a lock (opened 1855) designed to enable imports, especially coal for Brighton, to be brought in closer by ship.[38] He was 'a great favourite among the navvies'[39] but more importantly was again within an easy commute of Anna and his parents. On 10 November 1851 his second child, Margaret Amie, was born and Anna surely travelled down to see her new niece, probably also visiting the Royal Pavilion which was opened to the public that year.[40]

Unless her health had been very poor she would almost certainly that summer have visited the Great Exhibition at the Crystal Palace in Hyde Park, London. There was much to fascinate Anna on show: a penknife with eighty blades, sculptures in various substances, textiles, furniture, china and glassware, musical instruments, early photographs, clocks, all sorts of steam-driven machines, new foodstuffs such as condensed milk, canned food, and champagne produced from rhubarb, laces and velvets, a stained glass gallery, hastily fig-leafed erotic art, an alarmed bedstead by which 'the sleeper, without any jerk or the least personal danger, is placed in the middle of the room: where at the option of the possessor a cold bath can be placed',[41] stuffed animals, and dazzling displays of jewellery including the Koh-i-Noor diamond. Especially worthy of her attention was the special display of beehives including one designed like a town house which contained four different bee families demonstrating industriousness and working harmony. The model dwellings for the working classes would have sparked interest as would the crowd-pulling medical display which included an 'artificial leech', the much looked-at artificial hand, and a collection of glass eyes.[42]

Like many visitors Anna probably took in other London sights that flourished on the coat-tails of the exhibition: cycloramas, dioramas, panoramas, the British Museum, Madam Tussaud's, Kew Gardens, Sir John Soane's Museum, Brunel's new tunnel under the Thames, churches, and art galleries.[43] She may have been one of the 145,000 visitors to London Zoo in August 1851 where one of the main attractions was a four-ton hippopotamus, which Thomas Babington Macaulay described as 'the ugliest of the works of God'.[44]

In 1852 Philip and Sarah moved to Santander, Spain,[45] where Philip helped construct the Santander–Logrono and Bilbao–Tudela railway lines. Philip spent twelve years in Spain where he was a well-respected engineer. While there 'he was the means of the release of two Englishmen who had been unjustly imprisoned at Toledo'.[46] He also became friendly with some nuns to whom he occasionally lent money[47] and became owner of an iron factory.[48]

At around the same time, Isaac was running into difficulties with the brewery. 'I wish very much that I could be of any use to thee in advising about the Brewery', Philip wrote to him, 'It weighs very heavily now I am sure.'[49] Isaac may have been coming under public, financial, and familial pressure to sell. Just nine months later William Lucas was to write: '*Our* trade is doomed and denounced and we must give over any expectations of increasing our substance this way.'[50] Isaac realized that he was unlikely to increase his substance that way, and had already bought a boat or ship, christened the *Mary Grace* after his eldest grandchild. This may have been connected with his role as a coal merchant, or for other international trade on which Philip gave him advice.[51] How far Isaac pursued his shipping interests is unknown (he would give his occupation as ship-owner in a will of 1861), but by early 1853 he had sold his Brighton brewing concerns and was looking for a more secure livelihood.

Anna's health had again worsened and at the beginning of 1853 she was undergoing treatment. 'Although her sweet and helpful influences were felt wherever she might be,' Bayly wrote:

> there is no doubt that a considerable portion of her life was spent mainly in repression. Her varied capacities enabled her to enter with unfeigned interest into a great variety of subjects. She could see at once how a picture should be composed, a fact or sentiment expressed, a garment cut out; how flowers should be arranged; what a committee should or should not do – but with all these mental resources, the frail body refused to do its part, and days and weeks had often to be spent in enforced idleness.[52]

Most of 1853 would be physically ennervating for Anna, and her concentration frequently failed, as Bayly reveals: 'Her hungry nature longed for food of many kinds – political, social, philanthropic – all these departments teemed with interest to her; yet there were periods when to read a short paragraph in a newspaper, or the Report of a Society, was for days together an impossibility.'[53]

Sad news had also come that Anna's grandfather had died on 14 January, Philip's birthday. This was a sore loss to Mary especially who hero-worshipped her father, 'Oh what a thing it is', she said, 'to have looked back, all one's life, on parents whose walk was *perfect*!'[54] Up until three years earlier gravestones and mourning dress were against Quaker rules,[55] but when John Wright senior was buried in the Lammas Quaker burial ground a headstone marked his grave. Mary went into mourning, and it may have been on this occasion that the crêpe on her skirt was limited to within two inches of her waist by a pious dressmaker who told her with no trace of irony, 'Worldly people have it brought up quite to the waist.'[56]

Meanwhile Sarah Stickney Ellis had been hatching a plot to have Anna, Isaac, and Mary come to live with her at Rose Hill in Hoddesdon, Hertfordshire, during the two years that her husband was engaged in missionary work in Madagascar. Sarah chose to remain in England to superintend Rawdon House, the boarding school for young ladies she had opened in 1845. Her stepdaughters were not living in the house and she wanted some – but not just any – companionship. On 19 March 1853 she wrote: 'Once I had hoped that Isaac and Mary Sewell and Anna might be induced to come and live with me, as Isaac has given up his business at Brighton; but I am afraid the plan is too good to be realised.'[57]

Around October of that year the Sewells moved instead to Graylingwell, which was situated on high ground on the north-eastern outskirts of Chichester. Anna was typically away from home during the shift, but this time she was undergoing medical treatment. The move was prompted by Isaac's June appointment as manager of the Chichester branch of the London and County Bank.[58] Located on East Street, where then as now banks congregate, no. 5 is still home to its descendant, the National Westminster Bank, which commemorates its predecessor with a stonework '1836 London and County Banking Company 1899' above its door. In the midst of moving, Mary visited Rose Hill, as Sarah Stickney Ellis reported:

> I have had a delightful little visit of only one night from Mary Sewell, on her way to their late residence, where she was going to pack all the furniture up, sell two cows, some pigs, a chaise, and what not, besides colouring and painting the whole house, and depart with all her furniture for Chichester in three days. She gave a sad account of Anna, worse instead of better for the treatment; she is coming to me after a while, but I think not for long.[59]

The Sewells almost certainly settled at Graylingwell Farm House, earlier known as Graylingwell Manor House. The 'Manor of Graylingwell' is listed in 1854 as being leased by John Abel Smith,[60] MP for Chichester and son of the John Smith who helped found the America colony near Anna's Haywards Heath home. Smith was a Quaker and Isaac undoubtedly knew him, probably subleasing from him the farmhouse and a small bit of land while Smith remained lessee of the whole farm estate which was owned by the Church.

Graylingwell Farm House was attractive, spacious, and set by itself down a long carriage drive, east off College Lane. Built during the seventeenth century or earlier,[61] it was surrounded by tracts of open farmland, had an orchard next to the house, its own meadow, and a large pond which was *the* Grayling Well. The son of one of Mary's friends recalled it as an 'old-fashioned country house . . . standing in its large garden, where bulrushes grew in the pond, and there was a crab-apple tree laden with bright-cheeked fruit'.[62] Mary and Isaac always felt that having a gracious garden was important so that Anna, if she was not able to walk far, might at least make her way out into pleasant surroundings.

In its afterlife the farmhouse became part of the West Sussex Lunatic Asylum, built in 1895–7 and later renamed Graylingwell Hospital.[63] During the violent winds of 16 October 1987 the house was badly damaged and in following years was boarded up.[64] In 1999 local newspaper articles appeared in which the city council and the public objected to the neglect of Anna Sewell's former home.[65] Two years later Graylingwell Hospital closed and in September 2002 its Victorian buildings, including Anna's old home, lie boarded up and abandoned, threaded over with ivy, brambles, and desolation. Because Graylingwell Farm House is a listed building, however, it is likely to have a future and in time Anna's residence there may be commemorated.

Near the house were Chichester barracks, so the sight and sound of soldiers must have been familiar to Anna. There was also plenty of open land for her to ride across and, it might be thought, a pleasant ride along the narrow River Lavant near their home. But riding beside the river may have been risky. Until 1856 the Lavant was 'the receptacle of privy soil from all adjacent houses', and realistically thought to be the source of much disease.[66] During Anna's Graylingwell years there was great concern at the high rate of fever and disease in the area. When the Sanitary Nuisances Act was passed in 1855, the Sewells, like all other Chichester residents, would have received a notice from the city council advising them of 'the propriety of immediately and closely inspecting their . . . premises and the removal of . . . noxious accumulations, the judiciously providing and keeping in good and clean condition sufficient drains, the providing of receptacles for filth of every kind'. They were also warned that as well as keeping their house well ventilated and cleansed, 'pains [should] be taken to provide ample supplies of wholesome water'.[67]

For health and activity Anna went out daily in her pony-chaise, often accompanied by Mary who remembered these as very 'pleasant drives'.[68] They surely explored the soft surrounding countryside of the Great Downs to the north and must regularly have gone down into Chichester. An ancient Roman town with a population of about 8,700, Chichester offered an ornate cruciform medieval cathedral and many fine Georgian buildings. Its city walls were lined with elms, markets were held on Wednesdays and Saturdays, and a centuries-old Market Cross marked the centre point of the four main roads that diverged from it west, east, north, and south.[69] The Sewells made some good friends at Chichester, and Mary and Anna possibly attended St Paul's church, to the north of the city, or visited at the workhouse not far from Graylingwell.

In January 1854 Philip probably paid a brief visit en route to France where he was anxious to raise: 'a Loan of £100,000 upon a Lot of Debentures of the Santander Railway . . . as I believe it will save me a very great deal of anxiety & be the stepping stone to success in opening the first part of the Line'.[70] He had no time for sight-seeing in Paris, he told Mary, but he did buy books including Macaulay's *History of England* and Elizabeth Gaskell's novel of the previous year, *Ruth*, which he particularly recommended: 'I like it very well indeed and do not feel at all called upon to join with the "Mr Bradshaws" of society in condemning its tendency – If it comes round in your Library you would like to read it very much.'[71] Anna surely read *Ruth* which controversially focused on a 'fallen' woman with an illegitimate son, presenting her as good and pure-hearted while attacking her judgemental persecuter Mr Bradshaw. Copies of the novel were burned by members of Gaskell's husband's Unitarian congregation, but Anna was likely to have admired Gaskell's true Christian aim. The typically Gaskellian reconciliation between characters at the novel's end, however, was probably a softer result than she would have meted out given the harsh punishments she later dispensed to some of the wrongdoers in *Black Beauty*.

Another novel Anna undoubtedly read around this time was Harriet Beecher Stowe's celebrated 1852 anti-slavery novel, *Uncle Tom's Cabin*. With its exposure of human injustice, its abolitionist message, its staunch Christianity, as well as its Quaker characters, it was a book she must have admired. Although she would never know it, Anna's own novel was to be forever linked with Stowe's when *Black Beauty* was published in America in 1890 subtitled *The Uncle Tom's Cabin of the Horse*.

Philip had commented from France in January 1854 that 'French English Turks & Russians are making all the use they can of [time] to be ready to send the greatest possible quantity of one another into Eternity on the shortest notice.'[72] By autumn reports of bloody Crimean War battles filled the newspapers: Alma, Balaclava, Inkerman. Most disastrous was the mistaken charge of the Light Brigade on 25 October at Balaclava, and Tennyson was not the only one to memorialize the charge in his celebrated poem. Over twenty years later it would make its way into Anna's account of the old war-horse Captain in *Black Beauty* who experienced the charge.

Margaret Sewell notes that Mary and Anna 'were always keenly interested in politics, and were diligent readers of the newspapers'.[73] The newspaper reports Anna now read of the appalling slaughter of men and horses were brought even closer to home by the fact that some of these victims of war were likely to have been sent out from her own neighbouring barracks.[74] It was not only the horrors of battle that Anna would have read about, but the appalling condition of cavalry horses during the bitter Crimean winter. Major Philips of the 8th Hussars wrote in November 1854 that having no hay their mounts were starving: 'at least ten horses have lost their tails in consequence: they have literally been eaten off. Some horses have lost their manes also'.[75] One night 150 horses died on board ship in a gale, the remainder disembarking so emaciated that their saddles did not fit.[76] By December the Cavalry Division had been reduced from 2,000 to about 200 horses, with many of those too sunken and skeletal to be ridden at any speed. Only a few horses ever made it back to England.[77]

Anna must avidly have read reports on her compatriot Florence Nightingale who was thirty-four like herself and whose life shared some similarities. Both had experienced years of spiritual crisis, both strove in their life's work to alleviate suffering, and on her return from the Crimea, Nightingale, too, like Anna, would suffer years of invalidism. 'It was not high position, or extraordinary genius, or [ladies'] "accomplishments," that made a Florence Nightingale,' wrote Mary, in words equally applicable to Anna, 'but it was a firm and faithful devotion of the talents [she] possessed, to objects worthy of women, and of Christians.'[78]

In 1856 Philip and Sarah with their now five children – Mary Grace, Margaret Amie, Lucy Edith, Helen Ada, and John Wright, ranging in age from six to a few months old – came for a long visit to Graylingwell. The grandchildren delighted in Isaac who kept them entertained with playful antics including putting little pieces of cheese on their biscuits which he called 'horses with riders'.[79] Their memories of their Aunt Anna on this visit are not known, but Mary seems to have appeared rather earnest. 'With all her wise thoughts about the care of little ones, and her delight in watching them, Mrs. Sewell did not attract very young children', Bayly writes, 'I think she was never enough of an old lady for them, and she was more sought by their caretakers, who found her a delightful counsellor.'[80] Indeed, it was while at Graylingwell that Mary wrote a series of letters on education at the request of a friend.[81] She certainly grew close to her grandchildren in later years and may have been reserved during this particular holiday through grief as on 2 May 1856 her mother had died and was duly buried in the Quaker burial ground at Lammas.

Anna's health continued to deteriorate and she was forced to give up riding. Painting and reading, too, may have already fallen into desuetude. In summer 1856 she travelled with Mary to Marienberg[82] in Germany to undertake further medical treatment. Mary soon returned to Graylingwell but Anna remained in Germany for almost a year.[83] Marienberg (or Marienburg) was a hydrotherapeutic spa at Boppard (or Boppart), on the Rhine south of Coblenz. A contemporary guidebook described Boppard as 'a very ancient walled town, with 3500 inhab[itants] and dark narrow streets, no better than lanes', which Anna would have grown to know well. In these 'picturesque streets', the guide states, 'the antiquary, architect, and artist will find much to interest them'.[84]

When she had energy, Anna's own artistic impulses no doubt inspired her to sketch or paint local scenes, perhaps the unusual bridged spires of the Hauptkirche or scenes along the Rhine where she may have sat or taken boat trips. Marienberg itself, built in 1738, was a large convent behind the town which had subsequently been a cotton mill and a girls' school before becoming the 'medical boarding-house for the *Water-cure*' where Anna stayed.[85] She made some close friends during her time there although again no trace of their names exists. Bathing in and drinking the waters and undergoing cold-water treatments as during her time with Tennyson, she seems to have had a social and beneficial time. It was probably here that she learned German and the many German songs that her niece Margaret recalled her singing in her 'very sweet and true, though not strong' voice.[86]

Copious correspondence must have been exchanged during these months between Anna in Germany, her parents at Graylingwell, and Philip in Spain, but none has been discovered. Although this was to be a happy time for Anna, for other members of the family it was fraught. On 2 April 1858 Philip and Sarah's sixth child, Philip Edward, had been born in Santander, but Sarah was worryingly ill after the birth. 'I have had many a trouble since I wrote to you last', Mary told her friend 'Mrs R' on 19 April, 'deep anxiety about Sarah . . . [and] I have been very unwell myself'.[87] One of Mary's troubles related to the pecuniary implications of the unexpected decision Isaac had taken, or had thrust upon him, earlier that month.[88] 'My good husband has resigned his position in the Bank', Mary told Mrs R, 'We are able to live without his being in much more business than attending to his own; but I am afraid he will find leisure wearisome. We shall have to be more careful, of course, than we have been, and that is never pleasant, is it, dear?'[89]

Although Isaac had some ongoing business interests in shipping and coal, and probably enough investments so that destitution did not lie in their doorway, having to face real money worries again when she was about to turn sixty would have been far from pleasant for Mary. There were also, of course, Anna's medical expenses. Although treatment on the Continent was cheaper than in Britain, an almost year-long sojourn must have been costly and can only have added to Mary's concerns. Nevertheless, Anna was seeing some benefit, as Mary told Mrs R:

Anna's back and chest are better, feet quite lame, and her head not much better: still, in many ways it will have been a great benefit. She has made dear and valuable friends, and gained a great deal of experience, and seen much variety, which, to such a prisoner as she is, is a great advantage. I expect she will return in May, should nothing unforeseen prevent it.[90]

During Anna's absence, daytime solitude fell heavy on Mary, and it was now that her literary career began. As Bayly records: 'in her sixtieth year she began to write verses, and felt the power growing as she wrote. It was the discovery of a new existence – a new era, though it came as quietly as the leaves unfold in spring.'[91] This sounds like a gloriously inspired blossoming, but it can be no coincidence that this move to authorship coincided with Isaac's leaving the bank. When Mary had written *Walks with Mamma* thirty-two years before at Dalston, it had been because she needed money and there were few other ways she could earn it. Now, too, financial motives undoubtedly encouraged the versification whose origins Mary ascribed to 'the emptiness of her life in Anna's absence'[92] and her desire to contribute 'simple, descriptive poetry' to 'the working man's library'.[93] It was after Anna returned and became Mary's clear-seeing editor that Mary's literary career was truly to flourish.

Anna's health had improved so much by the time she arrived back from Marienberg – probably as planned in May 1857 – that she was walking quite well. She and Mary went to Dorking in the rolling, wooded Surrey countryside for a two-week holiday which they later remembered as a time of unalloyed happiness. For perhaps the only time in her adult life Anna could once more take 'walks with Mamma', and mother and daughter took full advantage, strolling together about this pleasant market town and venturing along some of the many walks through its verdant environs. 'The weather was delicious', Bayly writes, 'all day long they walked and sat among the spring flowers, revelling in the beauty of that lovely place.'[94] In the evenings at their lodging they were so engrossed in Thomas Carlyle's *Past and Present* that they stayed up long into the night drinking coffee to stave off sleep so they could continue with it.[95] Today Carlyle's book is more likely to be found a serviceable soporific than a reason not to dream, but to Anna and Mary this 1843 work of social criticism reflected many of their own concerns. Perhaps they felt as uplifted as Quaker diarist Caroline Fox who wrote on 5 August 1843 'Finished that wondrous "Past and Present," and felt a hearty blessing on the gifted Author spring up in my soul. It is a book which teaches you that there are other months besides May, but that with Courage, Faith, Energy, and Constancy, no December can be "impossible."'[96] Margaret Sewell records that Anna and Mary 'read prose and indulged in a good deal of hero-worship, their heroes being chiefly social reformers, or contemporary writers of fiction and biography'.[97] Carlyle was undoubtedly one of those worshipped.

After the Dorking holiday Anna began helping Mary revise the poems she had written, but in autumn of the same year she was off travelling again. This time she went with Mary and Isaac to visit Philip in Spain or, as an 1845 guidebook described it, 'the most romantic and peculiar country in Europe'.[98] Spain was a less tamed country than others in Europe and fears of highway robbery were widespread. Even twelve years after Anna's visit, when measures to halt such crime had been instituted, an 1869 guidebook advised: 'never attempt resistance against Spanish robbers, as it is generally useless, and may lead to fatal consequences; whereas a frank, good-humoured surrender . . . [and a] courteous appeal to them as *Caballeros*, seldom fails to . . . chloroform the discomfort of the operation'.[99]

Anna, Mary, and Isaac reached Philip's Santander home safely. Apart from her deep enjoyment of time spent with her brother and his family, Anna must have been taken on drives to explore this thriving seaport town with its bustling quay and its attractive new houses. She would have seen the orchards of orange and lemon trees in the surrounding area and have been driven along the town's fashionable promenades. She also surely tried the national breakfast of very thick drinking chocolate, the best of which a guidebook advised was 'made by the nuns, who are great confectioners and compounders of sweetmeats and sugar-plums and orange-flower water and comfits.'[100] There were also bath-houses and the mineral spring *de la Salud* two miles distant whose cures she may have tried.[101]

Back in England again, life continued its usual pattern and Anna's health seems to have remained stronger. Sometime during 1858 preparations began once again for another house move. For reasons unknown, probably economic, perhaps related to Isaac's business interests, the Sewells shifted to a hilltop Wuthering Heights of a house in a tiny Gloucestershire village.

EIGHT

Anna Amazone

1858–64

I could not live without horses, of course I couldn't.
(*Black Beauty*, Chapter 15)

It should not be thought that Anna toiled not neither did she spin, for when strong enough she literally did both; never more so than during her six years at Blue Lodge, the isolated hilltop home at Abson to which she and her parents moved in late 1858. These were whirlwind years of work – domestic, charitable, and editorial – during which Anna innovated and achieved, making a real and felt impact on her world. Although still plagued by lameness and other ongoing symptoms, she enjoyed a period of comparative strength and her truest years as an *Amazone* – as contemporary horsewomen were sometimes known – were upon her.

Set roughly eight miles north-west of Bath and eight east of Bristol, Abson was a little Gloucestershire village one-and-a-half miles north of and above the busier village of Wick, through which ran the old London-to-Bristol road. An area of mining, agriculture, and 'mills of different kinds',[1] Abson-cum-Wick had a population of only 833.[2] As usual Anna was away visiting during the move, and although they were once again, as Mary phrased it, 'out of the way of *temporal* prosperity',[3] funds were found for Isaac's typical house alterations. These included what 'Mrs F', a new poet friend, described as the addition to the 'otherwise very modest house', of 'a large and lofty' drawing room which

> swallowed the Chichester furniture at a mouthful, and gaped for more. But a skilful use of Indian matting, a judicious placing and draping of spare chairs and tables from other rooms, and above all the introduction of Anna's spinning-wheel, had banished all bareness, and given the same air of distinction and simplicity to the room which was so striking in its inhabitants.[4]

While the construction was under way Mary attempted to train an incorrigible maid, and sometime before December, 38-year-old Anna arrived at her new home. Situated down a long driveway off the north side of Lodge Road, the only modern clue to its whereabouts, Blue Lodge still exists, although it has been altered since Anna's time by the addition of a high middle section and division into two residences. It is still an enchanting site with lovely gardens and open rural vistas in an area abundant with horses.

Located a mile west of Abson's centre, Blue Lodge was (and is) ecclesiastically within the parish of Siston,[5] a small village below Abson about a mile and a half west by bridle paths, a bit further by road. In the Sewells' time Blue Lodge was alternatively known as Siston Cottage[6] where the 1861 census lists retired bank manager Isaac aged sixty-seven, Mary sixty-four, Anna forty-two and two house servants, Elizabeth Ashby fifty-six and Ann Ashby twenty-one, as living. Residents are given for the adjacent 'Blue Lodge Farm' comprising 100 acres, so it seems probable that, as at Graylingwell, the Sewells rented a few acres and the main house themselves and another tenant ran the larger surrounding farm.

In the tenth century a Saxon hunting lodge within the now centuries-since deforested royal Kingswood Forest, Blue Lodge in 1858 was a wide two-storied house built of local stone to which a Georgian front had been added at the beginning of the nineteenth century. Near the south-facing front of the house were eighteenth-century out-buildings and a high stone wall which served as a wind break.[7] Beyond that were gardens and views on towards the valley in which Wick nestled and the nether end of the Cotswold hills in the distance. 'Oh, such lovely views', wrote Sarah Stickney Ellis visiting in summer 1859. 'The house is charming amongst old, old trees with a sweet garden; but Mary Sewell and Anna always make everything charming.'[8] Mrs F shared this view of their ability to charm, noting that although Blue Lodge lacked a greenhouse, even in winter the drawing-room vases were filled with 'tasteful arrangements of ivy-sprays'.[9]

For all its grace, Blue Lodge had its drawbacks, as Mary described to Mrs R on 5 December 1858:

We are situated . . . on a high hill which is frequented more by the wind than fogs – though a number of fine trees round us offer a pretty good screen: it is remarkably healthy, and almost as inconvenient as it can be. It is a long way from *everything*, with neither postman, carrier, omnibus, nor rail, neither shop, needle-woman, nor charwoman to be had, so that everything has to be done and obtained with the greatest difficulty. For instance, our letters every day take two good hours to get and post. We are two and a half miles from the school, &c., and the roads almost impass-able in some parts for our chaise, and entirely for foot-passengers in winter wet. And adhesive clay and ruts to break the springs, which was the case last week! You will naturally say, Why did we come here, almost 'out of humanity's reach?' Well dear, humanly speaking, it was a great mistake, a mistake through and through.[10]

If they had moved here to economize, it was an error for, as Bayly recorded, 'the inconveniences of the place made it anything but cheap'.[11] Yet, despite initial misgivings, life at Blue Lodge was to offer Anna some of the happiest, busiest, and most productive experiences of her life.

Anna and Mary immediately embarked on a raft of charitable tasks and tried to stir up philanthropic activity and community spirit in a disenchanted and divided area. These two clear-sighted, deep-hearted, plain-spoken women who lived on the hill made a strong impact on the villagers they befriended. An indomitable pair who pulled as a team, they were a calm, effectual, practical force that, when working to alleviate suffering or improve life for others, allowed no one and nothing to stand in their way. 'We have settled in a thoroughly neglected parish', Mary told Mrs R:

There is *one* sermon from the curate on Sunday, and that is all he does for the souls of seven hundred parishioners. There is a Sunday and day-school, but which no one but the poor discouraged master ever entered. This broke our hearts, and we determined to put forth our strength, with the Lord's help, to do something for them. There was not a tract or book for any one to read, nor any Bible to be purchased. This we felt must be mended also, and therefore, dear friend, as we have taken all this upon us, you will not be surprised, with writing, needlework, and all the *et-cæteras* of housekeeping, that we should have little leisure time.

We are rather afraid that we have engaged with too much for our
strength, but the cry seemed so loud 'Come and help us,' that we
were anxious to try.[12]

Although Wick was set in what Kelly's 1863 *Post Office
Directory of Gloucestershire* described as 'a beautiful and romantic
valley, through which runs the river Boyd',[13] romantic existence was
not the lot of local cottagers. Poverty was evident and conditions
were harsh. Mary roundly condemned the tendency of poets 'to
write sweet fictions about our "rustic hinds," as though they might
live upon the breath of morning – always rosy; and the perfume of
flowers, always in blossom'.[14] Anna and Mary had always been
concerned about the plight of working women and their children,
but here they increasingly, perhaps because of Isaac's own coal
interests, became involved in the lives of the men who delved for
long, gruelling hours in the 'black sepulchre[s]', as Mary called
them,[15] of the great Bristol coalfield, or laboured in all weathers and
states of health on the local farms.

Using their blunt diplomacy and a pertinacious dedication to task
they quickly established a lending library which opened on
6 December 1858, as Mary reported,

with a good number of subscribers, and beautiful books. It has
been a difficult business to set it off. We were strangers, and the
clergy were very suspicious of us, fearing we were Dissenters, and
as we have taken in three parishes, we have three clergymen to
deal with. We determined to hold to broad catholic foundations –
they were no broader than the Church of England. We are
surprised at what we have gained, though James's *Anxious
Inquirer* was cast out, from the name of the writer. We feel that
we have had more help and wisdom than our own, so we thank
God and take courage.[16]

The book purged from their library was *The Anxious Inquirer
After Salvation Directed and Encouraged*, a famous evangelical
work, still reprinted today, by John Angell James (1785–1859), an
eminent Birmingham Congregational minister who had a large
following among dissenters and those with low-church leanings.

Although Anna and Mary's religious views were now broad and non-sectarian, they seem to have attended the Church of England services of the Reverend Thomas Boucher Coney who alternated Sundays between the Norman St James's parish church at Abson and the new, 1850-consecrated church of St Bartholomew in Wick.[17]

Anna's own spiritual voyage continued on a fairly even keel with the occasional capsizal; as Mary revealed to a friend, she was reeling back from the faithless depths: 'I wish you were fully escaped from Doubting castle – It is a miserable place . . . Anna will keep a little dark room in that same old castle, where she sometimes goes and bemoans herself; and I scold her, because the place is let to quite a different sort of people to you and to her!'[18]

Although the improvement in her feet evidenced on her Dorking holiday had regressed, Anna's health at Blue Lodge seems stronger than it had been for the previous twenty years. She began teaching at the neglected village school and was once again strong enough to ride. 'Dearest Nanny is quite lame, and her head very weak', Mary reported to Mrs R that first December, 'but according to her measure she is very active; and her back being strong now, she can ride alone on the pony to the school often in the week.'[19]

Anna had horse sense in more ways than one, and her astute equine understanding was enhanced during her years as an Abson *Amazone*. '[O]f all the recreations . . . none creates more real and heartfelt enjoyment . . . in all ages, than the exercise of riding,' claimed Mrs J. Stirling Clarke in her 1857 *The Habit and the Horse; A Treatise on Female Equitation*: 'for, seated, as we are, high in air, surrounded by the pure atmosphere, and inhaling it, our elasticity is increased, and an indescribable sense of happiness pervades the whole frame. But to feel this exquisitely, proficiency in the art is indispensable.'[20]

Anna certainly possessed what Clarke set out as the 'essential attributes of the lady-like and accomplished horsewoman':

to sit a horse equally well through all his paces – firmly, yet gently, to control his impatient curvettings; fearlessly, yet elegantly, to manage him at speed, with a hand firm, yet light; steadily, yet gracefully, to keep the seat; preserving the balance with ease and seeming carelessness; to have the animal entirely at command,

and, as if both were imbued with one common intelligence, the rider vieing in temper with her steed in spirit; to unite courage with gentleness, and to employ energy at no cost of delicacy.[21]

Although Anna was not among the ladies who rode purely to display the elegance of their forms, she probably did follow current trends in riding wear. Clarke advises that tight lacing, 'pernicious' in pedestrian life, is even more dangerous in riding as it 'lays the foundation of an insidious malady, which either renders [the horsewoman's] life one of lingering misery, or hurries her to a premature grave'.[22] 'Riding stays', she directed, 'should be made elastic over the hips, with particular attention to having the "busks" very short.'[23]

Anna is likely to have also shared her views on underclothing, all 'superfluity' of which was to 'be dispensed with . . . At the same time, the error of extremes into which some ladies run, by the absence of all petticoats, must be carefully avoided.'[24] Petticoats, Clarke advised, should be of 'black satin or silk', not white.[25] 'Trousers', similarly, 'are indispensable both for modesty, and comfort: dark colours are preferable to white; for if the Habit flies up, which is almost certain in cantering, particularly in windy weather, the white immediately catches the eye of the spectator, whilst by being dark, the trousers appear as a portion of the Habit, and pass unnoticed.'[26] The riding habit itself, Clarke directed, should be simple and elegant, with gaudy colours, anything fluttering, and 'everything masculine carefully avoided'.[27] A tip she gave that would have been particularly useful for Anna was that 'Ladies who suffer from cold feet in winter should make a point of warming them before mounting, as it is much easier to keep up the circulation, than to create it. Lamb's-wool socks, or warm soles in the boots, will be found very comfortable.'[28]

Anna had since childhood talked to her horses as she rode or drove and the expert Clarke, as well as approving of the petting of horses constantly indulged in by women riders,[29] recommended communication: 'The voice, soothingly applied, has always a peculiar charm for the horse, and his sagacity and retentive memory soon enable him to distinguish that of his rider . . . The fair equestrian cannot avail herself too much of this characteristic.'[30] In

turn Anna recommends this in *Black Beauty* where ideal groom
John Manly guides Black Beauty 'by the tone of his voice or the
touch of the rein'.[31]

Riding undoubtedly gave Anna, as it gives many women, a sense
of power and independence. Women were advised for their own
safety not to travel by themselves when they could avoid it, but a
horse was sometimes considered a suitable chaperone and protector.
Even more importantly for Anna, on horseback she was free
temporarily from lameness and dependency; she was strong,
powerful, fast, and untouchable. As well as riding for work and
transport purposes, she doubtless carved out time for leisure rides.
She appears to have visited Tracy Park,[32] the estate of the locally
prominent Davy family on the southern edge of Wick. Now a luxury
golf club and hotel, 'The Gloucestershire' in the ancient Tracy Park
Estate boasts in its advertising that Anna was a frequent visitor, and
it is likely that she knew this centuries-old stately home, enjoying
rides through its gracious grounds or taking tea in its lofty rooms.
The Gloucestershire's claim that Anna 'was so inspired that she
based her book Black Beauty around [Tracy Park's] stables', is
probably over-eager, but the 1856 courtyard stable block possibly
influenced some scenes.[33]

Not everyone was as fortunate with horses as Anna. In August or
September 1859 the Sewells' seventeen-year-old groom was killed in
a freak accident when out with Anna's pony. Sarah Stickney Ellis,
who was visiting at the time, reported:

> as we were sitting reading in the afternoon, a loud knock came to
> that almost untouched door, and tidings that he had had an
> accident. Isaac and Mary both went out in a tempest of rain;
> Anna and I sat alone wondering. Presently another knock, and
> tidings that the poor boy was quite dead. He had been trying to
> pass a cart; the pony slipped on the wet ground, and the boy fell
> with his head on the hard road, and the wheel of the cart went
> over it; and three days afterwards, when I walked over the spot,
> the stains of the blood were all about the place to such an extent
> as seemed almost impossible. In the stillness and solitude of that
> out of the world place thou mayst suppose what a sensation was
> created. Mary and Anna were greatly troubled, and the servant

wept night and day; nobody liked to be left alone . . . every poor person we met stopped and talked sadly and solemnly about it.[34]

Blue Lodge's isolation had advantages in that regular callers did not, as Mary put it, 'cut up' their time 'into bits . . . Every one who came to see us had to climb up a long steep hill, so that they had to be very much in earnest to do it. We could take our own times for going to them, and so we got through something.'[35] One of the things they 'got through' was producing most of Mary's literary works. Mary composed verses as she paced their long, straight hazel-lined[36] path which suited her exactly: 'A crinkle-crankle walk is dreadful,' she said, 'it cuts off all one's rhymes.'[37] Anna read and advised on everything that came from her mother's pen and took over the housekeeping. '[I]t seems to suit her well,' noted Sarah Stickney Ellis in 1859, 'she is very brisk, but her feet still useless.'[38]

Anna's Aunt Wright, who would die on 18 January 1861, had been publishing regularly throughout the 1850s, and her Aunt Maria Wright in 1859 produced both *The Anchor of Hope; or, New Testament Lessons for Children* and *The Bow of Faith; or, Old Testament Lessons for Children*. It was Mary, however, who was to find the greatest literary fame in the family until Anna's own novel was published. In her sixties and seventies, Mary wrote verse designed for the moral and practical edification of the working classes and children. She used simple language that reflected both her readership's needs and her own dislike for fancy phraseology and affected manners[39] (years later when a friend referred to her beehive as an apiary, Mary responded indignantly: 'It's a *bee-hut*'[40]). Her verses encouraged the following of God's will, condemned cruelty, unkindness, sloth, alcohol, and wastefulness, and promoted sound moral behaviour, charity, and love for one's neighbour. They also offered practical instruction in housekeeping, parenting, and dealing with hardship. Although a contemporary reviewer stated, '[Mary Sewell's] works are printed by hundreds of thousands, and have a world of readers',[41] she herself made no exalted claims, readily accepting that she wrote verse rather than poetry. Her skill was, as she put it, 'a knack of a rough sort of rhyming that serves my purpose . . . all the Byron at Friends' Meeting trained me well in rhythm'.[42] Her 'straightforward, unflinching attack on literary self-love', Mrs F maintained, 'was a compliment to sense and temper'.[43]

After writing her first ballads at Graylingwell, Mary in 'fear and trembling' had shown them to their old Brighton friend, Henry S. King.[44] He was now a partner in the London publishing house, Smith, Elder and Co.,[45] and after reading them over in her presence, he announced: 'This will do.'[46] Mary's *Homely Ballads for the Working Man's Fireside* were duly published in 1858.[47] Mary admired Henry's professional acumen, but Anna possibly still held a more personal admiration for him. After his wife died in childbirth in February 1860,[48] she may have once more let thoughts of romance ripple through her mind, but again it was not to be. In September 1863 Henry married Harriet Eleanor Baillie-Hamilton, a poet half his age, 'noble-minded, red-haired and pre-Raphaelite-looking', and Anna's junior by twenty years.[49]

'[The Sewells] have indeed other troubles, but amidst all Mary Sewell is doing wonders with her little poems', Sarah Stickney Ellis noted in 1859. 'Two publishers are wanting to have them, and they bid one against another so that she enjoys the full pleasure of her own plentiful pocket-money, which is no small cause for rejoicing.'[50] Because of outbidding, a Norfolk connection, or because Mary favoured their temperance connections, Jarrold and Sons (now Jarrolds) of London and Norwich, who were 'publishers for the people',[51] became her permanent publishers.

Mary's most famous work, *Mother's Last Words*, came out in November 1860. It was soon 'in everybody's mouth',[52] and from then on she was dubbed 'Mrs Sewell, Author of *Mother's Last Words*', The ballad tells of two young orphan boys who in obedience to their mother's dying words choose to suffer as crossing sweepers rather than turn to crime. It had 'a sale unprecedented in the history of ballads', selling over a million copies within Mary's lifetime,[53] doing well in America, and being widely translated in Europe. The tear-inducing qualities of the poem were lauded. Dora Greenwell in 1865 wrote, 'We have seen a class of adult criminals . . . follow its course with eager, attentive eyes, with broken exclamations, with sobs, with floods of tears.'[54] Jarrold and Sons' advertising claimed, '[t]he Superintendent of the Lambeth Ragged Schools writes: – "I read 'MOTHER'S LAST WORDS' to 260 Boys in our School; many were melted to tears, and all listened with breathless attention, requesting that I would read it again another night."[55]

Mary soon followed this success with other popular works[56] such as *Our Father's Care* (1861), a ballad about a poor London watercress girl,[57] and her epistolary novel *Patience Hart's First Experience in Service* (1862),[58] narrated by a spirited kitchen maid. Mary's ballads were widely reprinted and were read aloud to prisoners, the sick, dying children, the poor, sailors, and anyone they might edify. Hundreds more people heard them than bought them, and they were sometimes read with accompanying lantern slides. Many were initially published individually in Jarrold and Sons' 'Household Tracts For The People' series, which sold for 'Twopence each, or in enamelled wrapper, Threepence' or could be bought at two shillings per dozen. Charitable organizations bought by the dozen and distributed copies to schools and the poor. Mary was soon besieged by fan mail, as a friend recalled: 'So much was she made of just then, that I said to her quite playfully, "I hope they won't spoil you." "My dear," she replied, turning on me almost reproachfully, "I have *nothing* to be proud of; it all came in answer to prayer." "Yes," she added immediately after, "even the rhymes."'[59]

As an author Mary achieved celebrity in the charitable circles that mattered to them, but it is clear that Anna's editorial role was crucial. 'All Mary Sewell's work was subjected to Anna's very honest criticism and approval,' Margaret Sewell recalled, 'and no doubt gained much by it.'[60] 'My Nannie has always been my critic and counsellor', wrote Mary, 'I have never made a plan for anything without submitting it to her judgment. Every line I have written has been at her feet before it has gone forth to the world . . . Oh, if I can only pass my Nannie, I don't fear the world after that.'[61]

Anna was at once her mother's keenest admirer and most uncompromising critic. She was 'exacting in her love'[62] and would, with what Mary called 'her usual frank criticism', point out anything that was not good enough.[63] 'I was once with Anna when her mother read aloud to us something she was preparing for the press', writes Bayly:

It was beautiful to witness the intense love, admiration, and even pride which beamed in the daughter's face, but this in no wise

prevented her being, as I thought, a very severe critic. Nature had
bestowed on her a remarkably sweet-toned and persuasive voice.
I think I hear her now, saying 'Mother dear, thee must alter that
line,' or 'Thee must put a fuller word there, that will give out
more of thy meaning.'[64]

Their intense involvement in Mary's writing was one of the ways
in which Anna and Mary led lives that by now were almost one.
Margaret Sewell remembered her aunt and grandmother as:

not only mother and daughter, but close friends. As far as I can
remember, Anna had no friends apart from those who were also
friends of her mother. She and her mother lived one life. Anna
practically never left home, and all their interests were in common
. . . Anna was idolized by both father and mother. Though visibly
dependent upon them, they in their turn were in many ways
dependent upon her.[65]

Elisabeth Boyd Bayly echoes this view: 'Never could there be a more
perfect love than existed between this mother and daughter – the
never-ceasing joy of each other's lives; but in their union, it was the
active, impetuous mother who leaned: she originated, and the frail,
ripe-judging daughter weighed the product.'[66] Bayly agrees, noting:

In many respects the lives and interests of Mrs. Sewell and her
daughter were so closely associated that the story of one
describes the other . . . the usual relative positions of mother and
child were reversed in them. I cannot say that the daughter led,
for the impulse to action came usually from the mother, but the
daughter pronounced judgment upon it. The enforced sedentary
habits of Anna's life were favourable to early maturity of
judgment, and Mrs. Sewell was by nature quick to bend to the
opinion of one she trusted.[67]

'There was about them both such a rare distinction', writes Mrs F:
'It was not mere intellect, or mere goodness, or even mere nobility,
though it had much of all these in its composition . . . it was the
general effect produced by uncommon intellectual powers,

combined with still more uncommon integrity and simplicity, and directed by a [supreme] "charity".'[68] She added that Anna and Mary were an:

> unconventional . . . pair of twin souls. . . . They could not be anything but dignified and courteous. . . . The 'plain living' which they loved to associate with 'high-thinking' was marked by exquisite order and nicety, such as one rarely sees. Yet all seemed to spring up naturally around them, with no petty anxieties or fatigues to themselves, and no worrying of dependents. All was lovely calm, yet full of cheerful activities that never jostled each other.[69]

Mary was effectual, determined, and enthusiastic. She was friendly and outgoing and had a strong faith in others, sometimes disappointedly so. Anna, as well as being highly intelligent, tenacious, practical, and passionate in her beliefs, was more clear-sighted, more self-critical, and exercised more judgement and reserve than her mother. This was not the reserve of a shrinking violet. 'Physically weak, [Anna] had a very strong character and was quite fearless', wrote her niece:

> many instances of her courage were told to us. The sight of cruelty to animals or to the helpless, or even thoughtlessness and indifference to suffering, roused her indignation almost to fury, and wherever she was, or whoever she had to face, she would stop and scathe the culprit with burning words.[70]

Philip's family seem to have been living near London for at least some of 1859 and 1860 and in 1861, perhaps before their return to Spain, Anna's four nieces, aged from seven to eleven, came on a visit. Her two nephews were probably in school. Philip and Sarah's third son, Henry Eustace, had died aged nine months the previous December. Anna and Mary enjoyed the visit, as Mary told a friend: 'It is something quite new to us to have so much young life about us, but it is very charming to see the ever-hopeful elasticity, and boundless expectation, and simple faith of children.'[71] 'She could not only tell stories, but *play* stories', Margaret remembered of Mary:

There was a rocking-boat in the hall, which was a great feature. We remember the delights of the afternoon play-hour; she would play at going on journeys, when an enemy would come after us, and we all had to jump into the boat and row for our lives – just what children delight in.[72]

Anna undoubtedly took her nieces for drives in the countryside and drew pictures for them just as she so often would in later years. By 8 October 1863 when Isabel Gertrude, Anna's youngest niece, was born, Philip and his family were living in France.

Mary's authorship income provided a level of freedom that she and Anna had never before, enabling them to make financial decisions of their own. They embarked, as they always did when the freedom to follow dreams allowed, on some intensive charity schemes. They did not simply give money away; their help was always practical, use was made of what was available, and nothing in their own household was wasted. Mrs F's comments of Mary apply equally to Anna:

> She had a profound appreciation – an appreciation which cost her unspeakable suffering – of the miseries of others. The miseries of biting poverty, still more those of vice and ungodliness, were terrible to her heart and imagination, and she found no rest save in using her powers to the utmost in remedying them when they came within reach of her living presence or her pen . . . She was no socialist, no democrat; – but she courageously recognised the grains of truth hidden in socialism and democracy at a time when such recognition was rare in religious circles and involved loss of caste, and loss of confidence among many whose good opinion she highly valued.[73]

Together with regular district visiting, Anna's teaching at the day school, the founding of the library, and work on Mary's writing, by 1862 Anna and Mary were also involved heavily in the cause of temperance, the flourishing anti-alcohol movement. 'My unspeakable hatred to our liquor laws, and all that pertains to strong drink', wrote Mary, 'is, that drink has done so much to fill our country with these two extremes – on the one hand, the vulgar pride of wealth, and on the other, the most abject, degrading, soul-destroying poverty.'[74] Anna would later inject a temperance message into *Black Beauty* and Philip would turn down £10,000 rather than have a pub run on land he owned.[75]

Drunkenness was a visible problem in Abson-cum-Wick, and Anna and Mary repeatedly saw the damage it did in absorbing money needed for necessities and its contribution to domestic violence. Early in 1862 Mary also spent an evening visiting the gin-palaces of London with a city missionary as she described in the chapter titled 'The Monster Evil' of her book *Thy Poor Brother*:

> I looked on into those dull, half-alive faces, at those half-stupified bodies, which had crept from the cold and wet outside, into a warm, dry and cheerful place – the like of which, they could not find in their own homes. They were not all talkative, nor intoxicated; the larger number of those I saw, looked under a spell, stupid, apathetic, drowsy; some few were noisy and argumentative . . . As I stood there in the warmth, and light, and thought of the rain outside, and of the miserable homes, in alleys, and attics, I said to myself, 'I should come here, and do as they do, if I did not know better.'[76]

Their own area had, Mary wrote, 'three public-houses and three beer-shops', but no other place where a man could go if far from home 'to rest himself, to eat his dinner, protect himself from the weather, spend an evening, or transact his business. For all these necessities, he is obliged to go to the public-house, and then, as a matter of course, he must drink for the good of the house.'[77] This limitation extended from men to beasts as Mary pointed out:

> There is also a considerable traffic through our village, in the conveyance of goods to large adjacent towns. The roads are hilly, and the horses often require to stop. In the distance of eight or ten miles, there is not a place where a man can sit down, or get a drink of water for his horses, except at the public-houses.[78]

In order to 'arrest the inveterate drinking habits of our villages', Anna and Mary founded a local Temperance Brotherhood. As Mary described in a May 1868 paper she wrote for a Ladies' Temperance Conference in London, she and Anna called on villagers and 'solicited co-operation, and, failing that, deprecated opposition.'[79] They soon had a core of eight working men who wanted to help. Anna and Mary met with their little band, prayed for God's guidance, and split the area into eight districts. Each man was responsible for a district of about one hundred people and fortnightly delivered to every home one of Jarrolds' temperance tracts and sought 'by conversation to awake interest in the subject'.[80] Every two or three weeks for the first four months Anna and Mary met with their 'brothers' to discuss progress, pray, read Scripture, sing a hymn, and partake of 'coffee, cocoa, and currant cake'.[81]

Soon enough interest had been raised for a public meeting to be held in the village schoolroom where more than sixty villagers pledged to abstain from alcohol.[82] Anna and Mary also founded a Band of Hope, a temperance group for children, and in June 1862 Mary told Mrs R that success continued:

> on Whit-Tuesday, we gave a Tea-meeting to our pledged abstainers – I suppose about a hundred and twenty. We had tables on the lawn, and a capital cake and bread and butter. After tea we adjourned to the little spacious barn which had been prepared for the occasion, and had an excellent meeting . . . we are not sectarian, and I hope and trust we may not be so, or else I feel that the large measure of blessing that we have received in working together as brethren will be likely to leave us. Love and union is all my aim.[83]

Anna and Mary may have been encouraged into temperance work by Sarah Stickney Ellis who like her husband was a staunch supporter of teetotalism, but their zeal was also influenced by Julia [Mrs Charles] Wightman's temperance book *Haste to the Rescue; or, Work While it is Day* (1860).[84] Learning while on a visit to the area that the author of *Mother's Last Words* lived in the vicinity, Julia Wightman called on the Sewells just as they were establishing their brotherhood and to their delight offered them plenty of first-hand advice in their 'little cause'.[85]

In July 1863 Mrs F visited Blue Lodge. Although thirty years
younger, Mrs F developed a close friendship with Mary whom she
idolized, although she kept up a regular correspondence with both
Mary and Anna, Anna often writing on her mother's behalf as well
as on her own account.[86] Mrs F commented of Mary: 'No doubt
the fact that the reigning friendship of her life had been with her
own daughter made it natural to her to put herself on a level with
the comparatively young and inexperienced.'[87] Mrs F's visit was
filled with literary talk and, for Mary and Mrs F, garden walks.
Mrs F's journal account of her blissful, yet productive, four-day
visit gives an idyllic description of Blue Lodge and its inhabitants at
that time:

Monday, July 27, 1863. – Pony-chaise met me at Keynsham
station. Lovely drive through quiet and sunny country. After
dinner commenced reading [Mary's] 'Thy Poor Brother,' and went
on for an hour, Mrs. Sewell reading, and I offering criticism. Her
genuine modesty struck me greatly . . . To the MS. again before
tea. Tea on the lawn, under wide tree-shadows, with beds of
brilliant flowers spread all about. After tea more MS., till
moonlight drew us again to the garden. A long talk there on
things in heaven and earth and ranging between the two . . .
Delightful company!
Tuesday, July 28. – The window of my room gave me the view of
a sunny, park-like, upland field, sprinkled with calm tree-
shadows, under which newly-shorn sheep rested here and there.
Birds singing softly all about. Breakfast in a sunny parlour . . .
Walked in the garden for a quarter of an hour after breakfast with
Mrs. Sewell. Then she established me in her private sitting-room,
with letters to write, and Bushnell's 'Inner Life.' At twelve we met
in the drawing-room, Mrs. S., Anna, and I, and went on with
'Thy Poor Brother' . . . Tea again on the lawn . . . After supper,
recited Wordsworth's 'Ode on Intimations of Immortality.' Talked
of his poems generally.
July 29. – Mrs. Sewell claimed *my* promise to read her parts of my
MS . . . Drove in the evening with Anna to Wick. Saw their
cottage, taken for Mothers' Meetings, &c. Afterwards another
spell at the MS.[88]

'On leaving,' Mrs F reported, 'Mr. Sewell drove me to the station. He was a most kind and courteous host, ever ready to welcome the friends of his wife and daughter. Both then and afterwards, I was struck with the patience and cheerfulness with which he bore the reverses of life.'[89] She also offers insight into Anna's household role. While she and Mary strolled outside, Mrs F recalled:

> Anna would appear from time to time at the garden door of the house, shading her eyes with her hand, and trying to discover our whereabouts, anxious to meet any possible want or wish of her mother's . . . At the time I speak of, Anna was unable to stand for more than a few seconds at a time, though she moved freely about the house. Wherever Mrs. Sewell and I might be working at our proofs, or discussing questions they suggested, if household affairs brought the daughter to her mother's side, she was obliged to kneel on the nearest support for the minute she remained.[90]

Bayly, having met Mary the previous year, also visited that summer when Mary was writing the final chapters of *Thy Poor Brother*, and she describes herself, Mary, and Anna sitting together in the drawing room: '[Mary] read me some of the earlier chapters. They were so suggestive, we talked and talked, complaining of nothing but the lapse of time. Anna was lying on the sofa – her mother sitting at her feet, with one hand rubbing the lame foot, with the other holding the manuscript out of which she was reading.'[91] 'The parting came all too soon', Bayly recalls:

> In the afternoon it poured with rain. When the carriage that was to take me to the station came to the door, Anna was standing in the hall, enveloped in a large mackintosh. The future writer of 'Black Beauty' was to be my driver. I found that she and her mother were in the habit of driving out on most days, without attendance, the understanding between themselves and their horse being perfect. The persistent rain obliged us to keep up our umbrellas. Anna seemed simply to hold the reins in her hand, trusting to her voice to give all needed directions to her horse. She evidently believed in a horse having a moral nature, if we may judge by her mode of remonstrance. 'Now thee

shouldn't walk up this hill – don't thee see how it rains?' 'Now thee must go a little faster – thee would be sorry for us to be late at the station.'[92]

During this drive Bayly spoke to Anna about Horace Bushnell's 'Essay on Animals'.[93] Bushnell (1802–76) was a Congregationalist pastor in Hartford, Connecticut and the author of a string of theological books and pamphlets including the intriguingly titled *Moral Uses of Dark Things* (1868). Given Mrs F's reference to being set up by Mary with Bushnell's 'Inner Life', Anna had probably that very summer already read some of his work. Mary would later write of her great admiration for him: 'such a great soul: such a powerful mind – so simple, affectionate, genial, and childlike'.[94] Bayly told Anna that Bushnell set forth a God–human–animal hierarchy in which humans were created to follow the will of God and animals to follow the will of humans. Animals, especially horses, were created by God to provide strength for human use. Bushnell argued that, according to God's will, animals would be very happy serving humans provided they were well treated; it was therefore incumbent on people to treat them kindly. Anna absorbed these ideas, as she told Mary Bayly after writing *Black Beauty*:

> The thoughts you gave me from Horace Bushnell years ago have followed me entirely through the writing of my book, and have, more than anything else, helped me to feel it was worth a great effort to *try*, at least, to bring the thoughts of men more in harmony with the purposes of God on this subject.[95]

Mary's *Thy Poor Brother* was published in December 1863. Written in the form of letters to a supposed friend who needs advice on helping the poor in her district, it recounts under the guise of a fictional 'lady' Mary and Anna's own experiences in helping the poor, drunken, crazed, and fallen.[96] Anna had been, as always, a tough and thorough editor, but she had also meanwhile taken on a new project of her own.

Anna had started evening classes for 'men and lads', in Wick.[97] In the 1850s and 1860s adult education was burgeoning and many villages started night schools for local workers. Anna's teaching, in which Mary soon joined, was closely bound up with their temperance ideals and took great determination to get under way at a time when their progress towards local sobriety had been scuppered. 'The public meeting and Band of Hope were allowed at first to be held in the schoolroom', Mary recalled,

> but the rector after a while withdrew his permission altogether, and our public meetings ceased. This was a great blow, and paralysed the work; our members fell away, and some found their way back to the public-house. After many months of anxiety and fruitless effort, occasionally holding a meeting in a Dissenting chapel, a house became vacant, which was immediately hired.[98]

'The last week we have opened a miniature Working Men's Hall in our village,' Mary reported to Mrs R on 30 November 1863, 'fourteen feet square. I am high busy, preparing lectures, addresses, &c. Nanny and I drive to Wick three evenings in the week at eight o'clock. Don't you think we shall get very brave and hardy before the winter is over? We have had such a very encouraging beginning.'[99] This 'Work-men's Reading-room' served not only as Anna's night school but as a place 'to which converts from the public-house could be invited'.[100] 'It was a great reward to us to find that, soon after our room was opened, the skittle-alleys were forsaken', Mary reported with gleaming satisfaction.[101]

Their Working Men's Club soon had forty members 'not exclusively abstainers' who paid fourpence a month.[102] They were assisted on probably three other evenings in the week by 'two valuable members who lived near the spot' who superintended reading, writing, and arithmetic.[103] Mary stated that she and Anna taught:

> any subject likely to awaken interest and inquiry, such as geography, natural history, biography, and, if I dare use the word, science. The evenings were closed at nine o'clock, by reading a portion of Scripture and singing the Doxology. I often feared that our simple lessons would not be sufficiently attractive to keep up the attendance, and several times I inquired if the introduction of draughts, dominoes, &c., would not be an advantage, but that

was always met by a decided rejection of them. They were considered QUALIFICATIONS for PUBLIC-HOUSE company.[104]

Some evenings en route to Wick Anna would stop at the butcher's to collect a bullock's or sheep's eye which she would then dissect for her 'astonished' students in order to reveal the amazing mechanism of sight. Or she might explain that wheat's deep fibrous roots enabled it to flourish in seasons when other plants perish from drought. The miraculous nature of God's creations was often the subtext of her lessons.[105]

This teaching was, Mary recalled 'replete with interest and full of sweet reward' but necessarily

> somewhat laborious; the lessons required considerable time in the preparation to render them very simple and easy to be understood, and in all seasons we had a drive of two miles to the reading-room in an open carriage by a very hilly and, in part, unfrequented road; but during our first winter we were only twice prevented from going out, and during the whole time that we journeyed to and fro no accident occurred to us and no molestation was offered.[106]

Anna was morally fearless and physically unafraid and was undaunted by this dark travelling, whereas Mary was sometimes fazed. Having 'very little physical courage',[107] Mary was often tremulous on these nights when Anna guided their pony chaise carefully down the unlit muddy hill into Wick and back home again when drunken men might be staggering near, but her faith in Anna's driving skill, was absolute. Mrs F wrote of these journeys:

> At that time a weakness of the limbs confined [Anna] much indoors, except for the almost daily drives with her mother to the village, to visit their cottage friends and superintend the working-men's club they had established. These drives often fell on cold and wet winter nights, and I remember Anna's gentle triumph in having falsified her friends' predictions of physical harm to herself from the exposure, her mother gaily adding, 'In fact, we've come to regard night drives in an open carriage in bad weather as a positive cure for delicacy.'[108]

In addition to evening classes there was also a monthly meeting to 'receive the pence' and discuss society matters including voting on whether to introduce or reject members. Attendees dressed for these popular occasions, taking 'a sociable cup of coffee before commencing business' and afterwards enjoying an 'amusement' such as a reading, lecture, or singing. 'Reading the Scriptures, a short religious address, and prayer, with a hearty shake of the hand', Mary reported, 'closed these meetings at half-past nine o'clock'.[109]

Mary maintained that while their evening meetings 'were never exclusively religious . . . a religious influence decidedly prevailed in them'.[110] Anna and Mary regarded transformation from pub attendance to Christian faith as the best way forward for temperance, while awaiting the introduction of stricter alcohol laws. They also felt strongly about the importance of mutual help within the community and were pleased when what they had taught was taken away by the men and pursued in conversations in the village and within families.[111]

They used their hall for night classes, temperance meetings, probably their Band of Hope, and soon also for a Mothers' Meeting. Mary regarded Mothers' Meetings as offering 'the fairest prospect we have, for the elevation of the lower classes'.[112] She and Anna knew that working-class women could not always attend religious services and, if they could, sermons often went over their heads, so simple explanations of Bible verses were one component of their meetings. This was something that Mary Bayly had suggested.[113] Bayly was possibly the 'Mrs Bayley' who is considered to be the founder of women's meetings which were held 'among the pigsties and brickfields in the Kensington Potteries in the year 1853'.[114] She was certainly the author of *Ragged Homes and How to Mend Them* and *The Story of the English Bible*, and with such interests it is easy to see why she became Mary's friend and biographer. Anna and Mary's Mothers' Meetings probably ran for about two hours a week and, as well as religion, attendees were taught practical skills in cooking, housework, healthcare, childcare, literacy, and how to maintain a moral household and deal with a drunken husband.[115]

The Blue Lodge years, so busy, productive, and rewarding for Anna and Mary, were less satisfying for Isaac. Involved only peripherally, if supportively, in the activities of his wife and daughter, lacking companionship apart from Quaker meetings at Frenchay near Bristol which he regularly attended,[116] and no longer having a career, he grew restless. Perhaps it was this imbalance in family activities that prompted Mary to comment: '[t]he wasted hours of most men would do almost half the work of women'.[117] As early as December 1858 she had written: 'My good husband is pretty well, but I often grieve over him in this very secluded place: there is no one to speak to but the ploughman.'[118] In 1863 Isaac was appointed as manager of the new branch of the London and South Western Bank in Brighton.[119] He does not, however, appear to have taken up the post because on 17 November that year, aged seventy, he became manager of the London and South Western Bank's new Bath branch.[120]

Anna and Mary felt stark defeat at having to disrupt their plans, halt all their busy activities, pack up their belongings, and sometime before July 1864 move into lodgings at Combe Down, near Bath until they could secure a new home. They determinedly continued to drive the eight to ten miles to Wick to teach three evenings a week, but during the winter of 1864–5, Mary suffered a period of poor health and this became impossible to sustain.[121] The Wick whirlwinds were forced to leave it all behind.

NINE

Arranging the Fruit Worst Side Out

1864–71

I could not complain, nor make known my wants.

(*Black Beauty*, Chapter 30)

'Dear Nanny is pretty well,' Mary reported to Mrs R from Combe Down on 4 July 1864, '[but] the fatigue of leaving all right at Blue Lodge knocked her down, and she has again lost a good deal of her walking power.'[1] Anna was affected physically and emotionally by the move from Abson, and these months in temporary lodgings were a period of desolate readjustment. 'It seemed very hard at first', wrote Mary, 'to be cramped up in little rooms with no garden of our own, and all strangers about us, and no welcome from the faces we met.'[2]

If it was a wrench leaving all their charitable endeavours behind, it was heartbreaking to learn that no one had taken up the reins. '[W]hen we were finally obliged to leave the neighbourhood and other helpers were also removed', Mary wrote, 'no one remaining to take up the work – our interesting Band of Hope and the Reading-room Society were necessarily broken up, to the mutual grief and deep regret of all parties.'[3] One of the many letters they received before they left, poorly spelled but heart-felt, reveals the revered way in which the ladies from the hill were regarded in Abson-cum-Wick:

> I understand to well that you are about to leave us, and I feel deep regret on account of it: tis always Good to have a friend and Bad to be without one . . . I have never forgott, nor never shall, your great kindness. Both you and Mr. and Miss Sewell has always a verry High Place in my affections . . . my heart is full while I write. I feel like the Disciples did when Jesus was going to leave them, but I hope the Lord will still Bless us all and Bless you most wherever you go. When I think how Benificial you have been to

the inhabitants of wick how they will all miss you and Miss Sewell when you are gone away.

I hope dear Miss Sewell got home safe – when I met her in the rood to wick, I was so overjoyed I felt like one lifted out of the Body. I couldn't help my tears after we parted . . . Please to pardon my faults. We send our united love to you, dear Lady, and Mr. Sewell, and dear Miss Sewell.[4]

To those who may doubt the fulfilments of Anna's life, testimony like this shows that her choice of selflessness and a life of charity brought its own rewards. The joy she gave this worker on the road is more than evidence of a life well led, it demonstrates Anna's gift of giving spiritual strength to others even as she dealt with difficulties of her own.

These months at Combe Down were testing ones. 'When cut off from the occupations and circumstances that to a great degree build up our personality, we almost lose ourselves', Mary reported. 'I am feeling . . . a poor, empty, barren, hard-hearted, pitiful wretch.'[5] Combe Down itself, situated three miles above and southeast of Bath's centre, was a village where Bath stone was quarried, and its air was thought beneficial for invalids. In Mary's words they were in 'a very high, healthy situation, and the surrounding scenery is most beautiful'.[6] Bath offered much to Anna, as Mary recorded: 'she has many advantages, with close proximity of church, chapel, schools, shops, &c., which she had not before'.[7] Isaac meanwhile entered his new life as bank manager with an eagerness the direct inverse of his wife and daughter's. 'My goodman is pretty well', Mary told Mrs R, 'and likes his work.'[8] Philip and Sarah with their seven surviving children that year returned to England, settling at Clare House in New Catton, a suburb of Norwich. Philip took a position in Gurney's Bank in Norwich and when it became Barclays Bank in 1896 he became one of the directors.[9]

Before the end of 1864 circumstance had brightened for 44-year-old Anna, and the family had moved into The Moorlands, which Elisabeth Boyd Bayly deemed 'the loveliest of all their homes'.[10] It took some work for its full loveliness to emerge due to the neglect of the previous tenant,[11] and it was perhaps this effort to which Mary was referring when she told Mrs R: 'Anna is much better; we are

The narrow three-storeyed house at 26 Church Plain, Yarmouth, where Anna Sewell was born on 30 March 1820. Seen here in 2002, it is graced with bunting for Queen Elizabeth II's Golden Jubilee. *(Adrienne Gavin)*

An oil painting of Anna Sewell in her youth. *(Reproduced by kind permission of the owner)*

A drawing by Louis George Dudley, dated November 1935, of Dudwick Cottage (left), where Anna often stayed with her maternal grandparents, and Dudwick House (right), home of her Aunt and Uncle Wright. Beyond the properties is Dudwick Park with a carriageway through it leading out to Buxton. *(Reproduced by kind permission of the owner)*

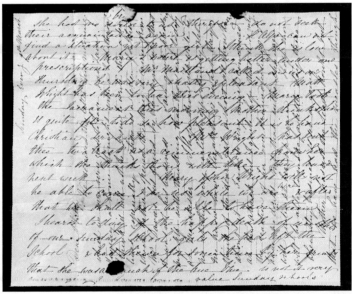

A letter from Anna Sewell in Brighton to her brother Philip in Yorkshire, dated 9 March 1845, in which she writes 'how pleasant it is to have Christian servants'. The crossed writing is typical for letters of the time. *(NRO MC 144/33, reproduced by permission of the Norfolk Record Office)*

Anna Sewell, probably in her late twenties or thirties, in a photograph that she gave to her brother Philip and signed 'your very loving Sister Anna Sewell'. *(Reproduced from Mrs [Mary] Bayly,* The Life and Letters of Mrs Sewell, *London, James Nisbet and Co., 1889)*

An oil painting of Isaac Sewell, the only known likeness of Anna's father. *(Reproduced by kind permission of the owner)*

Anna's mother Mary Sewell. *(Reproduced from* The House of Jarrolds 1823–1923, *Norwich, Jarrolds, 1924, by permission of Norfolk County Council Library and Information Service)*

Mary Sewell (seated) and Anna Sewell. *(Reproduced from* The House of Jarrolds 1823–1923, *by permission of Norfolk County Council Library and Information Service)*

An oil painting of Anna Sewell, probably in her late thirties or forties. *(Reproduced by kind permission of the owner)*

The White House (now Anna Sewell House), where Anna lived from 1867 to 1878 and where she wrote *Black Beauty*, photographed in 2002. The plaque commemorating Anna has been removed temporarily. *(Adrienne Gavin)*

Above left: A rare photograph of Anna Sewell taken around the time she wrote *Black Beauty*. *(Reproduced from A.A. Dent, 'Miss Sewell of Norfolk'*, East Anglian Magazine *15:10 (August 1956), p. 543 by permission of EDPpics and the Syndics of Cambridge University Library)*

Above right: Anna's brother Philip Sewell in later life. *(Reproduced from* Philip Edward Sewell: A Sketch, London, Jarrold and Sons, *[1910] by permission of Norfolk County Council Library and Information Service)*

Left: Anna Sewell's writing slope. A brass monogram 'AS' affixed to the desk can be seen when closed. *(Reproduced by kind permission of the owner)*

"The moon had just risen above the hedge, and by its light I could see Smith lying a few yards beyond me."—*Page* 121.

Above: Frontispiece and title page of the first British edition of *Black Beauty*, 1877. (*Reproduced by kind permission of the owner*)

Over One Hundred Thousand Copies of this Book have been Sold in England.

BLACK BEAUTY:
HIS GROOMS AND COMPANIONS.
By A. SEWELL.
THE "UNCLE TOM'S CABIN" OF THE HORSE.

AMERICAN EDITION PUBLISHED BY THE AMERICAN HUMANE EDUCATION SOCIETY.
GEORGE T. ANGELL, PRESIDENT. 19 MILK ST., BOSTON.

☞ Read the Introductory Chapter.

Right: Front cover of the first American edition of *Black Beauty*, 1890. (*Reproduced by permission of Norfolk County Council Library and Information Service*)

Cartoon by Tony Hall that appeared in the *Eastern Daily Press* on 6 September 1984 after Anna Sewell's grave was bulldozed. The caption read: 'The monument to Anna Sewell they cannot bulldoze away'. *(Reproduced by kind permission of Tony Hall and the* Eastern Daily Press*)*

IN
AFFECTIONATE REMEMBRANCE OF
ANNA SEWELL,
DAUGHTER OF
ISAAC & MARY SEWELL,
WHO DIED AT CATTON
APRIL 25TH 1878,
AGED 58 YEARS.

Anna Sewell's gravestone, 2002. After her grave was bulldozed in 1984 her gravestone was 'tidied up' and placed in a wall outside the former Friends' Meeting House in Lammas. It is flanked on one side by her parents' and on the other side by her maternal grandparents' gravestones. *(Adrienne Gavin)* getting on well, working like – Trojans, shall I say? Or English women? I think the last, because the cause is better, and *bloodless*.'[12]

Standing mid-way down the slope of the hills surrounding Bath and about two miles south-west of its centre, The Moorlands was an elegant, two-storied, double bow-fronted, south-facing house built of warm, sandy-shaded Bath stone. Originally built as 'Mr Mullens's Summer House' in 1740, it had been enlarged around 1800.[13] Surrounded by open farmland, the place was in Boyd Bayly's view a 'green Paradise', 'giving the impression of a place shut out from human ills, and open only to sweet flowers and sunshine'.[14] The house sat off the (old) Wells Road,[15] although its present address is Englishcombe Lane from which a long driveway meanders down beside a peaceful neighbourhood park that was once the Sewells' sloping meadow, to the front of The Moorlands below.[16]

Between the meadow and the house was a gently sloping lawn sprinkled with fruit trees where now (as probably then) a natural spring bubbles up. The upper rear windows offer panoramic views over Bath, and at the back of the house, where flats and houses now stand, were open fields through which there was a short cut down to Bath under magnificent trees.[17] Beside the house a level, terraced walk was added for Anna which was bordered by a long run of 'salvias and old-fashioned flowers' which Mary planted by meticulous plan to natural effect.[18] Mary was very fond of gardening, although they here also employed a gardener,[19] probably the 'gardener-groom' commonly hired by middle-class households which could not afford them (or, keeping only one horse and gig, did not need them) severally.[20] In gorgeous flower this 'green nest', as Bayly called The Moorlands, 'was a spot to dream of for its loveliness'.[21]

Locals today know that The Moorlands was once Anna's home, but, as in most places she lived, her years there are rarely mentioned in city guidebooks or local histories. Her Bath years are honoured, however, in the black horse logos of Moorlands Infant School and Moorlands Junior School, which were built on what was once Moorlands land and where Year Two pupils also do projects on Anna and *Black Beauty*.[22]

Anna's passion for animals was as strong as ever and the Sewells again kept a few pets and farmyard animals. 'Oh, it is charming, and looks so lovely! The grass as green as an emerald', Mary sighed one day watching their two cows, Fanny and Daisy, graze in the meadow.[23] There were also pigs, chickens, a pony, a brown dog named Lion, and undoubtedly bees.[24] Anna is likely to have had dogs and cats for much of her life. Mary had written from Stoke Newington almost thirty years earlier, telling her: 'We have now a famous dog which I am sure would soon be a great favourite with thee.'[25] Cats were likely to have been indoor pets, as Mary's love of birds fuelled her 'corresponding objection to out-door cats'.[26]

Although it had more elegance and history and was inland, Bath was, like Anna's former Brighton home, a busy watering place frequented by the fashionable, the ill, and the fashionably ill. With its courtly Georgian architecture and stylish streets and crescents, it was a world away from Blue Lodge where the nearest neighbours lived lives of poverty and graft not moneyed leisure. Anna's day-to-day existence here fell quieter although she regularly took drives with Mary through the surrounding area, delighting, as Bayly describes, in the 'banks and hedgerows around Bath [which] are rich in varied colouring at every season of the year'.[27]

Anna could have been in no better place for dwindling health. Bath was no longer in its glory days but was still esteemed for its 'cures'. In 1866–7 the famous Pump Room and Baths offered a year's worth of water-bibbing (drinking) for a £1 subscription. Baths 'at any Temperature, to 115 degrees Fahrenheit' were also available: at 1s. 6d. for a first-class bath, 6d. for a second-class, and 1s. for a second-class with a fire. Shower baths, vapour baths, combination shower and vapour baths, douches, 'Pumping in the Bath' or 'one additional Bather in each Bath' were all also advertised, as were portable mineral water baths for home plunges.[28] Anna may have tried the galvanic bath which was particularly recommended for lameness,[29] but even without electro-magnetism, one Victorian treatise claimed, Bath's waters 'in the form of a bath or douche' could be 'efficacious in removing pain, and restoring pliability to the limbs'.[30]

To optimize the benefits of treatment she might have followed contemporary medical advice to have a bed 'comfortably warm', but 'not too luxurious or enervating', to wear merino rather than flannel underclothes and cotton rather than worsted stockings, and to throw away all 'unnecessary wraps' and 'bandages of every description'.[31] Dietary advice for those undergoing treatment was to take breakfast and tea of 'as much stale bread and butter, or toast', as manageable 'with not more than two cups of black tea, or coffee and one egg: but no meat or fish of any description'. Luncheon was to be 'of biscuit, with one glass of good white wine' if required. Dinner should be 'mutton, lamb, or beef, roast or boiled; boiled or roast fowl', and supper 'of the lightest description, consisting entirely of farinaceous materials'. All 'highly-seasoned dishes, green vegetables, and fish' were to be avoided as were stimulants of any kind.[32]

Anna and Mary characteristically turned their attention to what local suffering they could lessen. Even at Combe Down they had had some thoughts of helping the quarrymen who needed, Mary observed, 'something more done for them than is at present the case'.[33] There was abundant philanthropic activity in Bath, with *The Post-Office Bath Directory 1866–7* listing fifty charitable 'religious societies'.[34] They perhaps joined some of these, but they were also charity innovators who liked to fill gaps rather than toe lines. On 17 August 1865 Mary wrote to 'JS' regarding some unnamed charitable endeavour she was to embark on which required an agent adapted to the work, otherwise she 'should not dare to begin in this neighbourhood'.[35] Anna generally supplied daring so it is likely that they soon had some project under way.

The year 1865 brought a change that perhaps made Anna and Mary resentful that they had moved to Bath at all, although by then they loved The Moorlands and had made new friends: Isaac was forced to resign from the bank. Although not himself dishonest, he was found 'culpably negligent' for 'defalcations by a cashier'.[36] This unfortunate end to a dedicated career meant that Isaac was now truly retired.

Living in a more accessible environment, Anna and Mary received regular morning calls from new friends and acquaintances. One such visitor was Mrs Williamson who Mary described as not 'at all like the general run of our callers'.[37] Possessed of 'large executiveness and organising power', she was also a charity innovator and it is not surprising that she became a close friend, especially of Mary with whom she corresponded until they both died in 1884.[38] Anna and Mary followed the progress of Mrs Williamson's later projects: 'a Free Registry for servants, shelter for them when out of place, and other things' and emigration work.[39] While in Bath, however, it was

Mrs Williamson's orphanages – for girls at Macaulay Buildings in
Bath and for boys at Claverton Down,[40] near Bath – that engrossed
them. Orphans were usually brought up in barracks, but Mrs
Williamson used the new 'family system', giving them an upbringing
as close to family life as possible, with good results.[41]

At least once, probably in 1866, Anna and Mary held a tea for the
orphan girls at The Moorlands, as one of Bayly's daughters describes:

> Mr. Sewell [was] very busy and concerned about the provender, and
> while Miss Sewell went to attend to his wishes, the other visitors
> appeared – Mrs. Williamson on her little pony, the children skipping
> about her, and a carriage for Mr. Williamson and two orphans . . . It
> *was* a pretty sight when Mrs. Sewell stood before the house to
> receive them, in her black silk dress without a furbelow, and quilled
> net cap, and with her duchess look – Mr. Sewell bending down his
> tall white head to the little ones and making them so heartily
> welcome. In a few minutes they were scattered about the grounds to
> do just what they liked . . . They were to have seen the cows milked,
> and had tea on the lawn, but it came on to rain . . . [but] there was
> all the fun of running to and fro from kitchen to barn with the tea-
> things . . . At tea the great excitement was to coax Lion . . . to eat
> from their hands. Proud was the little girl whose cake he gobbled up
> . . . It seemed like Eden, everybody so good and happy.[42]

The Bayly daughters had met Mary just a few days before, when
they saw her 'with girlish briskness of movement' at almost seventy,
learning the newly introduced game of croquet, to please a house
guest.[43] If they noticed Mary's youthful enthusiasm, they found
Anna a little more reserved: 'Miss Sewell is not as *unstiff* as Mrs.
Sewell, but very kind.'[44]

Anna continued as her mother's ruthless editor, although Mary's
literary output here slowed despite incessant requests from magazines
that wanted her verse. Her most famous new piece was her
temperance ballad *The Rose of Cheriton* (*c.* 1867), which described a
household ruined by alcohol. Used and admired by brigades of
charity workers and praised even by Matthew Arnold,[45] Mary's
didactic poems did not gratify all tastes. Anthony Trollope, no lover

of what he labelled 'small pietistic books' which were 'preachy-preachy for preaching sake',[46] gave *The Rose of Cheriton* a scathing review. Although he admits that 'Mrs Sewell must be put in a very different category from that in which we should class the general writers of such books', he condemned this ballad for factual errors, poor argument, impracticable remedies for drunkennesss, and 'flat and prosaic' versification.[47] Despite her purpose being primarily didactic, harsh criticisms naturally stung, as Mary later indicated:

> There are few persons I believe who, like the [present] author, know the intense gratitude and satisfaction which arises from being understood and sympathised with; or the anguish of being misapprehended – reviewers would hardly use their stinging & unfair whips with such remorseless levity as they sometimes do were they aware of what they inflicted upon the creature which had ventured openly to manifest its heart or opinions.[48]

Capacious thinkers, Anna and Mary weighed carefully whatever they themselves read and strove to avoid prejudgements. In *Black Beauty* Anna states, 'people don't always like to go to the bottom of things',[49] but she always tried to herself. Knowing of other people's shock at John Robert Seeley's controversial *Ecce Homo* (1865), which discussed Christ's humanity, one of Bayly's daughters was intrigued to hear the Sewells calmly 'discuss[ing it] *pro* and *con*'.[50] Religio-literary discussions were a mainstay in the Sewell household and some of these they enjoyed with Elizabeth R. [Mrs Andrew] Charles (1828–96), a writer of historical Christian novels, most notably *The Chronicles of the Schönberg-Cotta Family* (1863) about the life of Martin Luther.

Mary, and probably Anna, also became involved with the Moravian Brethren who Anna had been interested in when she was twenty. They would have attended services at Bath's Moravian Chapel in Charlotte Street under the Reverend Francis Scholefield[51] and may have become involved in the Moravian Missionary Society. Like their earlier denominational experiments this did not mark any permanent or formal allegiance and when they left Bath they also left Moravianism. They seem to have decided that their spiritual home was, as Mary put it, 'in "the blessed company of *all* faithful people"'.[52]

On 23 December 1866 Anna's sister-in-law, Sarah Sewell, died. If they were not there already during Sarah's final days, Anna and Mary travelled immediately to Norwich to help Philip through this difficult time. In a letter that probably dates from January 1867 the ever-practical Anna wrote to Isaac from Buxton where she and Mary had taken the children: '[t]he snow is very heavy & we think Philip will not return from Norwich to-day, as it is a great exposure. The dear girls are all with chicken pox but getting on pretty well . . . I hope thou art have a fowl for dinner sometimes,' she advised him, 'it is no use saving them only do not kill both the young cocks there are poulets which must be killed.' She told him that she had hoped to return to be with him after the holidays but that the plan:

> had to be given up & now all the children will have [to] be undertaken until quite the end of the month when Miss Alexander will come & lessons will begin again. I fear this will be too much for Mother alone & cannot quite see my way home soon as I had hoped it is a very heavy business altogether that this New Year has brought us, & will call for sacrifice all round but if we can only stand in one right place that will be the great thing & the only way to peace & blessing. Be sure to let us know how thou art getting on – does the snow come into the roof very much over the end room or the attics? Pray take care of my plants. Mother is so glad her fern looks well . . . she has quite lost her cough & is looking a little better. Farewell, father dear . . . We are very glad thou art in the spare room, hast thou got any nice book to read? Is it very lonely for thee. We are often thinking of you & talking of thee & wonder how thou art. I wish enough to be at home with thee. Farewell. Thy loving child. Anna Sewell.[53]

Devastated by Sarah's death and worried by his now sole responsibility for his seven children as well as seven orphans he had become guardian to in 1865, Philip's health failed.[54] Anna and Mary surely cared for the children while he travelled alone to Panticosa, Spain, to recover his health and spirits.[55] To be near Philip and the children, 47-year-old Anna and her parents in September 1867[56] returned permanently to Norfolk, moving into The White House in Old Catton.

Three miles north of Norwich on a Norwich-to-Buxton route, Anna's new home was a mile or so out from Philip at Clare House and about seven miles from her aunts and uncle at Buxton. '[D]reary and commonplace enough' when they arrived,[57] their transformative zeal soon made the house lovely, as Bayly describes:

> exquisite perception of the effect of colour was seen in every part of the house – or rather, felt: all was too simple and harmonious to have any striking effect. The paper on the walls was of the quietest tone – no showy patterns, no one piece of grand furniture to spoil the look of the rest, but plants at the windows, and flowers in vases arranged lightly, never in solid clumps.[58]

Now known as Anna Sewell House and bearing a plaque that commemorates her residence, Anna's home at 125 Spixworth Road has had several names since her time.[59] What were once out-buildings now form 2 and 4 Church Street, and the old stables provide garaging and above them 'The Mews Flat'.[60] A seventeenth-century two-storeyed house set close to the road, Boyd Bayly called it a 'pretty white house'.[61] It now has red brick frontage but is painted deep cream at the rear. When, on 2 August 1878, the house was auctioned with Anna's father as sitting tenant, it was described as:

> pleasantly situate in Gardens and Pleasure Grounds next the Road from Norwich to Spixworth, in the occupation of Isaac Sewell, Esq., a yearly tenant, at the low annual rent of £45.
>
> It contains Entrance Hall, handsome Dining and Drawing Rooms opening to Gardens and Balcony, Breakfast Room, Five Bed Rooms, Box Room, W.C., well-fitted Kitchens, Scullery, Storerooms, Pantries, &c.
>
> In Yard adjoining are Stable, Carriage House with Loft over. Large Cistern, Pump, &c.[62]

The small front garden between the house and road was 'Anna's garden', and was, Mary wrote, 'designed and kept up for the pleasure of the toiling artisans of Norwich, whose Sunday afternoon walks led them in large numbers to Old Catton'.[63] Across the road

was Samuel Gurney Buxton's deer park where horses now graze.
From the rear were views over the garden, fields, and trees to the
village church.[64] Both the dining room and the drawing room had
views to the front and rear. French doors from the ground-floor
dining room opened onto a paved verandah at the rear, a small lawn
rising steeply beyond it, and at its crest were two large beech trees
and 'a straight, level walk, running the length of the garden', which
Mary paced while composing.[65] Above the dining room was the
drawing room (now remodelled into bedrooms) with a splendid
floor-to-ceiling window giving onto a balcony which overlooked the
garden. Underneath the leafy lattice fence Mary introduced between
them and their neighbours was a wide bed of 'treasures' she
'transplanted from the woods and hedgerows'.[66] These gave
pleasure in all seasons: 'primroses, wood-sorrel, speedwell, wild
geranium, lilies of the valley, and climbing things full of blossom in
spring and berries in autumn'.[67] There were also aloes transplanted
from The Moorlands.[68]

A small well-kept village with an old history, Old Catton in 1864
had a population of around 650,[69] and was home to many Norwich
merchants.[70] Church Street, on whose north-east corner The White
House stood, was the centre of the village and contained a manor
house, the Magpie Inn, and St Margaret's church which Mary and
Anna probably attended and in whose churchyard Sarah Sewell had
been buried.[71] The Catton Hall estate, owned by the Buxtons who
the Sewells came to know well, comprised most of the land on the
south side of Church Street. Workers in the area served on the estate
or were employed in brick-making, lime-burning, and market
gardening.

Anna regularly visited Norwich, a textile centre no longer at the
height of its boom. Harriet Martineau, writing in December 1853,
had noted, 'the extinction of the celebrity of ancient Norwich, in
regard to both its material and intellectual productions. Its
bombazine manufacture has gone to Yorkshire, and its literary fame
to the four winds.'[72] It did, however, still have 'its numerous Gothic
churches and quaint streets, its towering Castle and beautiful
Cathedral', as well as a bustling atmosphere.[73]

Travelling into Norwich, Anna's steely will met its match when
her Bath-accustomed pony baulked at going over the city's pebbled

streets. Learning that there was an alternative, non-cobbled route, his demurrals became absolute and no coaxing or castigation could move him; Anna was forced to take the long way round.[74] Anna drove herself everywhere, but driving alone could have its risks. Even apart from horse obstinacy, fright, or injury, shafts might break, the vehicle hit a rock and overturn or become stuck in mud – all the more awkward if one were lame. The unexpected encounter might also occur. In 1874 a man was tried at Norwich Assizes for seizing a woman driver's reins and pressing a pistol to her head.[75]

Anna and Mary felt a sad contrast between afternoon drives they had taken through the combes (small valleys) around Bath and the 'high banks and stiff hedges' that shut in the Norfolk lanes through which they now drove.[76] But they must have gloried in the never-ending Norfolk skies and in being able to drive to visit relatives. Family life now encompassed Anna, not only her brother's family but her relatives at Buxton. Her Uncle John Wright (now seventy-two) was living at Dudwick House.[77] Her Aunt Maria (sixty-five), who for a time ran John's household, may now have been back at Dudwick Cottage living with Anna's Aunt Elizabeth (sixty-eight) and Aunt Ellen (fifty-three). All these Wright relatives were still active in local charitable concerns, in which Anna may also have joined and she would have spent time regularly with her aunts in their beautiful, so familiar surroundings.

Anna's prime responsibility in these early Catton years lay with her nieces (known to the family by their second names or diminutives thereof: Grace, Amie, Edie, Ada, and probably Gertie).[78] Her two nephews (Johnny and Ted) seem to have been away at school. She drove or rode often to Clare House, Philip's elegant three-storied home on St Clement's Hill. Built of grey brick, the house had about nineteen acres of land including a large garden divided by a ha-ha from a field which sloped down to a V point where St Clement's Hill meets Constitution Hill. After Philip's death his children, in 1909, gifted the field, known as Sewell Park, to the city of Norwich. Outside the park gates at the southern end is a noticeboard headed: 'Sewell Community Power Group', symbolizing the community spirit that Philip, like Anna and Mary, regarded as so important. In front of the sign is a triangular horse trough, now planted with flowers, its inscription reading: '1917. This fountain was placed here by Ada Sewell in memory of her Aunt Anna Sewell authoress of Black Beauty and of her sister Edith Sewell – Two Lovers of Animals.'

In 1929 the Blyth School for girls was built on the site of Philip's former garden, and Clare House, by then known as 'The Grey House', was used as an ancillary building. During the Blyth School days Philip's barn was used as a bicycle shed, and Blyth schoolgirls, knowing that Philip's black horse Bessie may have inspired *Black Beauty*, 'by tradition regarded the stall in the stable area as that occupied by . . . Black Beauty'.[79] The house was demolished in 1970 to make way for the expanded co-educational Blyth-Jex School which now stands on the site.[80] In November 1977, on the centenary of *Black Beauty*, a local appeal was launched to raise funds to transform the barn into its present incarnation as the Sewell Barn Theatre.[81]

Philip's children already had a nurse, one 'J',[82] who had begun working for Philip when she was eighteen. She was 'wise and careful' and 'brought up all the family with devoted care'. Even Mary, despite her disinclination towards servants as child-raisers, thought highly of her.[83] But these children were not to be raised by servant alone. Anna and Mary had the considerable role of overseeing the moral and practical education of Philip's daughters. With five nieces to care for, ranging in age from almost four to seventeen, it was as well that Anna's health seems to have been reasonably good. She had great fun with this young company, taking them for long drives in the countryside. As Margaret recalled, they loved to hear her talk 'about trees and flowers and all animals – especially horses; we liked to listen to the conversations she held with the horse she was driving'.[84]

Anna entranced her nieces not just with her talk of and to horses but through her drawing. Margaret regarded Anna as 'no mean artist' and recalled that she 'used to draw with great facility for the amusement of her nieces, and competent critics have expressed the opinion that had she been trained she would have done notable work'.[85] Boyd Bayly also testifies that Anna:

had the artist instinct for form strongly developed. Her pencil drawings from nature, full of truth and spirit, are remarkable for excellence of composition; if she did not edit her landscapes, she had a genius for seizing the right point of view, and figures and objects were put in exactly the right spot.[86]

Anna painted copies in oils of work by artists such as Edwin Landseer, as well as her own originals.[87] It is fitting that she admired Landseer for, like her, he was passionate about animals. He was a vice-president of the Royal Society for the Prevention of Cruelty to Animals and refused to paint a docked horse or a cropped dog – two things that *Black Beauty* also inveighs against.[88] If Anna had spent time with London relatives in 1861 she may have seen Landseer's popular if controversial *The Shrew Tamed*, exhibited at the Royal Academy, which depicts a dreamy woman seated on straw, leaning back against the flank of a black horse.

Anna enjoyed outings with her nieces, but she also took her role as surrogate mother very seriously. While Mary had a natural sympathy with children, and never herself forgot what it was like to be young,[89] the nieces found Anna a little less elastic and more firm of mien and morals than their grandmother. They were, however, extremely fond of Anna. 'I have no recollection of being afraid of her', wrote Margaret. 'On the contrary, we used to like being with her. She told us appealing stories, and found interesting jobs for us to do. She was a very good needlewoman, and taught us to sew, and we had to do it very well!'[90] Anna's story-telling was clearly good practice for the novel she would soon write, but her particularity over her nieces' sewing reflects her own perfectionistic tendencies. Her nieces knew that Anna would never demand more of them than she asked of herself, but they also knew that, being Anna, this could be a 'big ask'.

'[S]he had a very high moral standard, and her code was exacting', Margaret recalled of Anna. 'Nothing but absolute truthfulness would do with her. Thoughtlessness, carelessness, or indifference to the feelings of others – especially with regard to the poor – were always rebuked. But she was just, and we knew it.'[91] Her nieces found her 'very strict, if not stern' and as her charges grew older, Margaret remembered, 'she expected more of us'.[92]

'Anna . . . had no acquaintance with fear – not even enough for mercy,' writes Bayly, 'it was impossible for her to understand the terror that would make others, children especially, tell lame falsehoods simply from want of presence of mind. She . . . [was] naturally stern in her judgments of others as well as of herself.'[93] Anna and Mary could both be harsh in their comments, but a friend of Mary's claimed that because their honest good intentions were so clear, this never rankled: 'I remember Mrs. Sewell's pulling me up sharply for advocating forgiveness of a personal injury which involved cruelty to an animal. "*Forgive* him!" she said. "I'd have roused the town against him."'[94]

Anna's own sweet-voiced firmness was connected to her passionate belief that the truth must be upheld at all costs, but her sense of honesty could at times be taken to bathetic extremes. She would not, as Margaret writes,

> suffer the most innocent deception. She would never hide a blemish. 'If I ask Nanny to arrange the fruit she will always turn the worst side out,' complained her mother, who from aesthetic reasons quite disapproved of this procedure. The daughter had aesthetic sensibility too; she was not unconscious of, or indifferent to, beauty or seemliness, but she could not bear that anything should be made to appear better than it really was.[95]

Anna's insistence upon truth in all things reflects her moral beliefs and her desire to control her own life. She was always, until her last years, very severe upon herself and was true to her ideals, even if that meant emotionally brutalizing herself. For Anna truth was beauty and God's will was the way. Yet unlike the fruit whose blemishes she deliberately displayed, she presented her own best side out and kept her worst hidden away. To the world she seemed a mixture of sweetness and strength and it was evident to anyone who met her that she was very high-principled. Her 'general appearance', too, Mrs F noted, 'had little or nothing of the invalid, and the calm radiance of her expressive face was remarkable. My husband chancing once to meet her in a shop in Bath, came home saying, "I've just seen Anna Sewell's beautiful face." And beautiful indeed it was, with the beauty of nobility and purity.'[96] When personal anger, despair, or physical pain flared she kept them concealed under a serene exterior. When her feelings were provoked on behalf of others, especially the poor or animals, she gave them far freer rein.

Anna was now in 'the seventh septennial' of her life, a period Edward John Tilt, author of *The Change of Life in Health and Disease* (1857), regarded as 'an extremely critical period of [a woman's] existence'.[97] The 'change of life' was most likely to occur, Tilt stated, between the ages of forty-two and forty-nine.[98] Anna's 'dodging-time', as Tilt termed the perimenopausal years, probably occurred during her Bath or early Old Catton periods and must have caused some disruption to her life physically and emotionally. The fact that she seems during these years to be driving more than riding may have been connected to advice such as Tilt's: 'horse-exercise should be left off at cessation; indeed, its utility in favouring the m. flow sufficiently points to the discontinuance of the practice during the time preceeding and following the change, for then it is likely to cause flooding, piles and leucorrhoea'.[99]

If she sought treatment for menopausal symptoms she was probably offered remedies such as morphine, exercise, travel, iron tonics, bandages for the limbs, abdominal belts, or mineral water. Bleeding (about twelve ounces) was recommended for headaches and to relieve flushing, perspiration, and dizziness, and leeches placed behind the ears or at the nape of the neck were thought to ease discomfort.[100] It is unknown whether Anna felt this an emotionally fraught time of life or if she shared the feelings of suffragist Eliza Farnham who, 'writing in the 1860s, saw menopause as a time of "secret joy," of spiritual growth, of "super-exaltation"'.[101]

Anna and Mary had taken on what charity work their familial duties allowed time for. They set up a Mothers' Meeting, Anna undertook the 'care of schools', and poor visiting identified individual cases for help.[102] Samuel Gurney Buxton, the 'benevolent squire' of Catton Hall, saw to most of the charitable needs of Old Catton, so Anna and Mary worked from the outset in Philip's neighbourhood of New Catton, an industrial area whose population of around three thousand was mostly working class, many involved in weaving and shoe-making.[103] They surely became engaged in some of the many charities with which Philip was or would became connected. He was to be secretary of the Norwich City Mission, a member of the Discharged Prisoners' Aid Mission, and as well as giving temperance talks in surrounding villages, he served on the

Council of the Church of England Temperance Society.[104] He taught
Sunday school for many years and was a church warden at Christ
Church, which lay just across the road from his field. Philip had
accepted the Church of England in a way that Anna and Mary never
completely did. Like Anna and Mary, he was independent,
outspoken in the face of wrong, very hard-working, and his faith lay
at the core of everything he did.[105]

Anna and Mary developed a wide acquaintanceship in the area,
but callers swallowed time they would, in less social environs, have
used working. In a memo to herself Mary urged 'be more in the
habit of working during long calls'.[106] Guests also often stayed at
The White House where they were welcomed with an 'absence of all
pretension and fuss-making' and with the 'graceful, heartfelt
hospitalities' Bayly attributed to the Sewells' Quaker back-
grounds.[107] 'If ropes and pulleys have been necessarily set to work in
preparation for a visitor, refined feeling keeps them out of sight',
Bayly recalled.[108] Guests were served 'no profusion of dishes, but
simple delicacies daintily served' and the little inviting guest
bedroom was clean and white with 'flowers and books placed
exactly in the right position'.[109]

Leading a busy social, familial, and charitable life meant that
Mary's writing fell away, something Bayly regarded as a good thing
given that 'declining vigour called for hoarding and accumulation of
force, in order to keep up the old standard'.[110] In 1869 Mary's
Stories in Verse was published containing many ballads which had
long been circulating as individual Household Tracts.[111] In 1870 she
considered writing a guidebook on Mothers' Meetings but could
find no time to do so.[112] Instead, she invited women from their own
Mothers' Meeting to come to tea at The White House in groups of
three or four each week and chatted with them in the 'summer-
parlour'.[113]

Anna and Mary's own relationship remained paramount, and
Margaret Sewell states that they:

formed a mutual admiration society, and were, indeed, singularly
adapted to supplement each other. My aunt's appreciation of her
mother's gifts was profound, while her intimate journals display a
humility and self-depreciation that are remarkable in so strong a

character, and certainly not warranted. To outsiders the mother must have seemed to eclipse the daughter, for my grandmother was a woman of singular charm. She was enthusiastic, imaginative, sympathetic, an idealist, and deservedly popular. Anna, on the other hand, was practical, critical, and far-seeing, and, while fundamentally as much an enthusiast as her mother, possessed a larger fund of common sense and a balanced judgment. No one recognized this better, or as well, as her mother, who was aware how much she owed to her daughter.[114]

From 1870 to 1877, in what Bayly describes as '[l]ess than fourteen pages of an old, haggard-looking account-book', Anna kept a journal.[115] In 1870 she recorded her life as busy with involvement at schools, poor visiting, trips away to stay with friends, and a holiday at the seaside.[116] The few entries Bayly records give an idea of family, charitable, and world activities:

January 1870. – At Old Catton. Father is in his seventy-seventh year, well and active. Mother in her seventy-third year, very well and wonderfully active and competent. I in my fiftieth year, as well as usual.
April 8. – Mother is now engaged in getting signatures to Miss Preusser's Memorial to the Poor Law Board about pauper children.
October 28. – Metz capitulated, 173,000 troops laid down their arms with Marshal Bazaine.[117]

Anna's close contact with her nieces and nephews must have brought great joy into her life and a clear sense of worth and purpose. Not only could she teach and morally guide these young Sewells in the way her mother had trained her to do, but she could instil in them her own love for the natural world, enjoy their company, and delight in their chatter. Her role became even more important when in 1869 Philip contracted a 'long and serious' illness.[118] The family thought that they might lose him and the children be orphaned, but Philip recovered and in 1870 married Charlotte Jane Sole.[119] This was, like his first marriage, a happy one and pleased the family greatly. It also lightened Anna and Mary's responsibilities, as Charlotte took over 'mothering'. Although Anna was happy for Philip, and her older nieces were virtually adults, she must have felt some pangs of loss.

The summer of 1870 was nevertheless a blissful one. 'I think we have done little but be happy,' Mary told Mrs Williamson on 8 August, 'and no harm of any kind has come near us.'[120] It was during this season that the summer-parlour was built for Anna. The hedged-in rear of The White House's garden had been a vegetable patch, but Mary had transformed it into a lawn with flower-beds. Now, against the garden wall, Anna's summer-parlour was built: a large, unheated greenhouse, in season full of light and sun.[121] The family's hope that Anna would spend many happy hours there was not to be, however, for this crystal time was about to shatter.

On 26 December 1870 there was an eclipse of the sun clearly visible in the Norfolk skies.[122] It seems an omen of the shadows that now started to fall over Anna's family. In November Isaac had started to suffer from attacks of faintness and dizzy spells which the doctor thought indicated 'something serious'.[123] Just four months later Anna herself fell seriously ill.

TEN
A Troublesome Case
1871–7

[H]orses are used to bear their pain in silence.
(Black Beauty, Chapter 25)

'I have not been well', Anna recorded on 1 March 1871, 'Dr. R[1] thinks it is a troublesome case.'[2] Just weeks before her fifty-first birthday, Anna was given only eighteen months to live.[3] Never again would she sit in her summer-parlour or venture beyond the garden gate. Her nights and mornings would be spent in bed and her afternoons and evenings on a sofa in the drawing-room. She was terribly weak and suffered much pain, but her symptoms would wax and wane in severity. 'This has hindered us in our own work,' Mary told Mrs Williamson early in Anna's illness, 'but we do not know what kind of work carries us the most surely forward.'[4] This was the beginning of Anna's end, but the work that most surely carried her forward was not yet begun.

Her 'troublesome case' may have been a combination of concurrent or consecutive ailments or may be more wholly traceable to the SLE form of lupus. Anna's official cause of death is listed as 'Chronic Hepatitis' and 'Phthisis Pulmonalis' (tuberculosis), both of which may well have overtaken her. Patients with SLE can have hepatitis as part of their lupus, but lupus itself can also affect the lungs. Given that her basic state of health was poorer than ever before, but that she still suffered from comparatively better or worse periods, what seems most likely is that the severe effects of SLE precipitated this deterioration in 1871, compounded in later years by other ailments.[5]

'I have been thinking a good deal lately about Christian discipline, and how wonderfully the Blessed Lord can *alter* afflictions without removing them', Mary wrote.[6] From being plagued with ill-health that sometimes kept her at home, but for periods allowed reasonable if limited mobility, Anna's afflictions now kept her housebound. Mary grew climbers and rambling flowers in boxes on the drawing room balcony to create an 'upstairs garden' for her and hung there a 'tempting lump of mutton-suet' to attract the tom-tits.[7] Anna was effectively trapped in this drawing room for most of the rest of her life and it was here that *Black Beauty* would be written. 'The room itself', wrote Bayly, 'had an old-world look, a low, subdued harmony of colour, and a scent of pot-pourri, in keeping with the quaint speech, the silver hair, and antique, old-world courtliness of the lord and lady of the home'.[8]

Anna's 'ever-deepening trial' was now fully realized by the family, Bayly recalls, 'darkening the future with anticipations of increased suffering'.[9] There was no real hope of improvement and thoughts of the afterlife shaded their minds. Something greater than 'even patience and hope', was needed, Bayly writes: 'I have often heard [Anna and Mary] speak of this time, and how by degrees they learned more perfectly the Divine lessons taught by suffering, and consented, with their whole hearts, that their training should be as the Master's, "perfect through suffering."'[10]

Anna's illness was 'severe and distressing', Bayly reports, and Isaac, too, was becoming 'increasingly feeble'.[11] He was probably in the early stages of senile dementia and the long, slow deterioration of her beloved father must have caused Anna great sadness. Nurse to both daughter and husband, Mary strove to maintain a household that Anna's nieces would still love to visit: 'I could not bear for the dear girls to think of grandmother's house as a gloomy place.'[12] At seventy-four Mary faced these new challenges, but her pace did not slacken. She continued with as much charitable work as she could, given Anna's condition, and she and Anna talked through the progress of their altruistic enterprises which, at least until early 1872, remained numerous.

Perhaps so that Anna could see some of the fruits first hand, in the summer and autumn of 1871 a string of benevolent entertaining was done at The White House, as Anna recorded:

August 9 [1871]. – Mrs. Riches' class of thirty girls came to tea.
Sept. 1. – We gave a tea and frolic to thirty-four children, Miss H.'s Band of Hope. G. and E.[13] helped.

Sept. 13. – Mother's Sun Lane Infants (50) had tea and play. A and A.[14] helped famously.[15]

When Anna was well enough to be left, Mary ventured out to her New Catton school, as Anna wrote:

Nov. 6. – Mother's Sun Lane School was inspected by Mr. S. The week previous she went every day, and since then goes one day each week, taking her dinner at Mrs. A'—s. She is trying a new plan of teaching to read without spelling, but making words with loose letters. She is also making clothes for the R'—s. Little Caroline R. comes three days a week. Mother gives her two lessons a day.
Nov. 11. – Mother also began a class for the girls of Miss H.'s Band of Hope on Saturday mornings every other week.[16]

Every second year Anna noted in her journal their gift of clothing to the value of 4s each to between sixty-five and eighty impoverished widows including all widows in New Catton aged over sixty as well as many younger. The gifts were biennial so that what the Sewells could afford would buy 'good' gifts rather than the thinner products of annual spending. Mary ordered samples of cloth from several suppliers and with Anna carefully chose which patterns they preferred. They then asked the Bible-woman to ascertain from each widow whether she would prefer her quota in linsey, flannel, calico, or in some years a shawl.[17] These gifts were given in November, Bayly writes, 'since Christmas presents give time for the cold to be felt before they come'.[18]

On 6 November 1871 Anna made a significant announcement in her journal: 'I am writing the life of a horse, and getting dolls and boxes ready for Christmas.'[19] Both activities indicate that Anna was not entirely prostrated by her ailments at this time, but Bayly reports that Anna's diary makes no further mention of *Black Beauty* until December 1876.[20] The novel seems to have been started in 1871 with Anna dictating it to Mary and then worked on it only sporadically, if at all, until 1876–7 when Anna was able to complete it by writing in pencil.[21] Mary states that 'the book took root in [Anna's] mind' near the start of her incapacitation 'and from time to time a few portions were dictated – reading or writing being equally impossible to her. Years went on, and no progress was made, except in her mind, where many pictures were clearly drawn and stored away in her memory.'[22]

A truism states that writers should write what they know. Anna knew horses. Despite tremendous physical obstacles, she was about to produce a novel that would do for horses what no other work had ever done, which would draw on her astute equine knowledge, and which would express the beliefs of her life. Her 'life of a horse' would also give her a project that was singularly her own in a way she had rarely had and provide a pivot for her thoughts on long weary days. Given that she was to outlive her doctor's fatal prognosis by five-and-a-half years it may not be mere fancy to suggest that Anna's desire to see *Black Beauty* completed gave her added impetus to live. She started writing it, too, when her own direct contact with horses ceased. During the summer of 1871 she loaned her pony to a girl who learned to ride on him.[23] When it became wrenchingly clear that she would never ride or drive again, she gave her pony and chaise to the Buxton Reformatory, which Philip now owned and managed.[24]

On 4 June 1871 their Uncle Wright had died[25] and Philip inherited his properties in Buxton, Brampton, Lammas, and Lambeth, becoming a landed gentleman. For convenience's sake he remained at Clare House rather than moving to Dudwick House, and his reputation as a philanthropist now grew exponentially until his own death in 1906. He had also inherited his uncle's charitable projects including the reformatory, with which the extended family in Norwich, Old Catton, and Buxton were all concerned. Anna's aunts at Buxton had already been involved with the reformatory for almost twenty years, and in 1888 Philip would report that at ninety, blind, and bedridden their Aunt Elizabeth's interest in it continued unabated.[26] One of Philip's daughters in future years would also give every reformatory boy a copy of *Black Beauty*.[27] After Philip's death Anna's nephew, Ted, and niece, Margaret, remained central to the running of the reformatory (from 1894 known as The Red House Farm School), until their own deaths in 1937.[28]

The reformatory boys learned to cultivate land and raise pigs and other animals as well as having a general education, some also learning tailoring, baking, and shoemaking (an expanding Norwich trade). The timetable was strict but offered some variety: prayers, singing, games, Saturday baths, Sunday church, and on Wednesday evenings 'sock knitting and darning for the whole school'.[29] Philip 'became all in all' to the reformatory,[30] and in company with his mare Bessie traversed the narrow country lanes to Buxton to visit it once or twice a week.[31]

Bessie was a family favourite who Margaret Sewell suggests was the original of Black Beauty.[32] Although Anna could no longer ride or drive, she and Bessie nevertheless became, in Margaret's words, 'very intimate'.[33] Like Black Beauty, Bessie was, 'a splendid creature, holding rank with the fastest trotters in the county, with any amount of go, courage, and spirit in her', but also, Bayly states, on dangerous or slippery evenings 'made up of caution and care. How in the pitch darkness and narrow lanes, where guiding must be impossible, she manages never to let a wheel get entangled is only known to Him who asks, "Hast *thou* given the horse his might?"'[34] Although Bayly thought Bessie shared the Sewell family spirit,[35] Bessie did not share Black Beauty's patience. In later years when Philip drove his daughters to visit The White House, after a mannerly fifteen minutes she would start pawing and fretting to be off. 'Come, girls, come; Bessie wants to be going', Philip would call. 'Then a number of heads would be thrust out of an open window, calling out, "Oh Bessie dear, do be quiet; we haven't half done yet. Do stand still, there's a dear; do."' This gave them an extra five minutes before they had to scramble out of the house and into the carriage as Bessie started to pull away.[36]

Philip regularly travelled to the reformatory on Monday evenings, stopping briefly at The White House en route and calling out 'Good-Night' as he passed between nine and ten o'clock on his way home.[37] He also came to tea with Anna and his parents every Sunday, a highlight of their week, and was a very supportive son and brother. Once reading aloud a letter of sympathy on her condition, Anna broke off to say, 'I don't think I can appropriate all this pity. No one need be pitied who has mother and Philip.'[38]

'Mother went, with our children, to St. Faith's Union, and gave toys and presents',[39] Anna recorded on New Year's Day 1872, opening a year that would see smallpox ravage Norwich and death visit Sarah Stickney Ellis and her husband William. This was to be a wretched year for Anna. 'I am quite poorly with pain', she wrote in her journal on 26 January.[40] At the year's end she was again writing, 'I am poorly.'[41] 'Quite poorly' was, Bayly states, the strongest expression Anna ever used for her suffering, yet her symptoms 'were mainly of a very painful and depressing character'. Had 'her face been marred with grief', Bayly reports:

> no one would have been surprised. It was a wonderful evidence of the triumph of the spirit over the body that her face was not only sweet and peaceful, but often radiant; and so evidently did this proceed from the power of the Spirit of God, that in her presence one had a feeling of being on holy ground; her face shone with the far-off light of the morning of the resurrection.[42]

Although Bayly's couching is a typically Victorian rendering of angelic suffering, it still gives a sense of the real struggle Anna was waging to keep what she endured to herself and to accept her afflictions as God's will. Incapacitation gave her time to fret upon faith, and must also have caused her periods of enormous frustration at the inability of her body to follow the will of her mind. Physical suffering, together with the guilt and aggravation that naturally arise from having to wait to be done for rather than doing oneself, must also have led to disconsolateness and a fraying temper that she had to work hard to suppress. That she managed to keep a calm demeanour while experiencing years of chronic pain was something at which those who knew her marvelled: 'She could bear pain without showing it in her face or voice', Mary wrote. 'Once I said "Do thee *never* break down or fret about it, darling?" She said, "Sometimes when I am alone in my room, I do say, 'Poor Nannie!'"'[43]

'It is a year and a half since she left the house, except occasionally for a few steps in the garden', Mary wrote of Anna, probably in 1872 or 1873. 'The disease which the doctors expected would have worn her out by this time from extreme suffering, is not manifestly worse, but by little and little the strength keeps wasting, and her capacity for any effort decreases.'[44] Anna's daily routine was as Mary describes it:

She is usually in bed till midday, and then dresses, resting between whiles. She lies on the sofa for the remainder of the day, sometimes sitting down to meals with us only for a very short time. She requires almost complete quiet; conversation and reading are usually too fatiguing for her.[45]

This was a horribly incapacitating illness, and a baleful experience for one who had already battled so hard with her health. Anna's body was wracked, but Mary maintained that she had 'perfect peace', and was 'the sweetest, most cheerful patient – the most unselfish sufferer I have ever seen – the expression of her dear face combines it all, and sometimes she has such a lovely colour,[46] and looks so animated and beaming, that no one would think she ailed much'.[47] Mary wrote that the doctor attributed Anna's endurance to her 'tranquillity and her courage, and the exceptional advantages she enjoys in the way of nursing'.[48] Mary was a very attentive nurse, and while her claims that 'I am her constant companion. Since she was confined to the house, I have only been out two days. We have no gloom',[49] seem exaggerated on all three counts, they do reflect the change that Anna's illness had brought upon both their lives. Mother and daughter, especially in light of Isaac's failing faculties, were all-in-all to each other as never before.

The pressure on Mary as chief care-giver to daughter and husband was enormous. She experienced 'turns of severe but seldom disabling suffering, brought on by the constant strain upon her' and, Bayly implies, fell into sloughs of depression.[50] Mary felt her own illnesses frustrating as she told Mrs Williamson: 'It has been quite humiliating to me to find how one misery in the flesh can absorb the whole nature, and let the zeal and power of life pass into warm clothes and a glowing fire.'[51]

During 1873 Anna's health rallied a little.[52] 'My darling maintains the slight improvement', Mary wrote:

It is just about this time two years since she left the house, but she is always my dear cheerful companion, and in our hardest days we have glad surprises . . . We lead by no means a solitary life. We have several young people round us who are earnestly desirous to lead a vital, practical Christian life, and we are deeply interested

in them. They are often here to question the old pilgrim, and all
this keeps my dear Anna full of external interest, which is so
wholesome and happy for her. To my astonishment she never
seems to find the time drag heavily, though usually lying
unemployed on the sofa.[53]

With the easing of Anna's symptoms Mary engaged in a little
more of her own work, Anna noting on 1 October 1873, 'Social
Science Congress. Mother and aunts went through the whole week. I
am very well.'[54] Later that year she could add, 'I keep good
nights.'[55] Mary in 1873 also wrote *Davie Blake The Sailor*, a ballad
for sailors, Anna commenting the following June,[56] '"Davie Blake"
has had some good reviews. The second edition is going off. It is
much liked by sailors' friends.'[57] Bayly recalled that when she came
to stay at The White House Mary would sometimes leave her to
tend to Anna while she went poor-visiting:

> Before leaving the house, she would return, in her walking dress,
> to have one more look at her darling, and would be greeted with,
> 'Mother dear, how nice thee look!' or, 'Mother dear, don't thee
> hurry back, I am quite comfortable. Couldn't thee call on Lucy
> Smith? – It is not her washing-day, and she would be pleased to
> see thee.'[58]

This slight fillip in her health also meant that Anna could very
occasionally indulge in some evening pursuits that had been
favourites with her and Mary for years. They had always loved
reading and reciting long passages of poetry, Anna favouring works
by Wordsworth, Shakespeare, and Tennyson.[59] Mary thought Anna's
recitation of modern poets such as Tennyson was wonderful whereas
she herself 'had only my old *Byron* . . . and *Moore* to come in
with!'[60] In a coincidental tangling together of the possible love
interests of Anna's youth, Henry King became Tennyson's publisher
in 1874, and she must have felt a poignant confluence of emotion
when she discovered the connection.

Anna and Mary's other favourite evening pursuits were, Margaret
writes, '"capping verses" or . . . games involving the stringing of
rhymes. They liked the young people to join in these exercises, but

we made a sorry show in comparison.'[61] Anna would also often
while away dragging hours by asking whoever was at hand to give
her a few random words which she would then weave into narrative
verse.[62] Bayly records two of Anna's compositions:

Prawn, Yawn, Tall, Wall, Missed, Kissed.
O Henry dear, don't *yawn* so loud,
　　The tea will soon be here;
But Jane has had an accident
　　Which might have cost her dear.

In coming up with that *tall* urn
　　She caught a sight of Jem,
She *missed* the step, and *kissed* the *wall*,
　　Instead of kissing him.

I do not think the girl is hurt,
　　But still she's vexed and fluttered;
So cook will bring the *prawns* and toast,
　　And tea-cake, when 'tis buttered.

Tomtit, Sooty, Fate, Butter
It happened one day that the birds went to dine,
　　By a special invite from the hawk;
The viands were excellent, so was the wine,
　　And each guest had a small silver fork.
Robin Redbreast was there, as of course you'd expect,
　　And *Tomtit* with a bow and a sputter,
His rev'rence the Rook, with a *sooty* black cloak,
　　And canaries as yellow as *butter.*
Ah! little they thought, as they strutted and chirped,
　　Of the *fate* that awaited them there;
For the Hawk with his kindred pounced down on his guests,
　　Whilst their pitiful cries rent the air.[63]

On 18 October 1874,[64] just ten days after her eleventh birthday,
Anna's youngest niece, Isabel Gertrude, died. Six years younger than
her next sibling, she was the baby of the family and her loss was

deeply felt. She was buried in her mother's grave in St Margaret's churchyard in Old Catton.[64] Anna, who, if she could not visit her grave, could see the churchyard trees from the drawing-room window, composed a poem in her memory:

> Seven young trees grew close together,
> All fresh and green in the summer weather.
> A little one, beautiful, tender, and tall,
> Grew in the middle, the joy of them all;
> And lovingly twining their branches together,
> They circled it round, in the fine summer weather.
> On the Sabbath eve of an autumn day
> The beautiful plant was taken away,
> And left a lonely and leafless space,
> And nothing was found to fill the place –
> Nothing of rich, nothing of rare,
> Could fill the spot that was left so bare;
> Nothing below, nothing above,
> Could fill this empty spot but love.
> Then closer the young trees grew together,
> In the chilly days of that autumn weather;
> And every branch put forth a shoot,
> And new life quickened at the root.
> They grew in the winter, in spring they grew,
> Silently nourished by heavenly dew;
> And when they came back to the summer weather,
> One beautiful group they stood together;
> And their greenest leaves hung o'er the place
> Where the youngest had stood in its tender grace.
> Nothing below, nothing above,
> Nothing can heal the hurt but love.[65]

Regarded by those who knew her as clear in her faith and glowingly religious, Anna nevertheless was still searching for absolute religious contentment. Much of her time 'unemployed on the sofa' was spent purely in thought, surely about *Black Beauty*, family, books, and charity work, but, most significantly for Anna, about her own spiritual state. Writing in *Life in the Sick-Room*

(1844) of her own five-year period of invalidism, Harriet Martineau comments on the honesty that invalids demand, their emotional changeability, and the spiritual elements of their lives. One of the great difficulties of 'long sickness and seclusion', she states, is 'that all old pains, all past moral sufferings, are renewed and magnified . . . every old sin and folly, and even the most trifling error, rises up anew, however long ago repented of and forgiven, and, in the activity of ordinary life, forgotten'.[66]

In 1874 Anna's grains of spiritual irritation were finally washed away when she experienced a transformation into deeper faith which echoed the conversion experience of her mid-twenties. This was induced by a booklet a friend had sent her entitled *A Word to the Wavering Ones* by Hannah Whitall [Mrs Pearsall] Smith (1832–1911), a Philadelphian ex-Quaker who was an influential figure in the Methodist Holiness Movement. This booklet forms chapter twelve of Smith's *The God of All Comfort* which promoted the idea that faith should bring joy, comfort, and peace into Christians' lives, not worry, fretfulness, and discomfort. Smith argued that it was a sin to doubt, that it was disloyal to God to waver in one's faith, that it was unconscious pride, not humility, to think one's self unworthy of God's love, and that salvation was a gift to be accepted not a task to be achieved. Anna told a friend that, although she had long loved the Lord, it was only during the summer of 1874 that she truly learned what it was to 'abide in Christ'.[67] 'I had always taken my petition and request to Him', she wrote:

> but then I knocked from without, somewhat in the spirit of a beggar. Now He has shown me that I have a place in the household, I belong to the family of God, and my very frailty has given me a place among the weak ones in whom His strength is perfected. I know now the meaning of that word, 'Now no longer a servant, but a Son.'[68]

Anna's friends and family 'who had watched her perfect patience and uprightness before God and man', as Bayly writes, were stunned that Anna had thought herself a 'wavering one'. 'It was difficult for us not to feel almost hurt, as though she were doing dishonour to the Grace which had so wonderfully upheld her; but so it was.

Her victory had been gained by a constant inward struggle, known only to herself and her Lord.'[69]

Anna had crucified her 'self' in the way that in youth she had feared, but now it brought her peace and spiritual rejuvenation. 'The last remnant of the old severity against herself passed away,' declared Bayly, 'for the rest of her life, it seemed to outward eyes to be with her, "None of self, and ALL of Thee."'[70] Given Anna's strict, uncompromising qualities it was all the 'more remarkable', Bayly thought, 'that in her last chastened years all took notice of a more entire gentleness of spirit in her than even in her tender-hearted, impetuous mother'.[71]

In early summer 1875, with 8,000 others, Mary attended the international 'Brighton Convention for the Promotion of Scriptural Holiness'. 'I feel as if I had been into a land of fountains and brooks of water, and seen all the figs and pomegranates and honey, and drunk a little of the wine – oh so sustaining', Mary told a friend of the experience.[72] Hannah Whitall Smith preached at the convention, her sermons so highly regarded that she became dubbed 'the angel of the churches'.[73] Anna must have longed to see and hear the woman whose work had so changed her life, and the books, papers, and ideas Mary brought back from the convention brought her a period of 'peculiar joy'.[74] 'How good it was of those people to make such an effort to share with many others their own good things!' Anna often said. 'How they poured themselves out to do us good, and kept back nothing, delighting to spread forth all they had seen and handled!'[75] 'I cannot tell you how thankful I am for the four days I had at Brighton', Mary wrote to a friend:

> you truly divine that Nannie and I have been feeding on the feast ever since. We are *very happy*; even these cold, wet days cannot make more than skin-deep impression upon us. My darling has more assurance than ever, so full of cheerfulness and sweetness – the drawing-room is always bright.[76]

Anna and Mary were both on a spiritual high, but religion also continued its day-to-day function in the household. Family prayers were not recited as spoken prayer was against Quaker custom and theirs was still essentially a Quaker household. A nightly religious reading for the household had, however, long been Sewell practice. With Isaac no longer able to conduct this, Mary now did so as Bayly, then a frequent guest, described:

> At half-past nine the servants came in; Mrs. Sewell read a chapter, occasionally making a few remarks as she went on, and then a hymn or piece of poetry. Now and then she read a short extract from a magazine or paper . . . Now and then, but rarely, the sweet voice from the sofa was heard, always beginning with 'Mother dear, don't thee think' so-and-so . . . When the servants rose, the master rose also, and remained standing until they had closed the door, saying in his courteous way, 'Good-night, Emily. Good-night, Jane.'[77]

Mary told Mrs Williamson that Anna claimed never to feel 'the nights long; she has so many things and thoughts to hold communion with'.[78] On one of her visits Bayly recalled that the evening reading was drawn from Matthew 'the Gospel of the Kingdom'. After the servants had gone 'and the weary master had retired for the night', she and Mary sat around Anna's sofa and the three chattered happily about 'the coming Kingdom and its exceeding glory'. Visiting Anna in her bedroom the next morning Bayly asked her how she had slept and Anna replied, 'Oh . . . I have had such a happy night; it was nice to be awake and ready to listen to His teaching about the Kingdom. He not only gives me "songs in the night," but "instructs me in the night season".'[79]

Mary maintained her old habit of taking pre-breakfast walks, now often confined to the garden.[80] Instead of composing as she strode, she now considered verses from a favourite book that Bayly identifies as *Daily Light*. This was probably *Daily Light on the Daily Path: A Devotional Text Book for Every Day in the Year; In the Very Words of Scripture*, which was divided into a volume for 'The Morning Hour' and one for 'The Evening Hour'. These page-a-day, palm-sized volumes offered a daily thematic statement, and included relevant biblical quotations. After her walk, as Bayly recalls, Mary would join Isaac and any guests for breakfast and pour out her thoughts on the *Daily Light* verse she had been reading. After breakfast she would take the verse into Anna's bedroom: 'where I often had the privilege of joining them', Bayly adds. 'They both knew that a trying and suffering day lay before them, and they together hid away some heavenly words in their hearts, that they might not faint by the way.'[81]

Anna had undoubtedly received much medical treatment and opinion, but eventually Mary confessed:

We have no doctors now. They gave no hope, and did no good, and therefore were exceedingly discouraging, so I gave my darling into the hands of the Great Physician, and He does not discourage. We wait in patience, trusting to see Him work a perfect work for us of the best kind, of which He only is the judge. My sweet one is so cheerful – so charmingly patient, that the days are not wearisome, and just now she is not suffering so much – indeed her general health is better now than it was some months ago. Sometimes she really looks well.[82]

In 1876 Anna was well enough to return to *Black Beauty*. '[S]he was so far improved in strength as to be able to write in pencil her clearly arranged thoughts,' Mary recalled, 'I immediately making a fair copy.'[83] There can be few books so painfully and slowly produced. Every sentence fatigued Anna but any surge in energy she used profitably. She 'always uses what little power she has,' Mary reported, 'never hopelessly giving up because she can do no more, never wishing or complaining, but cheerfully submissive'.[84] She now had her title and on 6 December 1876 pronounced, 'I am getting on with my little book, "Black Beauty."'[85]

The novel seems to have been finished during the winter of 1876–7 and at around the same time Anna expressed her intention in writing it: 'I have for six years been confined to the house and to my sofa, and have from time to time, as I was able, been writing what I think will turn out a little book, its special aim being to induce kindness, sympathy, and an understanding treatment of horses.'[86]

Not only was Black Beauty probably inspired by Bessie, but Margaret Sewell also suggests that Anna's own horses served as models for some of the other equine characters.[87] In writing her novel Anna drew on people, places, and ponies she knew as well as on her knowledge of horses and her imagination. She was also determined to get her beliefs across, and wove into her sad, exciting narrative of a horse's life messages not only about cruelty to horses and other animals, but also against drinking, hunting, irresponsible smoking, war, ignorance, blindly following party politics, and not keeping Sunday as a day of rest. Although her physical access to the world was now closed, her mind was not and even as she wrote her book she gathered new ideas and incorporated them into her purpose. On Sunday afternoons her conversations with Philip were now, as Margaret Sewell states, 'largely of horses in general and Bessie in particular'.[88]

Anna also sometimes sat at the window overlooking her garden at the front of the house and had conversations with passers-by – assuredly both human and equine. As any horse-lover knows the sound of hooves draws eyes to windows, and she must often have watched as horses trotted by, just as she must have spent long spells observing the deer graze in the park opposite. One particular conversation she had influenced the memorable scenes of Black Beauty's experience as a London cab horse. 'In thinking of Cab-horses, I have been led to think of Cabmen', Anna wrote:

> and I am anxious, if I can, to present their true condition, and their great difficulties, in a correct and telling manner.
>
> Some weeks ago I had a conversation at my open window with an intelligent Cabman who was waiting at our door, which has deeply impressed me. He led the conversation to the Sunday question, after telling me that he never plied on the Sabbath. I found that there was a sore, even a bitter feeling against the religious people, who, by their use of cabs on Sunday, practically deny the Sabbath to the drivers. 'Even ministers do it, Ma'am,' he said, 'and I say it's a shame upon religion.' Then he told me of one of the London drivers who had driven a lady to church – as she stepped from the cab, she handed the driver a tract on the observance of the Sabbath. This naturally thoroughly disgusted the man. 'Now Ma'am,' said my friend, 'I call that hypocrisy – don't you?' I suppose most of us agree with him, and yet it might not have been done hypocritically – so few Christians apparently realise the responsibility of taking a cab on Sunday.[89]

Anna set about making that responsibility clear in her novel.

Now that Anna was a writer she needed her own family editor and while Mary 'watched over every page',[90] and they must have talked over every stage of the book, she is unlikely to have been as critical as Anna was herself. Philip, too, was significantly involved in the project. 'Contemporary letters show that he saw and read carefully every chapter as the work proceeded,' Margaret wrote, 'my father had a definite share in the production of the book.'[91]

Early in 1877 Anna experienced respite in some of her symptoms. 'My jewel has been better this winter', Mary told Mrs R. 'The mildness of the weather has suited her well.'[92] Isaac, however, who was now eighty-three, was 'gradually becom[ing] weaker in body and mind'.[93] Whenever they envied the happy things that others were doing or seeing, Anna and Mary consoled themselves, Mary confided to Mrs R, 'by saying, "Well, we *have had* that," and have not to expect its continuance or renewal.'[94]

The comparative rally in Anna's health meant that in the early months of 1877, as well as completing her own book, she was able to indulge in some religio-literary discussions and reading with Mary. Spiritually, Mary stated, they were 'both very happy – hungry and thirsty as always, but with no fear of famine'.[95] One bite of spiritual nourishment they took was the evangelical Asa Mahan's *Out of Darkness Into Light* (1877), which recounted his struggles with faith and his spiritual life before and after baptism. They also read works by the Dean of Canterbury, Frederic W. Farrar (1831–1903), including his popular biography, *The Life of Christ* (1874), and his sermon collection, *The Silence and the Voices of God* (1874). They both also perused 'with deepest interest' Henry Dunn's *The Destiny of the Human Race* (c. 1863).[96] With 'intense delight'[97] they read *Charles Kingsley: His Letters and Memories of His Life* edited by his wife Frances, and published in 1876 by Henry King. They were both highly impressed: 'if you have not read it, do,' Mary recommended, 'it is worth anything; such thought, freshness, earnestness; such love and trust in God – such an affectionate admiration of nature and the beautiful earth and heavens. I feel my very soul fed and expanded and encouraged by it.'[98] Anna was so smitten that she used lines from the book as her epigraph to *Black Beauty*:

He was a perfect horseman, and never lost his temper with his horse, talking to and reasoning with it if it shyed or bolted, as if it had been a rational being, knowing that from the fine organisation of the animal, a horse, like a child, will get confused by panic fear, which is only increased by punishment.[99]

Anna was not the only family member then writing. Her aunt, Maria Wright, after producing her two books of Bible lessons for children in 1859, had taken up her pen again in her seventies and her new works must have formed part of Anna's reading during her years of illness. In 1872 Maria's biblical commentary, *The Beauty of the Word in the Song of Solomon*, was published but thereafter she turned novelist, in 1873 producing both *The Happy Village, and How it Became So* and *The Forge on the Heath*. Her final novel, *Jennett Cragg The Quakeress: A Story of the Plague*, was published early in 1877. This was a historical novel based on the true story of Jennett Cragg, a Quaker, who in 1687 rode alone over 200 miles to London to rescue her two infant grandsons after the plague had killed their mother, and their father had been banished for his Quaker faith. Jennett was the type of woman to appeal to the Sewell–Wright women, especially to Anna. Strong, determined, lovingly dominant in her own marriage, unashamed of her faith, and an excellent and fearless horsewoman, she travels despite risk and peril on her black steed, Midnight. It is interesting that Maria should be writing about a black horse at the same time as Anna, and possibly Philip's Bessie also inspired Midnight. Although not nearly as realized a character as Black Beauty, Midnight is mentioned often in the plot as an excellent horse who needs no whip or rein, can gallop for miles, and is admired by all who meet him, so much so that villainous King's Troopers try to seize him. Mary thought the novel '*pretty* writing and reading',[100] and Anna must have enjoyed this exciting tale of woman and horse risking danger, persecution, and plague.

Anna's cousin, Joseph Stickney Sewell, and his second wife came to stay at The White House early in 1877. Joseph had spent eight years as a missionary in Madagascar, and he was also one of the writers in Anna's extended family, authoring books on religious topics, missionary work, and Madagascar, including an

English–Malagasy Dictionary and the first ever Malagasy grammar. In 1878 he would become editor of the Quaker journal, *The Friend*. Anna must have been fascinated by his experiences. '[S]o good, so happy, so interesting!' Mary wrote of their visit. 'We have much enjoyed them.'[101]

Isaac's condition, like Anna's, had persisted since its onset almost seven years before. He was suffering from failing faculties and senile dementia which had been, until now, Bayly describes, 'more of a sorrow to those who watched him, and knew what he had been, than to himself'.[102] In June 1877 his condition worsened and he began experiencing 'mental impressions of a very distressing character, needing constant effort in those about him to divert his mind'.[103] There were 'faithful servants' in the household and Philip and his children and even the aunts at Buxton must have helped all they could, but with Anna herself ill and needing ongoing attention, Mary, at eighty, was overburdened. Isaac could be solaced by no one but her: 'it was always "Mary" that the sufferer wanted – and had'.[104] One thing that helped Mary through, as she told Mrs Williamson, was poetry: 'it seems so essential to certain states of mind and feeling. In the present exceeding monotony of our household existence, with my husband so feeble, and my darling often in too sensitive a state to bear a word, poetry comes to me like dew and sunshine.'[105]

Anna had now finished writing *Black Beauty* which she dedicated to her mother. Mary took the manuscript to her publishers, Jarrold and Sons, who accepted it for an outright sum, which seems to have been £40.[106] Single payments without a royalty provision were quite common at the time and this was a good price for a first novel.[107] On 21 August 1877 Anna reported, 'My first proofs of "Black Beauty" are come – very nice type.'[108] Thomas Jarrold, who 'took the warmest interest in all [Mary's] writing', and had become a dear friend, died suddenly just before *Black Beauty* was published,[109] so it was 'Mrs. Samuel and Mrs. Thomas Jarrold who 'took great interest' in seeing *Black Beauty* through the press.[110] Published by Jarrold and Sons' London office at 3 Paternoster Buildings just in time for Christmas 1877,[111] Anna's 'little book' entered the world.

ELEVEN
My Little Book
1877

[W]e have no right to distress any of God's creatures without a very good reason; we call them dumb animals, and so they are, for they cannot tell us how they feel, but they do not suffer less because they have no words.   (*Black Beauty*, Chapter 46)

'The first place that I can well remember was a large pleasant meadow with a pond of clear water in it.'[1] Thus opens Anna's novel, whose full title was *Black Beauty: His Grooms and Companions. The Autobiography of a Horse.* 'Translated from the Original Equine, by Anna Sewell.' Black Beauty recounts the rural idyll of his colthood with his mother Duchess on kind Farmer Grey's farm, his breaking-in, and his early observations of cruelty: boys who throw stones at horses, and hunting which pointlessly kills hare, horse, and man. Sold, aged four, to Squire Gordon of Birtwick Park, he meets the plump, plucky grey pony Merrylegs and the feisty chestnut mare Ginger who has received only unkindness in her life. Here, too, are ideal groom John Manly, gentle stable boy James Howard, and his later replacement little Joe Green. Revealing what it is like to be a horse and describing terrible instances of mistreatment, Black Beauty also recalls his adventures: saving lives by refusing to cross a weak bridge over a storm-swollen river, being rescued from a deadly fire, and galloping furiously for the doctor.

Sold, aged seven, to the Earl of W— at Earlshall Park, he suffers under the harmful but fashionable bearing-rein, races after a bolting horse, and when Reuben Smith recklessly rides him drunk, suffers the fall that reduces his prospects for ever. Changing owners frequently thereafter, he falls down the equine social scale, doing ever harder work and experiencing neglect and misuse. As a job-horse in a Bath livery stables he is driven by all types of inexperienced drivers, and while owned by a Bath gentleman his first groom steals his food and his second neglects his stable.

He vividly recalls his time as a London cab-horse working with ex-warhorse Captain and poor, kind owner Jerry Barker. In London he sees terrible cruelties to horses: flogging, overloading, excessive hours, careless accidents, and the effect of alcohol on masters. Worst of all he sees Ginger emaciated, ruined, and carted off dead. He is whipped brutally as an overburdened carthorse, and as a hired cab-horse he collapses on Ludgate Hill under the strain of too much luggage. Sold at a horse fair as a broken-down animal, he is bought by kind Farmer Thoroughgood at the insistence of his grandson Willie, and he finds a final happy home with the three Misses Blomefield and his old groom Joe Green. 'My troubles are all over', he declares, 'and I am at home.'[2]

This simple but powerful story initially provoked a tentative reaction, and the London booksellers bought just 100 copies on publication. Having strong faith in the book, however, Jarrold and Sons stepped up its marketing campaign, pitching it at schools as well as booksellers and the novel soon met with more success.[3] The first edition – which in 2003 fetches around £10,000 – was produced in red, blue, and green cloth in at least three variant bindings[4] and with a single illustration: a frontispiece of Black Beauty waiting injured in the moonlight beside Reuben Smith's corpse.

In January 1878 Anna inscribed a blue copy to her aunts at Dudwick Cottage,[5] and to Philip on his fifty-sixth birthday a red one:

To My dear Brother &
Valued critic, from his
Loving Sister
The author
14 Jany 1878.[6]

She had already sent copies to family and friends for Christmas and was receiving adulatory responses.[7] 'Read it! – I should think I did', wrote a cousin:

I am so delighted, so proud of my cousin . . . I do like the book exceedingly, it is *so good* . . . The story of poor Black Beauty and Ginger is most touching, and the different characters of the horses admirably carried out . . . were I to tell you of all I admire, I should not get this letter posted to-night. The best bit of writing . . . is the drive through the City – that is really wonderful. Are you sure you have never stood on the steps of an omnibus to collect passengers and watch the traffic?[8]

'As an imaginary entrance into and mastery of horse nature, it is extremely clever', another admirer told her, 'as a story it is thoroughly well planned and told; and last, not least, it must do good among all, high and low, who have the care of these noble creatures . . . My dear Anna, you have been doing angels' work in writing this book.'[9] 'You will be shocked to hear that a work intended to benefit mankind has been the cause of my neglecting all my duties', exclaimed a Norwich letter-writer, 'I *could not* leave Black Beauty till I left him safe in Joe's care . . . May it circulate widely, and may many a neglected Black Beauty find a resting-place in the kind consideration of some happy home.'[10]

Reviews which were, in Bayly's terms, 'laudatory enough to satisfy the vainest author', soon appeared.[11] On 22 December 1877 the *Eastern Daily Press* announced:

We have rarely read a book with so much genuine pleasure as this . . . The narrative is managed with no little skill and is full of variety and interest. The little book is especially valuable for the lessons of humanity which it inculcates, not only toward horses, but towards all living creatures . . . Such a volume as she has produced is an honor to her head and heart, and it is calculated to have a softening and humanising effect upon its readers . . . We heartily commend it to our readers, and we trust it will have a wide circulation.[12]

'Miss Sewell . . . writes with some humour; with keenly sympathetic feeling, and with a strong and noble purpose that pervades every page', the *Nonconformist* claimed on 9 January 1878:

It is all effective, but the most effective portion is when Black Beauty becomes a London cab horse – and that portion everybody who employs a cab should read. Had the Society for the Prevention of Cruelty to Animals published this, we should say it had published its best work. As it is, it would be difficult to conceive one more admirably suited to its purpose.[13]

The RSPCA's own organ, *Animal World*, noted: 'The more often we have turned over the leaves of "BLACK BEAUTY," the greater has been our delight.'[14] 'This Autobiography of a horse, his relations with grooms and companions', it asserted, 'is one of the best books recently published in support of our principles. The literary merit is excellent.'[15]

Anna had not intended *Black Beauty* to be a children's story, nor did its earliest readers regard it as singularly for the juvenile mind. It was written for those who dealt with horses – grooms, drivers, ostlers, stablehands – but a child readership had been envisaged even before the novel was published, and by February 1878 Anna was awaiting proofs of a School Edition. '[W]e have both a great desire that it should become a reading-book in Boys' Schools', Mary reported.[16] The 1870 Education Act had made education free for all and the 1880 Education Act would make it compulsory until the age of ten, so *Black Beauty* was timed ideally to meet expanded crops of child readers, and reviewers quickly recommended the book for a youthful audience. 'All boys and girls who are at all likely to have control of horses, or to be in any way connected with them, should possess this volume', the *Eastern Daily Press* stated,[17] while the *School Guardian* insisted: 'Wherever children are, whether boys or girls, there this autobiography should be.'[18] Later advertising urged:

> We strongly recommend parents to give their boys an opportunity of acquiring the valuable lessons which Miss Sewell teaches so pleasantly, that even the most abrupt of boys must be won over to follow the good and to shun the evil course in their conduct towards the dumb servants of man.[19]

Black Beauty was marketed not just for children but as an accessible horse-care manual, as a work of humane protest, and as an exciting narrative featuring an empathetic hero. In 1878 it was already in its fifth edition and the *Black Beauty* phenomenon had begun.[20] Anna was exhilarated by the acclamation her 'little book' was receiving, but her illness was worsening rapidly and she was destined to die before learning that within its first year *Black Beauty* sold over 12,000 copies.[21] 'No one would have been more amazed or more incredulous than my aunt had she been told that her book would attain world-wide fame', wrote Margaret Sewell in 1935, 'that it would be translated into practically every tongue possessing a literature, and that fifty years after her death its place would be unchallenged as the most loved of all books ever written on behalf of animals – one to be read with equal appreciation in castle and in cottage.'[22]

To say that *Black Beauty*'s success was galloping is no mere pun. By the mid-1880s it was in its 35th edition,[23] and by 1890 had sold over 100,000 copies.[24] These British sales, however, would prove as unwatered seed compared to the book's extraordinary flourishing in America. Pivotal to *Black Beauty*'s 1890[25] American debut (and ultimately for a common belief that the novel is American) was George Thorndike Angell (1823–1909), an indefatigable man of vision with a keen eye for what would serve his purpose and a strong sense of his own achievements. For years a successful Boston lawyer, Angell in 1868 founded the Massachusetts Society for the Prevention of Cruelty to Animals (MSPCA) after reading a newspaper report about two top Massachusetts horses who were driven to death after a forty-mile road race. The MSPCA agitated for anti-cruelty legislation, but Angell knew that prosecuting offenders was like shutting the barn door after the horse had been flogged beyond any capacity to bolt. He realized that prevention of cruelty through education, especially of the young, could do the most good. Consequently, he began publishing *Our Dumb Friends*, the first animal protection paper in the world; he set up in 1882 the first American Band of Mercy, which was a children's wing of the SPCA; and in the winter of 1888–9 he founded the American Humane Education Society (AHES).[26]

In early February 1890 Miss Georgiana Kendall of New York sent a copy of *Black Beauty* to Angell who immediately saw its educational potential as 'the best book ever written teaching kindness to the horse'.[27] For the past twenty years he had been seeking, and asking American authors to write, a book that would *'have as widespread and powerful [an] influence in abolishing cruelty to horses as 'Uncle Tom's Cabin' had on the abolition of human slavery'*. This book by an Englishwoman met his every wish.[28] Using the italicized emphases he would also introduce into the text of *Black Beauty*, Angell asked each reader of *Our Dumb Friends* '*who has ever loved or cared for a horse*, [to] send [him] as large a check as he or she can afford, to be used in the distribution of this book.'[29] On 1 April 1890[30] he published 10,000 copies '*at the marvellously low price of twelve cents each*' (eight cents extra by mail).[31] In re-titling it *Black Beauty. His Grooms and Companions. The 'Uncle Tom's Cabin' of the Horse*, Angell linked it firmly with Beecher Stowe's abolitionist novel.

Angell had ambitions for the novel and embarked on a fundraising campaign to secure its wider distribution. His stated aims were:

> to print immediately *a hundred thousand* copies . . . *to give away thousands of these to drivers of horses* – and in public schools – and elsewhere . . . to send a copy, post-paid, to the editors of each of about *thirteen thousand* American newspapers and magazines . . . to put a copy of it *in every home in America*.[32]

Had she been alive to seek a promoter, Anna could not have found a more enterprising or determined one than Angell, and his goals were not grand idlings: 70,000 copies were given away to stablehands and drivers during the first three months after its American publication.[33] He sent hundreds of copies to those he thought would contribute to wider production and claimed that 'probably not less than a thousand American papers, including those of highest literary standing and largest circulation' had published approbatory reviews of the book.[34]

The Critic of New York on 21 July 1890, although disliking Angell's 'Uncle Tom's Cabin' subtitle, extolled Anna's book:

> Miss Sewell may not have a mind as powerful as that of the author of *Gulliver's Travels*, but *Black Beauty: His Grooms and Companions* will do vastly more than that incomparable satire to convince mankind of the stupidity of treating the horse as an infinitely inferior animal. The happy thought has occurred to her, not of making a plea for the horse, but of letting the horse make a

plea for himself. And a still happier thought is that of robbing the plea of tediousness by making it dramatic . . . the story is . . . much *more* readable than the average novel of to-day. No wonder it has had so large a sale across the ocean. We should rejoice if its popularity in this country should prove to be even greater. . . . The tone of the tale is not namby-pamby . . . *Black Beauty* is a capital name, and will soon be a household word in this country.[35]

Angell maintained that he received 'but one criticism', and this was not of *Black Beauty* itself but of his enthusiastic use of it. A leading Boston newspaper condemned Angell's pirating of the novel, which paid the author nothing, and attacked the low price at which the AHES sold it. Angell's *Black Beauty* did list the author as 'A. Sewell' (probably de-gendered to create wider interest), but had been published without the agreement of either Jarrold and Sons or Anna's heirs. Such piracy was not uncommon at a time when American publishers often refused to recognize English copyright. Angell published a vigorous defence, stating:

(1) The author died *unmarried* shortly after the publication of the book.
(2) Her mother, a *widow*, died soon after.
(3) The English publisher paid Miss Sewell *just twenty pounds* for the book. By the payment of *twenty pounds* it became his property, *and no one but the English publisher gets a sixpence from the profits.*
(4) He has already sold 103,000 copies in England.
(5) He will receive thousands of dollars from its increased sale in Great Britain, Upper and Lower Canada, and other British provinces, which he would not have received but for its immense advertisement and sale in this country.[36]

Angell also explained that the AHES needed to undersell other American publishers '*even at a loss of thousands of dollars*' in order to get their anti-cruelty messages across.[37] As well as Americanizing spelling and terminology in *Black Beauty* (e.g. 'check-rein' instead of 'bearing-rein') and italicizing important passages, Angell also added his own introduction and pages of promotional material about the AHES.

To undersell was therefore to promote the aims of the society. One of his additional pages included illustrated directions on 'Killing Animals Humanely' which advised for horses:

> SHOOTING. – Place the pistol muzzle within a few inches of the head and shoot at the dot [front centre of skull], aiming toward the centre of the head.
> BLOWS. – Blindfold, and with a heavy axe or hammer strike just below the foretop, at the point indicated . . . Two vigorous, well-directed blows will make death sure.
> *Be careful not to shoot or strike too low.*[38]

In *Black Beauty* Anna also implies that shooting is the kindest end for a horse and humane thinking remains little changed today, adding only lethal injection as an alternative.

Other American publishers produced editions to satisfy their own agendas. Frank Miller's Harness Dressing, for example, produced fifteen tons of an edition of *Black Beauty* in which chapter headings were embellished with horses wearing rugs labelled 'Frank Miller's Harness Dressing', and their own advertising added at the ends of chapters.[39] Angell, however, was determined to undersell, and vowed to 'flood this whole country (1st) with "*Black Beauty*" and (2nd) with other publications of a similar kind'. 'Under Divine Providence', he stated, 'the sending of this book, "*Black Beauty*," into every American home may be . . . an important step in the progress, *not only of American, but the World's, humanity and civilization.*'[40]

His claims were again not entirely overstated for Angell was largely responsible for the extensive translation Anna's novel now underwent. It had been translated into French (*Prince-Noir*) in 1888, but Angell swiftly arranged for editions in German (*Schön Schwarzhärchen*), Italian (*Belmoro*), and Spanish (*Azbache*). *Our Dumb Animals* in October 1891 reported that Swedish and Volapük translations had been commissioned and a Japanese edition was planned.[41] In the same year Angell received a letter from 'Beirut, Syria', advising that it was being translated into Arabic and asking for his help in securing 'a cheap edition to be distributed gratuitously in *Syria*, *Palestine*, and *Egypt*, where terrible cruelty is inflicted on dumb animals'.[42]

As early as 1891 Angell's initial goal of 1 million copies had been met through AHES and trade editions. This was, Angell stressed, *'probably by far the largest number ever issued of any book in the world in the same length of time from publication'*.[43] In 1897 he claimed, 'probably *over two millions copies*' had been produced,[44] and in the same year Jarrold and Sons claimed total sales of 177,000 copies in Britain.[45] Dutch, Hindustani, Greek, Chinese, Turkish, Armenian, and Braille translations were produced, and in 1908 the AHES told a South Dakota correspondent who was begging for a Norwegian version that perhaps a Norwegian newspaper might serialize and publish it, although the AHES would be happy to provide advertising.[46] In 1909 *Our Dumb Animals* regularly advertised its own English, German, Modern Greek, Spanish, and Swedish editions for between 10 and 35 cents each and claimed that 10 million people had by then read the book.[47]

Black Beauty 'is to-day the sixth best seller of any books in the world', Jarrolds trumpeted in 1924.[48] Jarrolds alone published 150 editions before the copyright expired in 1927,[49] including 4 popular editions: the Reward Edition (for school prizes), the School Edition (for classroom use), the Popular Edition (gilt decorated cover), and the Paper Edition (paperback).[50] Post-1927 editions stamped ever faster through the presses of the world, and in 1935 world sales were estimated at 20 million.[51] In 1995 the approximation was 40 million as compared to 50 million for all of Dickens's works,[52] although Jarrolds prior to 1971 had already claimed 'the almost incredible number of not less than *fifty million copies*!'[53]

Clearly *Black Beauty* made considerable profit for some publishers and one can only imagine the modern-day court cases that might be instigated by an author seeking compensatory income. Anna would surely have acquiesced to Angell's altruistic pirating, and being a businessman's daughter would have expected publishers to benefit from their labours. Had she lived, however, she might have felt chagrin at the thought of the charitable good she could have performed with any income. She had not, however, written for money, nor did many of her readers have to buy the book.

From 1890 to 1910 the AHES distributed free to those who dealt with horses and to its Bands of Mercy children between 2 and 3 million copies of the book, 800,000 of which they published themselves, the rest by commercial companies.[54] Mirroring so many previous examples, in 1909 'the wife of ex-president Dole of Hawaii' ordered from the AHES hundreds of copies of *Black Beauty* for distribution to schools, kindergartens, poor settlements, and hack stands in Honolulu, and 2,000 more were ordered for distribution to boys in Cleveland, Ohio.[55] Early American humane success had also inspired the RSPCA in 1894 to add their endorsement, 'Recommended by the "Royal Society for the Prevention of Cruelty to Animals"', to the flyleaf of many British editions of *Black Beauty* where it remained for around fifty years.[56]

Not only the RSPCA, but also the Women's Christian Temperance Union and other societies promoted the novel.[57] Emma Saunders, a charity worker among railwaymen at Temple Meads Station in Bristol, distributed copies to all drivers of horse-drawn railway vans.[58] *Black Beauty* was also given to cabmen whose situation, as well as that of their horses, Anna had addressed empathetically in her book. Philanthropic campaigns targeted cabmen at the time, as their perceived behaviour – drunkenness, loitering, cruelty – was seen as disruptive and immoral. In Norwich on 4 February 1880 a dinner was held for between eighty and ninety cabmen who were each given several RSPCA publications and a copy of *Black Beauty*.[59] The London City Missionaries to Cabmen told Bayly that nothing, not even recent developments like cabmen's shelters or temperance work, 'has told so strongly for good among the men themselves, or induced such humane treatment of horses, as the influence and teaching they have gained from "Black Beauty" . . . many declare it to be "the best book in the world"'.[60]

'[T]han *Black Beauty* only the Bible has found a wider distribution', declared critic Vincent Starrett in 1923,[61] and biblical proportions were found not only in the proliferation of Anna's book but also in its content. Jarrolds claimed '*Black Beauty* is indeed a Bible for children',[62] and Angell termed it, 'the best missionary of its kind in the world'.[63] He believed it enabled his organization to reach:

perhaps hundreds of thousands *who seldom or never attend church or see a religious tract or newspaper*. On the subject of temperance it is perhaps on some accounts the best book ever written, because it reaches such multitudes of those who most need it and *yet will never read a temperance paper or tract.*

So on questions of *peace, observance of the Sabbath,* and, in fact, as one good bishop said, '*almost everything that goes to make a good Christian character,*' this book is preaching the gospel, day and night, Sundays and week-days.[64]

Anna had also included a topical protest against the use of the bearing-rein in driving. This extra fixed rein was attached to the bit (or in the Bedouin, or gag bearing-rein, to a more brutal gag bit) via a cheek ring hooked to a terret on the saddle pad on horses' backs and kept their heads pulled up high in the interests of fashionable equipage. The bearing-rein made it impossible for horses to lower their necks for an uphill pull, to correct a stumble when going downhill, or to rest when standing. It caused pain and physical damage, straining horses' backs, legs, necks, and mouths, causing breathing difficulties, and shortening their lives. J.G. Woods in 1881 wrote that it must be called the bearing-rein: 'I suppose because it is hard for the horse to bear.'[65] The RSPCA had been campaigning against the rein for decades and posted 'Please Give the Horse His Head When Going Uphill' signs, as did Angell in America.[66] When Anna was writing *Black Beauty* many letters were published in the press condemning the bearing-rein which, in the 1870s, like tail-docking,[67] had again become fashionable.

Although she suspected that if he noticed her book at all it would be only to point out errors, Anna with typical intrepidity had sent a copy to Edward Fordham Flower, a leading campaigner against 'the barbarous and senseless use of spurs, whips, curbs, gag bits, and bearing-reins'.[68] Anna would have known Flower's *Bits and Bearing Reins* (1875), which demonstrated that 'the high prancing step, and the toss of the head which scatters flakes of foam at every step', were not expressions of a horse's spirit but were 'occasioned by pain, and a vain attempt to obtain a momentary relief from their suffering' under the bearing-rein.[69] Although some drivers argued that it gave them better control, use of the bearing-rein was motivated largely by fashion, something that Anna, like Flower, castigated.

Mrs Toynbee, a mutual friend of Mary's and Flower's, reported his response in January 1878:

Mr. Flower [is] in a complete state of enthusiasm over 'Black Beauty.' 'It is written by a veterinary surgeon,' he exclaimed; 'by a coachman, by a groom; there is not a mistake in the whole of it; not one thing I wish altered . . . I shall show Mr. Bright that passage about horses in war. I *must* make the lady's acquaintance; she must come to London sometimes' . . . Is it being actively circulated? That was a point Mr. Flower was very anxious about . . . [he] could talk of nothing else . . . 'How could a lady know so much about horses! I should like to have a talk with her; do persuade her to come to London.'[70]

There was no hope of Anna going to London, nor of Mary – there was even another 'invalid friend'[71] then staying with them – but Anna treasured this report. When Mary took it into her she told Anna she 'was come to put her crown on . . . it was a triumphant moment . . . [bringing] indeed a full measure of gladness and confidence'.[72] Mary told Mrs Toynbee that Flower's comments were 'indeed a great encouragement both to me and Anna', and asked whether he might write 'a few lines expressive of his commendation' to help give the book 'a standing beyond what any one else could do.'[73] From the 1880s till the end of the century many British editions of *Black Beauty* included two illustrations from Flower's *Bits and Bearing Reins* which show a horse in comfort without the bearing-rein and in torture with it. These were also used in AHES editions until around 1910.[74]

It is often claimed that *Black Beauty* led to the abolition of the bearing-rein, but in fact the bearing-rein has never been banned legally in Britain or America and can still be found in use worldwide.[75] In Britain at least, however, its use tends now to be restricted to horse or driving shows where it is worn for short periods only.[76] Through its popularity, wide distribution, and empathetic depiction of horses' experiences, *Black Beauty* did, however, play a crucial role in discouraging use of the bearing-rein. An early reader told Anna that the book made her feel like cutting bearing-reins wherever she saw them and only fear of prosecution and being a woman prevented her from doing so: '[t]o induce fashionable ladies to forego the style of the bearing-rein', she told Anna, 'is simply to wait for an altered fashion; nothing short of that arbitrary foe will have any very evident effect, I fear; but the book is a thoroughly good step in the right direction'.[77] 'Bearing reins are less used every year,' Alfred Saunders, author of *Our Horses: or, the Best Muscles Controlled by the Best Brains*, reported in 1886, 'Miss Sewell's "Black Beauty," and the energetic appeals and well told facts of Mr. and Mrs. Flower, on this subject have done wonders.'[78] By the early years of the twentieth century the bearing-rein was falling out of fashion and under the 1911 Protection of Animals Act the RSPCA brought successful prosecutions for severe usage.[79]

Ignorance rather than deliberate cruelty was often why the bearing-rein was used, but ignorance is a folly Anna lambasts in *Black Beauty*. Kind-hearted little Joe Green who lets the steaming Black Beauty drink cold water and go without a blanket after his strenuous race for the doctor is treated harshly for almost killing him. John Manly tells Joe's father who has pleaded for his sorrowful son: '*Only* ignorance! only *ignorance*! how can you talk about *only* ignorance? Don't you know it is the worst thing in the world, next to wickedness? – and which does the most mischief, heaven only knows.'[80] Anna makes Joe bear the rational consequence of his ignorance just as she herself learned to in childhood, and Joe matures into an excellent and caring groom.

Turning a blind eye to cruelty, Anna also maintains, is almost as bad as cruelty itself and *Black Beauty* repeatedly entreats intervention. Her Quaker upbringing urged pacifism not passivity and, significantly, she gives the family name Wright to the 'real gentleman' who protests against the whipping of horses. '[T]his world is as bad as it is', he states, expressing Anna's ethos, 'because people think *only* about their own business, and won't trouble themselves to stand up for the oppressed, nor bring the wrong-doer to light . . . My doctrine is this, that if we see cruelty or wrong that we have the power to stop, and do nothing, we make ourselves sharers in the guilt.'[81]

Black Beauty did more than achieve fame and make effective protests. It broke gender, class, and readership assumptions about horse books. During the nineteenth century most books about horses were written *by* men *for* men of the horse-owning classes.[82] Anna was uncowed by such precedent, but the 'unfeminine' nature of her expertise was a point of notice with early readers. 'The author displays no small amount of knowledge of equine nature', the *Eastern Daily Press* commented, 'and she has evidently given more attention to the subject than ladies usually bestow.'[83] A cousin told her that the book was 'so unladylike that but for "Anna Sewell" on the title-page, and a certain gentle kindliness all through the story, no one, I think, would believe it to be written by a lady. Where you have obtained your stable-mindedness I can't imagine, but that you fully understand your business is a *fact*.'[84] Another admirer concurred, telling Anna, 'I cannot think how you could ever write such an Equestrian story. One would think you had been a horse-dealer, or a groom, or a jockey all your life.'[85]

Anna also broke with the tradition of addressing horse-owners. Instead she wrote for the working classes who actually cared for horses and who usually had learned horse care through word-of-mouth rather than written guidance. She attacked, too, that bastion of horse-writing at the time, hunting, and discussed the 'lower' equine roles that horse books generally overlooked: cab-work, coal-heaving, carting. Significantly, she made horses' suffering central, something most horse manuals marginalized.

Anna's equine concerns grew out of her Quaker-influenced stance against cruelty, her love of animals, and her own close relationship with horses, but her lifetime also coincided with the burgeoning of the humane movement. When Anna was two years old, Martin's Act of 1822 was passed in Britain, the first animal protection law in the world, designed to prevent mistreatment of cattle and horses. Two years later the world's first animal welfare organization, the Society for the Prevention of Cruelty to Animals, was founded, becoming Royal in 1840. As the animal that people had the most contact with, horses were the subject of early and sustained campaigns by welfare groups. By the 1860s the RSPCA was distributing booklets on horse care to drivers, coachmen, and carters and giving demonstrations of proper practice. It also protested against the use of sharp flint paving for roads which horses were expected to tread down and against brakeless omnibuses which horses had to stop by muscle-power alone. Welfare groups agitated for water troughs for horses just as the temperance movement campaigned for drinking fountains for humans. Anna's name became associated with these measures when, in 1891, a granite fountain donated by Caroline Phelps Stokes, an admirer of Black Beauty, was built outside the Public Library in Ansonia, Connecticut. Inscribed: 'Blessed are the merciful – Anna Sewell, Author of Black Beauty', it provided water for people and animals.[86]

Without horses Britain's industrial revolution and superpower status would not have been possible. Although railway expansion in the 1840s had swept away stagecoaches, the need for horses increased rather than lessened. Horses now transported passengers to and from stations, hauled goods from port to railway to end user, provided cab and omnibus transport in cities and towns, and serviced canals, mines, agriculture, and places untouched by rail. At the end of the nineteenth century there was roughly one horse for every eight people in Britain. In 1893 there were around 300,000 horses in London alone, over 100,000 of whom made their way through traffic chaos in the square mile of the City district of Anna's infancy every day.[87]

What Samuel Sidney in *The Book of the Horse* (1874) called the 'cavalry-consuming epoch' of the Franco-Prussian War had doubled the price of horses between 1863 and 1873,[88] and with owners determined to get their money's worth cruelty was widespread when Anna was writing. All the ill-treatment Anna describes in *Black Beauty* could be easily witnessed: flogging with anything from a stick to a shovel, whipping any part of a horse's anatomy, underfeeding, poor stabling, exhaustive riding, working injured horses, damaging styles of riding or driving, tail-docking, tight bearing-reins, the 'using up' of horses literally on their last legs, and persistent overloading. Cab-horses on average lasted only two years, their work and conditions were so hard.[89] Horse-traders also engaged in a range of swindles such as inserting a sharp substance between the hoof and shoe of a good leg to make a lame horse's gait look even,[90] painting a dark horse's grey hairs with ink to give a patina of youth,[91] 'figging up' a horse to go faster by inserting ginger into its anus,[92] or selling decrepit horses for use on night cabs where they were less visible.[93]

Like Black Beauty, horses commonly fell down the ranks from carriage-horse, to cab-horse, to cart-horse, to job-horse, to knacker's yard. Cities like London halved many horses' lives,[94] and horses regularly slipped and fell on the streets or collapsed from overwork. People would cluster around these fallen creatures but could not put them out of their misery until the owner was found. If impossible to cure or use any other way, the horse would be taken to the knacker's yard for slaughter where it was supposed to be killed within three days.[95] Often this was not the case and condemned horses might linger, maimed, unfed, and unwatered, for days. At the knacker's the horse's commodity value was literally anatomized. Pole-axed, flayed, and butchered, the horses' bones were boiled for oil used for leather-dressing, axle-grease and candle-making. Bone remnants were sold for button-making or ground for manure. Horse meat was boiled for catfood, the white 'tripe' for dogs, and the skin became leather for whips and carriage roofs. Hooves went for glue, old shoes to the farrier, tails and manes ended up as furniture stuffing or fishing-lines.[96]

Anna's detailed and accurate knowledge of horses came largely from her own close observation. Mary told Mrs Toynbee that Anna's 'thoughts and pictures' in *Black Beauty*:

> were the fruit of previous experience. When a child, she severely sprained both ankles, which ever after prevented her taking much walking exercise, and made riding and driving a necessity; and so it came to pass, between her and her own horse, and horses in general, a mutual confidence and friendship sprang up, and she learned all their secrets. She learned much through her ear, in this way quickly detecting if anything is wrong with a horse's foot, and through her eye she knows at once if anything annoys them.[97]

Anna may have augmented this knowledge by reading. One book she must have known was the RSPCA's *The Horse Book*, written by William Youatt in 1831 and subsequently revised by George Fleming, both respected veterinarians. The RSPCA produced thousands of copies of *The Horse Book* which advised on the care and good treatment of horses and attacked the bearing-rein and overloading.[98] Many editions of *Black Beauty* up until the end of the nineteenth century included at the rear a recommendation by 'The Translator' for those who 'wish to know more of the right treatment of horses, on the road, and in the stable . . . to procure an admirable little book, price fourpence, entitled "The Horse Book"' which has directions that are 'short, clear, and full of common sense'. Editions of *The Horse Book* published after *Black Beauty*'s appearance contained a reciprocal recommendation to read Anna's novel.[99]

Of course *Black Beauty* was not simply a horse-care manual, it was a work of literature. In Anna's day there was comparatively little in the way of equine fiction, and in writing literarily about horses Anna was again riding her own route. In form, however, she undoubtedly was influenced by the autobiographies and biographies of everything from baboons to pincushions that were available during her childhood and which had had their heyday in the late eighteenth and early nineteenth centuries. Equine examples of these which foreshadow *Black Beauty* are: *The Memoirs of Dick, The Little Poney: Supposed to be Written by Himself; and Published for the Instruction and Amusement of Little Masters and Mistresses* (1800), Arabella Argus's *The Adventures of a Donkey* (1815) and Argus's *Further Adventures of Jemmy Donkey Interspersed with Biographical Sketches of the Horse* (1821).

Black Beauty in turn, has had an enormous influence, inspiring imitations, sequels, illustrations, and movies as well as itself appearing in versions lightly abridged, severely condensed, or altered into forms almost unidentifiable with the original except for the title *Black Beauty* and the presence of a black horse. As early as 1885 a story entitled 'Dowse, the Gipsy' contained a horse called Black Beauty of whom his new owner says, 'I must change his name – it is too hackneyed.'[100]

In 1892 Angell advertised three 200-dollar prizes for 'the best and most useful stories of not less than one hundred "*Black Beauty*" pages' on kind treatment of domestic animals and birds in different regions of America.[101] Riding the tailwind of *Black Beauty*'s success, these were published by the AHES as 'sequels' to *Black Beauty* but were unrelated in content. The first was the anonymous 1893 *Our Gold Mine at Hollyhurst*, subtitled *'Duke': A Prize Story of Massachusetts* which told of the Gardner family, including Newfoundland–St Bernard cross, Duke, who act kindly to all animals. In the same year *The Strike at Shane's: A Prize Story of Indiana* was published anonymously[102] in which the brutal treatment of an old horse provokes other farm animals to go on strike. Third was Ellen A.

Barrows' Angell-revised *Four Months in New Hampshire: A Story of Love and Dumb Animals* (1894), which concerned a fictional animal rights association. Angell himself compiled *The Humane Horse Book* which the AHES sold for decades.

In 1891 Angell had also offered a $1,000 prize for 'the best equestrian drama of *Black Beauty*'.[103] It seems to have taken some years for the competition to close, but when Miss Flavia Rosser won, Angell paid her winnings and within twenty-four hours sold the play on for $1,200 to Boston theatrical managers Atkinson and Thatcher who mounted a 1908–9 tour of it throughout America.[104] The Massachusetts *Pittsfield Eagle* on 3 February 1909 reported, 'Everybody in almost every country on the face of the globe knows "Black Beauty" by heart, and truly it was a heart story that touched a tender chord in every breast toward dumb animals . . . the play . . . has made the greatest hit of any play put out in a decade . . . [it] closes with a grand allegorical scene.'[105] It clearly included significant alterations from the book, the Buffalo *Truth* reporting that it was a crowd-pleasing 'racing drama . . . The great scene, of course, is the winning of the famous English derby by "Black Beauty".' It also noted there was 'plenty of comedy sprinkled through its telling', yet it was 'a novelty because this is the first time . . . that a dramatist has attempted to make the humane treatment of animals the basis of a stage play . . . and it is not laid on with a shovel either.'[106] A shovel may have been needed at some point, however, as Black Beauty 'herself', Ginger, and Merrylegs were played by three real horses.

In 1954 Phyllis Briggs's *Son of Black Beauty* appeared, the autobiography of Stardust who experiences a series of adventures as Gipsy horse, circus performer, shipwreck survivor, and a wild horse for whom 'man was my enemy!'[107] 'In this book the art of the storyteller has been enlisted to produce what Black Beauty the horse could not,' the 'Publishers' Note' states, 'a son.'[108] Like most male working horses of the time in Britain, unlike in France, Spain, or Russia,[109] Black Beauty would probably have been – with clamps and a firing iron and without anaesthetic – gelded in the autumn of his first year just before weaning to make him more tractable.[110] Geldings were worth more than mares or stallions and were favoured for driving. Mares were popular for riding, while stallions could be hard to sell and railways charged almost double the fare for transporting them.[111] Anna never mentions Black Beauty's gelding, but given her strong rural experience and detailed knowledge of horses, this is not likely to be, as some have surmised, because she was ignorant of it. It may have been for reasons of Victorian propriety or because as a woman imagining herself into equine form it may not have occurred to her to do so, but in fact many horse manuals of the time also gloss over it.

Black Beauty's fictional family was further expanded by Josephine, Diana, and Christine Pullein-Thompson, themselves famous for their pony novels. Josephine recalls, '[a]s soon as I could read, I had devoured *Black Beauty* eight times, sobbing over Ginger and the hardness of human life'.[112] In 1975 their *Black Beauty's Clan* appeared (republished as *Black Beauty's Family* in 2000) which included Josephine's *Black Ebony*, the story of Black Beauty's youngest brother set in the 1880s and 1890s, Diana's *Black Princess*, the life of Black Beauty's great-niece during the First World War, and Christine's *Black Velvet* about a 1930s show-jumping great-great-great-nephew of Black Beauty. In 1978 they followed this up with *Black Beauty's Family* (republished as *More From Black Beauty's Family* in 2001), which comprised Josephine's life of *Nightshade*, a thoroughbred ancestor of Black Beauty, Diana's *Black Romany*, about an 1840s forebear of Black Beauty, and Christine's *Blossom*, the tale of his coal-horse great-great-niece.

Black Beauty's success had also inspired early imitations on both sides of the Atlantic. Canadian Margaret Marshall Saunders won an AHES competition for a companion book to *Black Beauty* with the bestselling *Beautiful Joe: The Autobiography of a Dog* (1894), which she dedicated to Angell. Jarrold and Sons also published echo works such as Dr Gordon Stables's *Sable and White: The Autobiography of a Show Dog* (1893) and *Shireen and Her Friends: Pages from the Life of a Persian Cat* (1894), both advertising *Black Beauty* at the rear. Horse autobiographies that have followed include Mark Twain's *A Horse's Tale* (1906) narrated by Buffalo Bill's horse Soldier Boy, John H. Burns's *Memoirs of a Cow Pony, as Told by Himself* (c. 1906), Michael Morpurgo's *War Horse* (1982), advertised as 'The *Black Beauty* of the Great War', and Richard Adams's *Traveller* (1989) told by Robert E. Lee's Civil War horse.

More significantly, Anna had claimed horse fiction for women
and when horse novels flourished in popularity in the 1940s, and on
into the girl-and-pony book boom of the 1960s and 1970s, women
authors dominated. In Britain these included the prolific Pullein-
Thompson sisters (and their mother Joanna Cannan), *Flambards*
author K.M. Peyton whose over fifty-year career includes the recent
Blind Beauty (1999), Ruby Ferguson and her Jill pony stories, and
Monica Dickens with her Follyfoot books. American examples
include Marguerite Henry's famous *Misty of Chincoteague* series
and Mary O'Hara's *My Friend Flicka* trilogy, and in Australia Mary
Elwyn Patchett's Brumby series.

Black Beauty itself has remained popular longer than any horse
book that came before it and all that have come after it, and its
hundreds of editions form the locus of searches by keen collectors.
The *Black Beauty* collection at the University of Connecticut, for
example, holds 450 different editions of the novel, spanning from
1877 to the mid-1980s.[113] Although nothing caps the power of the
actual story, from the late Victorian period onwards illustrations
have formed an important part of the book's popularity. The first
fully illustrated editions appeared in 1894: Jarrolds' British edition
with pen-and-ink illustrations by sporting artist John Beer (also the
first edition to carry the RSPCA recommendation) and J. Hovenden
and Co.'s New York edition with twenty-two illustrations by H.
Toaspern, Jr. In 1909 Jarrolds brought out two attractive editions:
the Prize Edition with illustrations by Winifred Austin and the
Presentation Edition with 150 illustrations, twelve in colour, by
Maude Scrivener.[114] *Black Beauty*'s particular appeal for women was
recognized early. Harriet Fowler, who has traced some of the
illustrative history of the novel, notes that several editions from
1900 to 1910 had women-focused decorative covers including
'fashionable women in large hats with Gibson-girl hairstyles'.[115] In
1912 Jarrolds published the now famous edition illustrated with
eighteen colour plates by Cecil Aldin,[116] and horse artist Lucy
Kemp-Welch produced what many regard as the finest illustrations –
twenty-four colour and many pen-and-ink – for the J.M. Dent
edition in 1915.[117] The 'Edition de Luxe' of this, including six extra
colour plates by Kemp-Welch and limited to 600 signed copies, is
the most sought-after twentieth-century edition.[118] A string of other

editions has appeared since, including Ellen B. Wells and Anne Grimshaw's abundantly illustrated and informative *The Annotated Black Beauty* in 1989.

Teaching editions also were produced early and are still appearing. In 1905 Mrs J.C. Gorham's *Black Beauty: Retold in Words of One Syllable* appeared, hyphenating many words – 'Ging-er', 'mast-er', 'hors-es' – to meet its subtitle strictures. Around 1922 Jarrolds produced a version 'Edited for School Use' which included an appendix of definitions, and at the end of each chapter comprehension, composition, and vocabulary work for students. In 1999 two slim school readers were produced by Stan Cullimore: *The Making of Black Beauty: A Biography of Anna Sewell* and *Little Joe Green*. The novel's historical value in portraying Victorian life has also been recognized since the 1920s, and the simplicity of its language and short chapters has served not only to teach children to read but also to teach English to speakers of other languages.

Not all readers, however, find *Black Beauty* agreeable, especially those who arbitrate over what it is best for children to read. A review of 1957 claimed it had 'long since outlived its usefulness as a children's book'.[119] In 1965 another reviewer claimed: 'By any standards, it is a poor book; yet on it goes . . . It is a book I would leave in [the library] but would never recommend to any reader.'[120] In the 1970s *Black Beauty*, like many children's books at the time, was attacked for offering a poor role model for children in having a passive, docile protagonist who was unquestioningly obedient.[121] Claims of 'maudlin sentiment' have also been raised as an objection, yet for a Victorian novel it is surprisingly unsentimental.

Heavily didactic novels have not appealed in recent decades, and the strong messages of *Black Beauty* are often a surprise to adults who recall from childhood only a sad story about the adventures of a horse. Abridged editions expunge *Black Beauty*'s more preacherly sections – first to go are those on electioneering and Sabbatarianism – in favour of scenes with more action. Some also delete harsher elements such as horses shrieking as they perish by fire.

Readers who come to the novel only knowing it from the myriad of forms that make up its culture text – the sum of a work's cultural impact – are often surprised to discover that it is not a story about the relationship between a horse and a girl or boy. Nor is Black Beauty a beloved family pet, a rescuer of children, a racehorse, or a secondary character in a human drama. Like some book versions, most film and television versions have departed almost entirely from Anna's story.

Early visual interpretations included Victorian lantern slides showing scenes from the book, produced by F. Newton & Co. of London and designed for public readings.[122] The first film versions were shorts directed by Lewis Fitzhamon and produced by Hepworth Company in Britain in 1906 and 1910.[123] American film versions began with Thomas A. Edison's *Your Obedient Servant* (1917). Vitagraph Picture Corporation then produced a film entitled *Black Beauty* (1921), as did Monogram Picture Corporation (1933, the first sound version), and Twentieth-Century Fox (1946). Alco Pictures made *Courage of Black Beauty* (1957), and *Black Beauty* (1971) was co-produced by Chilton/Paramount Pictures/Tigon British Film Productions. Educational film strips of *Black Beauty* were also produced in 1971[124] and in 1976.[125] In 1978 Hanna-Barbera Productions released an animated version, and in 1994 Caroline Thompson's Warner Brothers film appeared. Most depart widely from the novel, tending to focus on a boy and his horse, or girl and her horse, with the spotlight shone on the human story. Insofar as it makes horses central and gives Black Beauty his own voice and story, Thompson's is closest to the original.

Human characters and non-Sewell storylines also predominate in television series (and associated novelizations). London Weekend Television in two 26-episode seasons (1972–3 and 1973–4) produced the popular *The Adventures of Black Beauty* with its famous signature tune, 'Galloping Home', composed by Dennis Andrew King, now inextricably linked with the image of a galloping black horse. In 1978 Universal Studios made five one-hour-episodes entitled *Black Beauty*, and in 1990 the twelve-episode *The New Adventures of Black Beauty* appeared, set and shot in New Zealand.[126]

Black Beauty has played many roles and continues to see many permutations. In 1924 a Texas cowpuncher who was convicted of ill-treating his pony was jailed for one month and sentenced to read *Black Beauty* at least three times.[127] Presumably for fears over its positive black implications and on the basis of the title alone, the novel was banned in South Africa for a short period in 1955, and ironically it has been banned from some American school libraries because it depicts cruelty to animals.[128] In 1996 the spoof *Black Beauty According to Spike Milligan* was published, and in 1998 *Black Beauty* was staged as a children's musical in Manhattan.[129] A cornucopia of Black Beauty collectables exist: comics, annuals, read-along records, jigsaws, games, colouring books, paintings, posters, audio-books, interactive videos, and figurines of Black Beauty and his horse companions.

Black Beauty has inspired not only commercial products but humanitarian action. Given *Black Beauty* as a boy in the 1920s by an aunt who knew the book by heart, Cleveland Amory (a relation of Angell's) was inspired to found in America the Fund for Animals in 1967. In 1979 Amory established his Black Beauty Ranch in Murchison, Texas where horses and other rescued animals can live out their days not only kindly treated but also never ridden or driven.[130] A Black Beauty Horse Rescue Fund also exists in Glendale, California, and the Angell-founded MSPCA annually bestows its 'Black Beauty Award' upon 'a fictional, historic, or mythic animal who has improved society's relationship with animals',[131] the 2003 award going to Lassie. Indeed Anna's own county, Norfolk, has a preponderance of horse sanctuaries and organizations, being home to the headquarters of the International League for the Protection of Horses and to two Redwings Horse sanctuaries, some of whose horses until recently grazed in Dudwick Park.[132]

Black Beauty is a work of multiple capacities whose seemingly simple art, born of Anna's long hours on her sofa, is often underestimated. It provides practical education, moral instruction, narrative excitement, and emotional involvement. It is highly readable and survives where others of its time and style have long since obsolesced. A century after its publication it was rated the favourite book of ten-year-olds in a major 1977 survey of British children's reading.[133] Although its popularity has slipped from that pinnacle almost thirty years on, its classic status remains unshaken. In 2003 in Britain it still ranked 58th in 'The BBC Big Read' poll of favourite books of all time and in New Zealand 'The Whitcoull's Kids' Top 50' poll of children's favourites in 2003 ranked it thirty-nine and it was, by decades, the oldest book to rank. Many of the claims made for *Black Beauty* are not entirely accurate or have been used out of chronological context, but there is one that always rings true and is why the novel endures. It is, quite simply, loved.

The novel's strength lies in the sincerity and passion with which Anna wrote and in readers' empathy with its good-hearted, hard-working hero who, in the face of brutal injustice, sticks to his principles and comes through against all odds. *Black Beauty*'s real power is found in its emotional bond with readers. Although boys were the book's initial target audience among children – it is boys rather than girls who mistreat horses in the novel – it is usually girls to whom the book speaks on some deeper, indefinable level, provoking passionate loyalty and what May Hill Arbuthnot terms, 'Black Beauty vapours'.[134] Coral Lansbury suggests that 'its effect upon adolescent girls has always been one of unbearable anguish. Generally read at the perilously emotional time when a child crosses the threshold to adult life, *Black Beauty* is a work of inconsolable grief. It is read obsessively, as though it contained lessons which must be learned, no matter how painful.'[135] This is no new reaction. In 1878 a correspondent told Anna, 'It has made me cry more than twice or thrice. Poor Ginger! Then the fall on Ludgate Hill!'[136] Recollected in adulthood, it remains for many women 'such a sad book' despite its happy ending.

Black Beauty is the autobiography not only of a horse but also of Anna herself.[137] The opening of the novel and Birtwick Park were surely based on Dudwick Park, Farmer Grey on her grandfather Wright or Philip, the Gordons on her Aunt and Uncle Wright, the three Misses Blomefield (one even called Ellen) on her three aunts at Dudwick Cottage, and Anna herself and Mary as models for characters who step in to prevent cruelty. More subtly *Black Beauty* reflects the beliefs and pattern of Anna's life as well as its aims and constraints. Like Black Beauty who is sold on to a series of owners, Anna, too, had to move to various new homes for reasons beyond her control. Like her horse narrator she suffered permanent physical injury to her legs which restricted her life, and Black Beauty's periodic longing for companionship may well express the isolation which she often experienced. Anna can be seen as an amalgam of Black Beauty – the obedient narrator who suffers hardship without complaint, and whose good nature, despite physical damage, is recognized in the end – and Ginger who expresses the suffering, inner rage, and sense of injustice she must also have felt. *Black Beauty* is surely also Anna's expression of gratitude for the 'cures', companionship, and freedom horses had offered her. In writing her novel she aimed to do for horses what they had so often done for her: made life easier.

A classic is something the idea of which seems so simple and so perfect that to imagine a world where it no longer exists is impossible. This is the gift of genius: to fill a gap in the world that no one knew was there but whose existence is evidenced by its filling. *Black Beauty* is such a book. It has that ineffable something. Anna lived just long enough to see the first steps in what would become her book's phenomenal journey across time and the world, but that she did know of its very earliest success was the first and most precious diamond spilled from the treasure trove of its fame.

TWELVE

With Shining Feet

1877–8

I was now very ill; a strong inflammation had attacked my lungs, and I could not draw my breath without pain.

(*Black Beauty*, Chapter 18)

The desire to complete her novel and see it into the world may have lengthened Anna's life, but Mary claimed, 'the joy of the success of her book [was] almost too much for Anna's delicate frame'.[1] Her health had already worsened before *Black Beauty*'s publication, and completing it had been, in Bayly's words, 'as if the feeble flame of life had leaped up brightly for a last effort, and now flickered down again'.[2] In July 1877 Anna had written in her journal: 'I began milk diet two weeks ago, and hope for benefit.'[3] This invalid's fare did help slightly, but she was incapable of taking the advised amount and began to waste away. 'The darling has not been so well for the last few weeks,' Mary was soon telling Mrs Williamson at Bath, 'quite unable to work or do anything but be an angel of patience and sweetness in the house.'[4] Soon after *Black Beauty* appeared a 'cold settled on her lungs' and 'rapid decline set in'.[5]

For these past secluded years Anna probably had been in the advanced stages of lupus, with her flares as well as her baseline health being worse than ever before. Now in her final months her lungs were affected, possibly attacked by lupus in addition to either a severe lung infection, which in her debilitated state she could not fight off, or that number one killer of the nineteenth century, tuberculosis. Tuberculosis in conjunction with hepatitis is what her own doctor diagnosed.

Typical treatments for tuberculosis included many of those Anna would already have tried: bleeding, blistering, cod liver oil, calomel, stimulants, opium to ease coughing, rest, quiet, fresh air, and the milk diet she had started. Norwich pharmacies also offered all sorts of remedies for illness including the panacean 'Robinson's Original

Female Pills' which, if taken according to directions, promised to restore the 'sallowest complexion . . . to its natural clearness, the eyes become bright, with the radiance of animated health and spirits, the system purified, and all obstructions removed . . . they will soon restore Females of all Ages to sound health'.[6]

No pill or potion could save Anna. Her treatment from around the time *Black Beauty* was published was purely palliative, and even her afternoons on the sofa were soon replaced by total confinement to her 'little white bed'.[7] 'Step by step, day by day, the dear life seems to be slipping away,' Mary reported, 'gently just now, comparatively little pain, quiet and praiseful, taking medicine, food; – but the life goes. She can scarcely be moved without faintness.'[8] A nurse was hired and a water-bed obtained. 'The water-bed is a great comfort,' Mary wrote, 'she has not been moved to the couch for three days – it is all too much.'[9]

Still caring for Isaac whose own mental state was worsening, Mary was nevertheless Anna's constant companion and nurse. 'We do not talk of the future', Mary told a friend:

> the parting; it might unnerve us both, and we each know what the other thinks and feels. She has done the day's work in the day, and no arrears press on her tranquil spirit, which is resting in the arms of Eternal love. She never loses an opportunity of sending her love to her friends; all are affectionately remembered – thee most especially.[10]

The afterlife was naturally on Anna's mind, but her calm, positive faith continued as it had since her deeper conversion four years earlier. 'I wanted to tell thee myself of the goodness of the Lord,' Mary told Mrs Williamson, 'not in restoring bodily strength – but little more of this remains to be taken away – but in restoring the soul. We are both of us kept in such wondrous peace and trust. He is taking us down on the sunny side of the valley, where the dew lies still, and every sharp stone as we touch it is taken away.'[11] These stones were very sharp, and Anna was passing even beyond emaciation. 'There is now no acute pain internally', Mary wrote, 'but the poor bones, barely covered with skin, have passed through at the lower part of the back . . . The difficulty of raising the mucous phlegm is the most trying, but her sweet patience accepts all from the Hand of love.'[12]

Anna endured this final illness with her distinctive fortitude and the character Bayly always saw as 'remarkable',[13] but her days and the excruciating nights were exhausting and painful. 'The majestic grandeur of her countenance is never disturbed, excepting in sleep,' Mary maintained:

> then we see what she suffers, and how she restrains herself from showing it. Her thought is about me – we know each other's thoughts and feelings so perfectly, that words would be an intrusion, and might overcome us both. How long it may last I know not, but think it cannot be long – she now never rises from her water-bed. I have moved her into the drawing-room. The nurse always sleeps there, and I go to my own bed.[14]

Spring was always a special time for Anna and Mary, not only because of the pleasure they took in its lushness and sunlight, but also because it was their birthday season. The spring of 1878 was a heart-wrenching one. Mary as usual brought springtime flowers in for Anna's bedside, but they both knew that Anna's fifty-eighth birthday on 30 March would be her last and that Mary's eighty-first exactly one week later signified the final spring they would ever spend together. 'But oh! it is too touching,' wrote Mary, 'with all the sweet springing of the flowers, the joyous songs of the birds, and the sunshine, and she, fading away, never to look at them again with me.'[15] Mary could hardly bear to see Anna slipping away, but declared, 'I have freely given her to the Lord', and took comfort in imagining 'my darling drawn up to pass into the pure light of the Sun of Righteousness'.[16]

In April Mary wrote to one of the many friends and family who wanted news of Anna:

> You are longing, I know, to hear of my Jewel, but what shall I say? A little weaker, and a little weaker – two or three words at a time is all she can say, and all she can bear to hear. I dare not say a word that would touch her tender feelings. 'My dearest Jewel,' I say, and her response is, 'My dearest mother' – we neither of us

venture further. She has been sorely tried with her poor back – no ease . . . Her sweet patience is past description, and her thankfulness for any little change that promises ease, if only momentary, is truly touching. The dear Lord is putting on the last ornamental touches, and beautifying her exceedingly.[17]

A friend wrote a letter of comfort to Mary stressing that in the hereafter all Anna's hopes would be met: 'the desires and wishes of *such minds* as hers are not easily grasped, but she will be satisfied, and so will her mother. "Such high love" as you two have had for one another "is not of things to perish"'.[18]

On 11 April Anna put her worldly affairs in order by signing her will which appointed Philip, her nephew John, and her niece Margaret as executors. She left £20 for payment in small weekly sums to the poor people to whom she currently gave. She also left legacies of nineteen guineas each to three people who must have been very dear to her although no other traces of their role in her life exist: her 'dear friend' Margaret Taylor, her cousin James Hunton, and her friend Mrs Eyles. The remainder she left to Mary. Her property at the time comprised: '15 shares in the London & County Bank & Co. – 600£ [equal to about £40,000 in 2003] Utica & Ithaca Railway Bonds – 100£ Toronto Water Works Bonds' and some money Philip held for her.[19] She had just two weeks to live.

'Day by day the precious life is longing for its home', Mary reported to Mrs F on 23 April. '"Here in the body pent," weary and breathless; suffering night and day. *That* is one side of the picture – there is another – resting in the Will of God, without the shadow of a cloud between her soul and her Saviour. She is longing for the hour of her liberation, and I do not hold her.'[20] Mary passed on to Mrs F the message that, 'at broken intervals', Anna had asked her to send:

How we have loved her, mother, and how we have admired her! I have so often wished to write to her since I had her last letter. I have been waiting till I was stronger, and that has never come. Say to her from me . . . Do not mourn your 'dead Friend.' If God takes it away, it is because He has some other work *now* more wanted, and therefore more worthy of being done . . . I have many 'dead friends' in which I delighted – they were taken away from me one by one. They might have carried my heart away. I think they would, but I think they were taken away to be restored. I shall find them when the new life begins, and rise and enjoy them without danger. Meantime God has given me a few 'humble friends' to employ my small talents, and keep my thoughts from myself – little works for children and poor people, that have made me glad and busy, and thankful *now*.[21]

The bitter east wind that often rises up in spring was blowing across Norfolk during the last four days of Anna's life, and on 25 April its bite was 'worse than ever'.[22] In the earliest hours of that morning Anna's unceasing, wracking coughs woke Mary who came in to her at 4 a.m. In what Mary termed her 'bright sunny way' Anna sent Mary away saying, 'Oh . . . thee art not so good as thee said thee would be. Go to bed darling; I really have had some nice sleep.' At 6 a.m. Mary returned with 'something very soft' to put under her shoulders, but Anna, her back so tender that any movement was unbearable, had to refuse it until the nurse should move her again.[23]

At around 7 a.m. Anna felt faint. The nurse quickly called Mary, whose own account best reveals Anna's final hours:

I found her breathing with difficulty, but as soon as she could speak, she said, with one of her inexpressible smiles, 'I am not going yet, I am so strong.' She then asked the nurse if that was dying. For four and a half hours this painful breathing continued, becoming more and more difficult, and she was perfectly conscious till the last few minutes. She, as it were, girded herself to endure the pains of death, that she might spare the feelings of those around her. Her lips were often seen moving, and her clear, beautiful eyes raised upwards; then her face would become overspread with an almost luminous smile as she evidently received the answer. She did not move the whole time, but her sweet eyes were ever seeking me with inexpressible tenderness, as if with her whole soul she would comfort me. About a quarter of an hour before she passed away, she said, 'Pray,' and my Philip commended her into her Redeemer's hands, giving thanks for her full salvation, for all He had revealed to her, and for her perfect peace. She said 'Amen; it is all quite, quite true.' Then in a clear voice she said, 'I am quite ready.' Her eyes sought me again. I laid my cheek on hers; a few more long-drawn breaths and she had left me behind. The angel had gone out of the house, and left a void never to be filled till we meet again.[24]

In lines she probably composed about Anna after her death, Mary wrote:

> She died, yet is not dead!
> Ye saw a daisy on her tomb:
> It bloomed to die, she died to bloom.
> Her summer hath not sped.
> She died, yet is not dead!
> Through pearly gates, on golden street,
> She went her way with shining feet.[25]

Fifty-eight was a reasonably mature age to reach when, in 1878, the average age of death for Quakers was fifty-five and a half and for the general population only thirty-three,[26] but Anna's family on both sides were long-lived. Had she not suffered ill-health throughout her life, Anna could easily have expected to live into her eighties and may well have produced other literary works. As it happened, death was for her a longed-for release.

She had died, as she was born, on a Thursday, and her last horse-drawn journey took place the following Tuesday, 30 April 1878. As Mary's dear friend and neighbour Mrs Buxton recalled, Mary was watching from the drawing-room window as the hearse arrived outside The White House. 'Oh this will never do!' she cried when she saw that cruel irony and the undertaker's sense of occasion had harnessed all the horses in bearing-reins. Deeply distressed, she rushed out and had the drivers remove them from every horse in the cortege.[27]

Anna's body and the carriages of mourners followed the eight-mile route to Lammas, the site of her parents' marriage fifty-nine years earlier and the resting place of her Wright forebears for generations. The Quaker Meeting House had closed after Anna's grandmother's death[28] and had long been used as a Wesleyan chapel,

but the graveyard was still used by Quakers.[29] Although she had not
been a Friend for forty years, it was surely at Anna's own request
that she was here laid to rest near her maternal grandparents and
her Aunt and Uncle Wright. This was a place of the heart which
Mary described as 'a sequestered spot, surrounded by trees and a
high hawthorn hedge, where the birds are never disturbed'.[30]

Anna's death certificate listed her occupation as 'Daughter of Isaac
Sewell, gentleman'. Isaac's senility hopefully spared him some pain
on the death of his beloved daughter, but Mary was bereft. As
Margaret Sewell recalled, her 'grief and desolation were intense',[31]
and the tears she had so long held back now flowed.[32] She would let
no one but her sisters come and stay in the following months which
were surely the darkest of her life. 'Now, when I wake in the
morning – it's a burden,' she said. 'It was never so before.'[33] Much
of her time was spent caring for Isaac. His condition worsening, he
required 'little, constant, cheerful attentions' to distract his mind,[34]
but his 'failing mental powers ma[de] him a sorrowful charge'.[35]
A friend comforted Mary with the thought that her own death
might not be far off, but she was distraught at the thought of dying
while Isaac still needed her.[36]

Less than seven months after Anna, Isaac died on 7 November
1878, aged eighty-five.[37] It was not his inexorable decline but shock
resulting from a fracture to the neck of his thighbone that caused his
death. After so many years of deterioration his death came so swiftly
that Mary could hardly believe it had happened, and she still
listened for 'the heavy foot, and the ever-repeated question, "Mary,
are thee there?"'[38] Two nights before he died he experienced a
period of religious ecstasy, as Mary told a friend:

> I was standing by him at the bedside; suddenly his spirit was
> caught away from everything but joy and praise and thanksgiving,
> and for half an hour or more, as I stood amazed, he poured forth,
> in the most fervent and exalted language, a strain of praise to God
> – of perfect rest in Christ, and such an overwhelming sense of
> happiness that he said, 'I could shout for joy.' His passing away
> was as gentle as that of a child falling asleep in its mother's arms –
> the repose on the still face afterwards was perfect.[39]

He was buried next to Anna in the Friends' graveyard at Lammas, his will leaving everything to Mary.

'Still I am sad. The primroses coming, and no darling to carry them to,' Mary wrote a year after Anna's death, 'the birds beginning to sing to each other, and my bird is flown away, and will sing to me no more here; and I am deaf, and cannot hear her singing in that enclosed garden full of perfumes, though I am sure she is there; and I rejoice for that, but cannot help saying "How long!"'[40] When the anniversaries of both Anna's and Isaac's deaths had passed she wrote: 'I have not got over my double loss, but I have become satisfied to live with it.'[41] She undertook some redecorating of the house but felt it such a 'dry, heartless service' doing it for herself: 'I almost dislike the look of my clean walls and well-painted stairs. I have been wanting my Nannie; but oh, how sorry she would be to be recalled to this poor lean world . . . How near heaven becomes when your darlings are there!'[42] One morning during church singing, Mary reported: 'I could fancy I heard my Nannie's sweet voice among them, and I strained my hoarse little pipe to join in with her . . . In my own experience I do not know what is meant by getting over a deep heart-loss.'[43]

Longing for music and dreaming of the Lancing days when Anna, Philip, and his fiancée Sarah had sung together, Mary hired a piano: 'I thought if I could play, even in single notes, it might be music to me, though it wouldn't be music to anyone else.'[44] Despite her 'stiff old fingers', she learned two pieces 'and just in the notes "Excelsior" I could hear my Nannie's voice. But I *couldn't* express what I wanted: it was no use trying, and I sent the piano away.'[45]

Mary was nevertheless of a bright disposition and hid her sadness from all but those close to her. Anna's 27-year-old niece Margaret, who the family called Amie, came to live with her and provided conversation, laughter, and companionship. Mary also now had greater liberty although she claimed that her years of nursing Anna and Isaac had benefited her: 'The darling needing so very much care happily kept me from self-indulgent habits, for which I thank her, as I do for many other things – my jewel!'[46]

She continued her early morning walks and kept up many charitable roles and a busy correspondence. When she was almost eighty-four she took up embroidery of flowers on to satin, and her garden remained a delight, its flowers always connected with Anna, as she told Mrs Williamson:

> I filled my Nannie's own little glass vase with single white hyacinths and double white daisies, so fragrant and lovely. If the garden will afford a flower, I always put it in this vase by the side of her likeness in my bedroom, and then we talk together; at least, I talk as if she heard.[47]

Mary believed 'that my darling is often near me', but also told a friend, 'I should be frightened, you know, if I saw her.'[48]

In December 1880 Mary began dictating her reminiscences to Margaret for her grandchildren. Of Anna's birth she recalled: 'On the 30 March the little stranger came an unclouded blessing for 58 years the perennial joy of my life.'[49] Of Anna's invalidism she said:

> Though she is now safe in heaven with all her work done, I can scarcely bear to recall the beginning of this life of constant frustration – & constant success – but God has given her the victory. She has left an example to all who knew her, and all who knew her loved her, of the most persevering industry & cheerful patience . . . her own mind was always a storehouse of refreshment to herself, it was a rich garden, which her circumstances never allowed to be fully cultivated, but it was full of thought and a ready appreciation of the genius and talents of others. She was my sunshine always.[50]

Margaret, in her own memoir of Anna, recalled her life as 'in every way admirable, and probably its moral and intellectual level was above the average'.[51]

In 1881 Mary suffered a heart attack, but like Anna outlived morbid predictions, in her case by almost three years, although she was becoming slightly deaf and suffered from probably arthritic spells when she could not use her writing hand.[52] She thought a lot about heaven, writing: 'When I open my eyes in the "beautiful country," the bliss unspeakable to me would be to see my father standing with my Nannie beside him – his "little maid," as he used to call her.'[53] Her father and her daughter were the idols of her life, and Mary felt that when she and Anna had 'fought the battle of life with one heart and one soul' she had experienced a kind of paradise on earth.[54]

In 1880 the last of Mary's verse works, *The Martyr's Tree*, was published: 'It seems too ridiculous', she wrote, 'for an old woman of eighty-three to be publishing Ballads – don't you think so?'[55] In November 1883 she was making corrections to most of her verse for inclusion in her collected *Poems and Ballads* (which were published after her death). 'The prose works are to come afterwards', she told Mrs F, 'The "Mother's Last Words" are, I believe, to have an Apotheosis, having reached a million . . . Jarrold is printing a very small selection of my ballads just now, the profits to go to the aid of a mite of the distress in London.'[56] In the winter of 1883–4 she wrote *Sixpenny Charity* which urged the charitable to give weekly amounts, however small, to the poor so that they might budget on that income.[57]

A few days before her eighty-sixth birthday in 1883 she had told a friend, 'I can hardly believe that it is five years since my jewel left me; she is as fresh as ever in my heart and in my thoughts.'[58] Writing to Mrs F that November she reminisced over their happy Blue Lodge times,

> when she was there who had *not* written a book, but helped those who did write. Now I would fain hope she sees her own book doing for her dear Lord His work of mercy. I was much interested in hearing the other day that a man who holds an official position in China, but is now staying in Norwich, accidentally met with 'Black Beauty,' sat down and read it through, then went to Jarrold and ordered a hundred copies to give away. Besides this, he offered to give readings from it to an evening class of working men, which he is now doing.[59]

From Christmas 1883 Mary's health declined more rapidly,[60] and just a few weeks after her eighty-seventh birthday in April 1884 she suffered another heart attack and her breathing became laboured. On the lovely summer's day of 10 June Mary asked to be moved from her bed to a couch beside the open window. She gazed around at the nature she had always loved and then quietly passed away.[61]

Her cause of death was given as congestion of the lungs and senile
decay, although to the end she seems to have retained her faculties.
She was buried next to Isaac and Anna, near her parents, in the
Lammas burial ground. Her estate was a sizeable £6,223 (about
£435,000 in 2003) from which she left legacies to her sisters, her
cousins, and to charitable cases, the bulk being divided among her
grandchildren.[62]

Anna's aunts at Dudwick Cottage who remained active in charity
were, like Mary and their elder sister Anna,[63] long-lived. Maria died
in 1889 aged eighty-seven, Elizabeth in 1894 at ninety-five or
ninety-six, and Ellen in 1897 at eighty-three. Philip and his children
also continued to work staunchly in those charitable and evangelical
grooves Anna herself had known so well: improving the education
of children and the lot of the poor. Philip visited Spain again in 1880
where he had kept some property including an iron factory in the
village of Carril, near Vilagarcía de Arousa in Galicia where his son
John lived, worked, and encouraged local evangelicalism[64] until his
early death in 1898. John was the only one of Anna's nieces and
nephews to marry, he and his wife Mary having two sons, one of
whom, John, died in infancy. The other, Philip Edward, was
'mentally slow'. Dying in a care home in Norwich in 1972 he was
the last of Anna's direct Sewell line.[65]

Outliving his second wife Charlotte by seven years, Philip died
on 6 February 1906, aged eighty-four, after a short illness. His
busy philanthropic presence was missed after forty-two years in
Norwich and his funeral was well attended. The service was held
at Christ Church in New Catton where he was a churchwarden
and a stained-glass window was later erected there in his memory.
After the service his cortege and the chief mourners travelled the
snow-dusted route to Buxton where many others joined them. At
Dudwick Park the Red House Farm School boys joined the
procession and pupils from the Buxton schools flanked the path
from the church gate to his grave in Buxton churchyard.[66] While
Philip made provision for his daughters, daughter-in-law, and
grandson, the bulk of his substantial estate including the Dudwick
properties went to his son Ted, who had been a tea planter in
Ceylon for some years before returning to Buxton, and who was

their last Sewell owner.[67] Anna's nieces continued her interests in animals, education, and charity work. Grace became keenly involved in the local RSPCA and anti-vivisection movement, Ada left bequests to the RSPCA, the National Equine Defence League, and the National Anti-Vivisection Society, Edith attended training college in London, and Margaret studied at Newnham College, Cambridge, before becoming an influential figure in the development of social science and social services.[68]

On the centenary of Anna's death in 1978 a service in her honour was held at St Andrew's church of Buxton-Lammas, which concluded with a horse-led procession of schoolchildren and others to Anna's grave. Wreaths were laid during a graveside ceremony which included a reading of the final pages of *Black Beauty* while horses and ponies stood near.[69] Such memorials to Anna are rare. While her book went from strength to strength, Anna herself was little remembered after those who knew her had also died. Long grass grew up around her gravestone and its inscription almost wore away. A century after her death, nevertheless, there were still a few dozen people each year who came to Lammas seeking her quiet resting place. By the early 1980s the old Quaker Meeting House, by then privately owned, was derelict, but it was a listed building whose preservation was legally mandated. The graveyard similarly was protected by law, but that did not prevent the desecration that was about to occur.

Early on the morning of Saturday 1 September 1984, without warning or permission, bulldozers charged onto the burial ground, overturning tombstones, destroying graves, and uprooting the cypress trees that had so long stood there. Within a few hours the resting sites of Anna and at least fourteen members of her family[70] were destroyed under the directions of the site's owner.[71] Anna's gravestone was dumped among the ruined piles of tombstones on the edge of the old burial ground which was now nothing but bare earth and a few broken branches.[72]

Locals were horrified, enraged, and saddened by this shocking act. Public outrage and publicity were so intense that arrangements were made to move the tombstones to a 'safe place' to avoid them being stolen, and proposals were set in motion to have them restored.[73]

In October 1984 a petition was raised which 90 per cent of Lammas residents signed in support of replacing the gravestones in their original positions and preserving the site as a national memorial to Anna.[74]

The replacement never occurred. Retooled and cleaned, Anna's gravestone is now set into a flint-and-brick wall outside the old Lammas Meeting House. It is flanked on one side by her parents' tombstone and on the other by her maternal grandparents'. Underneath these three remaining stones are planters of flowers. The world that now literally passes Anna by races at speed along this often busy rural road, and planes from RAF Coltishall can often be heard above. In an engineless moment, however, this is still the place she knew so well. Her gravestone looks out over the road to open Norfolk fields where by night foxes and rodents run and by day horses and birds pass under overarching heavens where, for Anna, God and nature must surely be one.

(The Wright Family)

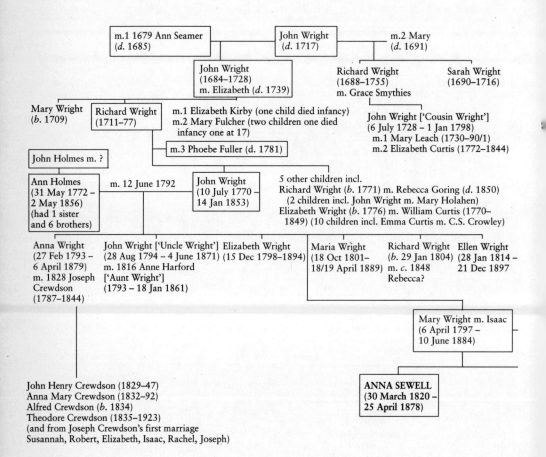

Anna Sewell's Family Tree.

(The Sewell Family)

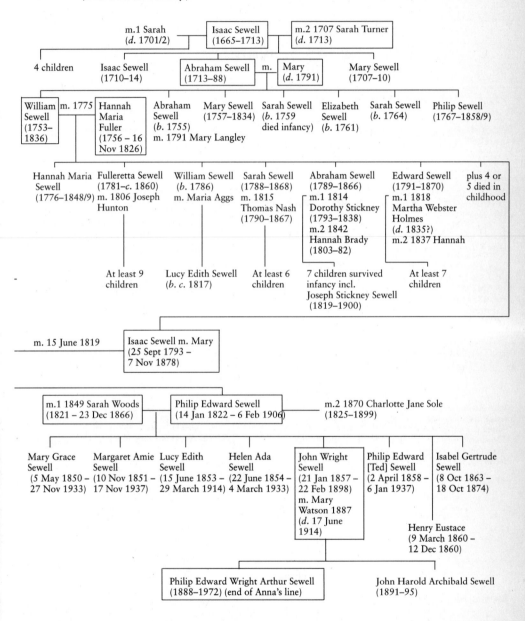

Notes

Abbreviations Used in Notes

AS   Anna Sewell

Bayly   Mrs [Mary] Bayly, *The Life and Letters of Mrs Sewell*, London, James Nisbet and Co., 1889

BB   Anna Sewell, *Black Beauty*, 1877. Peter Hollindale (ed.), Oxford, Oxford University Press, 1992

Chitty   Susan Chitty, *The Woman Who Wrote 'Black Beauty': A Life of Anna Sewell*, London, Hodder and Stoughton, 1971

DS   Dorothy Stickney Sewell

EDP   *Eastern Daily Press*

EBB1   Elisabeth Boyd Bayly, 'Literary Work' in Mrs Bayly, *The Life and Letters of Mrs Sewell*, 2 vols, London, James Nisbet and Co., 1889, pp. 130–63

EBB2   Elisabeth Boyd Bayly, 'Memoir', in *Poems and Ballads by Mrs Sewell*, 2 vols, London, Jarrold and Sons [1886], vol. 1, pp. vii–xxvi

ESRO   East Sussex Record Office

IS   Isaac Sewell

MAS   Margaret Sewell, 'Recollections of Anna Sewell' in *Black Beauty*, London, Harrap, 1935, pp. 1–6

MS   Mary Sewell

MSR   Mary Sewell, 'Reminiscences', 3 vols, unpublished manuscript in possession of owner

NRO   Norfolk Record Office

PRO   Public Record Office

PS   Philip Sewell

TPB   Mary Sewell, '*Thy Poor Brother': Letters to a Friend on Helping the Poor*, London, Jarrold and Sons, 1863

WSRO   West Sussex Record Office

Preface

1   See Chapter One, nn 6, 7.

Chapter One

1   MS to Mrs Toynbee, *c.* February 1878, qtd in Bayly, p. 277.

2   *Ibid.*

3   Bayly, pp. 274–8.

4   *Ibid.*, p. 273.

5   Unknown to AS, 24 December 1877, qtd in Bayly, p. 275.

6   *The House of Jarrolds 1823–1923: A Brief History of One Hundred Years* (Norwich, Jarrolds, 1924), p. 25.

7   Richard Dalby, 'Anna Sewell's "Black Beauty"', *Book and Magazine Collector*, 132 (March 1995) p. 14.

8   MSR provides a more detailed account of Wright (and some Sewell) family history and of Mary's childhood and youth.

These 'Reminiscences' (as they have been titled in a later typescript) were begun on 9 December 1880 when Mary was eighty-three and were left uncompleted at her death on 10 June 1884. They cover Mary's recollections of her family history and early life as well as Anna's up until 1836. The manuscript as well as a typescript copy of it are in the hands of an owner who wishes to remain anonymous but who has kindly allowed me access to them. The manuscript, which is what I have worked and quoted from, is written in three exercise books with marble-patterned covers. The pages have been numbered consecutively: volume I (pp. 1–39) is numbered one page per number, while volume II (pp. 40–66) and volume III (pp. 67–84) are numbered two pages per number, the number appearing on the right-hand page only. There are also two unnumbered loose pages probably connected with volume II. As pagination is consecutive I have not indicated volume numbers in my references. Volume I was dictated to one of Mary's grandchildren, probably Margaret Sewell who lived with her at the time. Volumes II and III appear to be in Mary's own (less legible) handwriting. Notation on the fronts of volumes I and II seems to indicate that they have also been copied into a 'big book', but volume III indicates 'not copied'.

Bayly reprints most of the 'Reminiscences' as 'Autobiography' pp. 1–76. She excises a few passages which she may have regarded as not serving Mary's (or Mary's ancestor's) memory well, including incidents related to whipping children, cruelty to horses, accidents, alcohol, financial difficulties, and Mary's helping in an elopement. Bayly's transcription is not always exact, some words and phrasing have been changed, and she generously adds punctuation which is sparse in the original.

9 See MSR, pp. 17–22.
10 *Ibid.*, p. 23.
11 *Ibid.*, pp. 25–7.
12 *Ibid.*, pp. 14–15.
13 *Ibid.*, pp. 25–30.
14 *Ibid.*, p. 47.
15 I am grateful to Linda Large for information about this sign.
16 Quoted in Bayly, p. 83.
17 MSR, p. 53.
18 See ibid., pp. 45–51.
19 *Ibid.*, p. 31.
20 MS, qtd in Bayly, p. 306.
21 Elizabeth Isichei, *Victorian Quakers* (Oxford, Oxford University Press, 1970), p. 150.
22 MSR, pp. 30–5.
23 *Ibid.*, p. 57.
24 *Ibid.*, pp. 57–8.
25 John Preston, *The Picture of Yarmouth* (Yarmouth, John Preston, 1819), p. 231.
26 MSR, p. 58.
27 *Ibid.*, p. 65.
28 *Ibid.*, p. 58.
29 Edith Sewell, compiler, *Joseph S. Sewell: A Quaker Memoir* (London, Headley Brothers, 1902), p. 9.
30 *Pigot & Co.'s National Commercial Directory: Norfolk & Suffolk* (London, Pigot and Co., 1830), p. 72.

31 MSR, p. 58.
32 *Ibid.*, p. 59.
33 *Ibid.*
34 MSR, p. 60.
35 *Ibid.*, p. 54.
36 *Ibid.*
37 MSR, p. 56.
38 *Ibid.*, p. 60.
39 *Ibid.*
40 MSR, p. 61.
41 *Ibid.*, pp. 62–3.
42 Mary misremembered this as occurring after the battle of Waterloo the following year, MSR, p. 61.
43 See generally *A Narrative of the Grand Festival at Yarmouth* (Yarmouth, J. Keymer, 1814).
44 MSR, p. 63.
45 Charles John Palmer, *Perlustration of Great Yarmouth* (3 vols, Yarmouth, George Nall, 1872), vol. 1, p. 215.
46 MSR, pp. 63–4, Mary states thirteen bodies.
47 *Ibid.*, p. 68.
48 *Ibid.*, pp. 64–5.
49 *Ibid.*, p. 66.
50 *Ibid.*, p. 62.
51 *Ibid.*, p. 65. Chitty p. 74 suggests that Anna's grandparents initially moved into Dudwick Farmhouse which is about half a mile north of Dudwick House and Cottage. My interpretation of documents I have had access to is that they moved into Dudwick Cottage from the outset and this seems certain from 1836 onwards.
52 *Ibid.*, p. 77.
53 *Ibid.*, pp. 65–6.
54 *Ibid.*, p. 66.
55 *The Home Life and Letters of Mrs Ellis*, compiled by her nieces (London, James Nisbet and Co., [1893]), p. 6.
56 MSR, p. 66.
57 *Ibid.*
58 MSR, p. 67.
59 *Ibid.*, p. 63.
60 *Ibid.*, p. 67.
61 *Ibid.*
62 His son Philip would also become a Freeman of the City of Norwich on 5 November 1874 on the basis of birth. I am grateful to Charles Briscoe for this information.
63 *Ibid.*
64 *Ibid.*
65 *Ibid.*
66 *Ibid.*
67 Often misreported as 25 Church Plain.
68 I am grateful to Robert Graham, who ran the Anna Sewell Restaurant, for information about the history of the house, and also to Danielle O'Hara.
69 MSR, p. 67.
70 *Ibid.*
71 MSR, p. 68.

Chapter Two

1   MSR, p. 68.
2   *Ibid.*
3   *Ibid.*
4   *Ibid.*, pp. 68–9. I am grateful to Michael Metford-Sewell for the Hackney location.
5   *Ibid.*, p. 68.
6   *Ibid.*
7   TPB, p. 19.
8   MSR, p. 69.
9   TPB, pp. 138–9.
10 NRO, 'From SF 199'.
11 TPB, p. 20.
12 MSR, p. 69.
13 *Ibid.*
14 *Ibid.*
15 *Ibid.*
16 This is the address given on Philip

Sewell's birth entry in *A Register of Births Belonging to the Quarterly Meeting of London and Middlesex*, PRO, RG 6/803.

17 See *TPB*, p. 21.

18 Quoted in Bayly, p. 80.

19 *TPB*, pp. 19–21.

20 Ben Weinreb and Christopher Hibbert (eds), *The London Encyclopaedia*, rev. edn (London, Macmillan, 1995), p. 217.

21 *TPB*, pp. 139–40.

22 MSR, p. 69.

23 *Ibid.*

24 *Ibid.*, pp. 69–70.

25 Isichei, *Victorian Quakers*, p. 136.

26 He may also have retained an interest in the Camomile Street house: MS to DS, [2] October 1825, NRO MC 144/16 makes reference to 'Isaac's tenant on Chamomile [*sic*] Street.'

27 MSR, p. 70.

28 Renamed Parkholme Road later in the nineteenth century. Its houses were demolished during the late nineteenth century and replaced by the red-brick homes that stand there in 2003. See Charles Booth, 'The Rhodes Estate,' *Survey of Life and Labour in London* (1886–1903), Charles Booth Online Archive, <http://booth.lse.ac.uk/images/not ebooks/b347/jpg/b347-055.jpg> 22 November 2003.

29 MSR, p. 70.

30 A poem Anna's aunt, Sarah Nash (née Sewell), wrote for her sister, Fulleretta Hunton (née Sewell), on 30 December 1824 includes lines that indicate that the extended Sewell family were very aware of Mary and Isaac's ongoing financial woes:

and next, the group at Dalston cheer,
And here, tho' crosses mark the scene,
And hope, but dimly shines between,
Yet Resignations genial ray,
Ere long may gild a brighter day,
And prove the friendly light that cheers
And guides them in succeeding years.

The crosses here are likely to be hardship rather than deaths. This quotation and information were supplied by M. Rigby to the Sowell Family Heritage site in 1998. <http://www.sowell.org/ annasewell.htm.> 5 February 2002. Attempts to discover further information about this material have proved unavailing and the site in November 2003 is untraceable.

31 MSR, p. 70.

32 *Ibid.*

33 Dorothy's sister, Sarah Stickney (later Ellis), regarded both Mary and Dorothy as very religious women. She wrote that Dorothy 'is so near the perfection of women's character that there always seems to be an atmosphere of comfort, quiet, and goodness about her'. Quoted in *Home Life*, p. 69.

34 The Wright family were early believers in vaccination. Mary recalled that her mother had tried to persuade the villagers of Felthorpe to vaccinate their children, even going so far as to take her young vaccinated children, Maria and Richard, into a home where the smallpox raged. 'The experiment was quite safe', Mary writes, 'but it is only fair to say, that Richard had the smallpox very badly when he was a young man.' MSR, p. 52.

35 MS to DS, 3 October 1825, NRO
   MC 144/16.
36 MS to DS, 14 November 1826,
   quoted by kind permission of
   Linda Steward.
37 *Ibid.*
38 Bayly spells it Nannie, and it is
   also in one place given as Nannie
   in MS's 'Reminiscences', probably
   in MS's hand, but earlier family
   letters use Nanny. It is possible the
   spelling changed over time, just as
   Anna alternated between 'A' and
   'a' capitalization when writing the
   first letter of her name.
39 MS to DS, [2] October 1825,
   NRO MC 144/16.
40 Ch. 2 of Bayly is devoted to
   Mary's 'Thoughts on Education'.
41 MSR, p. 73.
42 *TPB*, p. 55.
43 MS, qtd in Bayly, p. 103.
44 *Ibid.*, p. 104. This method of
   training, Bayly notes, echoes that
   used in the training of horses.
45 *Ibid.*, p. 103.
46 *Ibid.*, p. 104.
47 *Ibid.*
48 Marjorie Moon, *John Harris's
   Books for Youth 1801–1843*, rev.
   and enlgd, (Folkestone, Kent,
   Dawson Publishing, 1992), pp.
   6–7, 155–6, 174–5. A second
   edition of *Walks with Mamma*
   was published in 1829 and a
   'new and enlarged edition' in
   1839.
49 MRS, p. 70.
50 Bayly, p. 117.
51 MS [published anonymously],
   *Walks with Mamma, or Stories in
   Words of One Syllable* (London,
   John Harris, 1824), pp. 30–1.
52 MSR, p. 72.
53 MS, qtd in Bayly, p. 106.
54 MS, *Walks*, pp. 28–9.
55 MS, qtd in Bayly, p. 105.
56 *Ibid.*, p. 119.
57 MS, *Walks*, pp. 38–41.
58 Quoted in Bayly, p. 246.
59 MS, qtd in Bayly, p. 105.
60 *TPB*, p. 56.
61 MS, qtd in Bayly, p. 106.
62 Bayly, pp. 120–1.
63 MS, qtd in Bayly, p. 114.
64 MS to Mrs Brightwen, undated,
   qtd in Bayly, p. 306.
65 MS, qtd in Bayly, p. 111.
66 MSR, p. 71.
67 *Ibid.*
68 Bayly, p. 111.
69 MSR, p. 73.
70 MS, qtd in Bayly, p. 114.
71 *Ibid.*, p. 111.
72 *Ibid.*, p. 114.
73 *Ibid.*, p. 109.
74 *Ibid.*
75 MS, qtd in Bayly, p. 110.
76 MSR, p. 71.
77 Quoted in Bayly, p. 110.
78 *Ibid.*
79 MSR, p. 71.
80 *Ibid.*
81 Roy Porter, *London: A Social
   History* (London, Hamish
   Hamilton, 1994), p. 289.
82 Weinreb and Hibbert, *London
   Encyclopaedia*, p. 1006.
83 Possibly 'hobies'.
84 MSR, p. 71.
85 Isichei, *Victorian Quakers*, p. 66.
86 Material in this paragraph drawn
   generally from Isichei, *Victorian
   Quakers*.
87 Isichei, *Victorian Quakers*, p.
   146.
88 *Ibid.*
89 C. Willet Cunnington and Phillis
   Cunnington, *Handbook of
   English Costume in the
   Nineteenth Century* (London,
   Faber and Faber, 1959), pp.

578–80.

90 Chitty, p. 65 states that they had attended the Gracechurch Street Meeting ever since they left Yarmouth, but while possible this seems unlikely. Their official 'transfer' was from the Yarmouth Monthly Meeting to the Devonshire House Monthly Meeting (NRO 'From SF 199'), which was closer to both their London residences and their Dalston home. Devonshire House had taken on a more administrative role as the site for Yearly Meetings, but it seems likely that weekly meetings would still have continued there (I am grateful to Andrew Roberts for advice on this) and it seems probable that this was their regular Meeting.

91 Elizabeth Robinson, *Lost Hackney* (London, Hackney Society, 1989), p. 56.

92 Isichei, *Victorian Quakers*, p. 95.

93 Quoted in Isichei, *Victorian Quakers*, p. 90.

94 MSR, p. 84.

95 Isichei, *Victorian Quakers*, pp. 282–3.

96 Quoted in Bayly, p. 113. By 'toward' here Mary means the opposite of untoward.

97 MSR, p. 71.

98 *Ibid.*

99 MS, qtd in Bayly, p. 114.

100 MSR, p. 72.

101 *Ibid.*

102 *Ibid.*, p. 73.

103 MS, qtd in Bayly, pp. 85–6.

104 Bayly, p. 86.

105 MS to DS, 7 February 1830, NRO MC 144/15.

106 MSR, p. 71.

107 MS, qtd in Bayly, p. 118.

108 Mary's brother Richard was whipped at least once by a parent for repeatedly playing too near a pond, and Mary's father whipped a boy for slashing his horse, Rosinanté, MSR, two unnumbered loose sheets.

109 MS, qtd in Bayly, p. 105.

110 William White, *White's 1845 Norfolk*, Repr (Newton Abbot, Devon, David & Charles Reprints, 1969), p. 460.

111 MSR, p. 77.

112 Dudwick House was rebuilt in 1939–43. Dudwick Cottage with its Gothic windows and delightful garden was originally a four-roomed sixteenth-century flint cottage. It was expanded in the early nineteenth century and again in the 1870s, but it still stands much as it would have when Anna first stayed there. A public right of way leading through the park is used by riders who follow a route Anna herself would often have ridden, and a stable on the site later became know as Black Beauty's stable. I am grateful to Avril and Charles Briscoe and to Anne Cryer for information about the Dudwick properties.

113 MSR, p. 72.

114 *Ibid.*, p. 76.

115 MAS, p. 2.

116 MSR, p. 73.

117 *Ibid.*

118 Unnamed cousin to AS, *c.* December 1877, qtd in Bayly, p. 274.

119 MSR, pp. 71–2.

120 MSR, p. 72.

121 Material on Sandgate drawn generally from Linda René-Martin, *Sandgate: Rise and Progress of a Village* (Sandgate,

René-Martin, 1998) and 'Pigots 1840—Sandgate &c.' <http://freepages.genealogy.roots web.com/~shebra/pigots_1840_- _sandgate_&c_htm> 22 November 2003.

122 MSR, p. 71.

123 S.J. Mackie, *A Descriptive and Historical Account of Folkestone and its Neighbourhood* (Folkestone, J. English, 1856), p. 236.

124 MS to DS, 14 November 1826, quoted by kind permission of Linda Steward.

125 MS to DS, 7 February 1830, NRO MC 144/15.

126 MSR, p. 74.

127 *Ibid.*

128 MS to DS, 18 July 1832, quoted by kind permission of Graham Clark. It is possible that this letter was written after the Sewells moved to their next home, Palatine Cottage, but it is postmarked Shacklewell which is closer to their Dalston home.

129 *Ibid.*

130 *Ibid.*

131 *Ibid.*

Chapter Three

1 Isobel Watson, *Hackney and Stoke Newington Past*, rev. edn (London, Historical Publications, 1998), p. 63.

2 MSR, p. 74.

3 I have been unable to determine whether this building replaced Anna's home or is an extreme refurbishment of it.

4 MSR, p. 74.

5 *Ibid.*

6 MSR, p. 79.

7 Quoted in *Home Life*, p. 53.

8 John H. Ingram, *Edgar Allan Poe: His Life, Letters, and Opinions*, 1880, new edn (London, Henry Frowde, n.d.), p. 11.

9 *Pigot and Co.'s Royal National and Commercial Directory and Topography of the Counties of Bedford, Cambridge, Essex, Herts, Huntingdon, Kent, Middlesex, Norfolk, Suffolk, Surrey, and Sussex* (London, Pigot and Co., 1839), p. 438.

10 Watson, *Hackney and Stoke Newington Past*, p. 15.

11 *Ibid.*, p. 134.

12 Edgar Allan Poe, 'William Wilson' (1840) in Julian Symons (ed.), *Selected Tales* (Oxford, Oxford University Press, 1980), p. 80.

13 *Pigot and Co.'s Royal National and Commercial Directory*, p. 440.

14 MSR, p. 75.

15 *Ibid.*

16 MSR, p. 74.

17 *Ibid.*, p. 75.

18 *Ibid.*

19 MSR, p. 82.

20 *Ibid.*

21 *Ibid.*

22 MSR, pp. 82–3.

23 Quoted in Weinreb and Hibbert, *London Encyclopaedia*, p. 262.

24 Quoted in Porter, *London: A Social History*, p. 290.

25 MSR, pp. 79–80.

26 *Ibid.*, p. 80.

27 Bayly, p. 244.

28 MSR, p. 81.

29 *Ibid.*, p. 80.

30 *BB*, p. 103.

31 MS, *Walks*, p. 32.

32 MSR, p. 81.

33 Mrs Hemans, *Young Woman's Companion, or Female*

Instructor, new edn, London: Virtue & Co., *c*. 1830, p. 696.

34 MSR, p. 81.

35 AS to MS, 23 September 1835, qtd in Chitty, pp. 92–4, states that she went to 'Bridgmont'. The original of this letter has proved untraceable, but given that Anna's capital Rs could be mistaken for Bs and the fact that a Ridgmont known to her existed, Ridgmont seems plausible.

36 *Home Life*, p. 5.

37 *Ibid*., p. 6.

38 AS to MS, 23 September 1835, qtd in Chitty, p. 93.

39 *Ibid*., pp. 92–3.

40 *Ibid*.

41 *Ibid*., p. 93.

42 *Ibid*., p. 92.

43 *Ibid*.

44 *Ibid*., p. 93.

45 *Ibid*., p. 92.

46 *Ibid*., p. 93.

47 *Ibid*.

48 *Ibid*., p. 92.

49 AS to MS, *c*. 17 February 1836, NRO MC 144/21.

50 AS to MS, 23 September 1835, qtd in Chitty, pp. 93–4.

51 AS to MS, *c*. 17 February 1836, NRO MC 144/21.

52 MSR, p. 81.

53 AS to MS, *c*. 17 February 1836, NRO MC 144/21.

54 *Ibid*.

55 *Ibid*.

56 C. Willett Cunnington, *English Women's Clothing in the Nineteenth Century* (London, Faber and Faber, 1937), p. 124.

57 AS to MS, *c*. 17 February 1836, NRO MC 144/21.

58 *Ibid*.

59 MSR, p. 5.

60 *Ibid*.

61 MSR, p. 75.

62 *Ibid*., p. 78.

63 *Ibid*., p. 77.

64 MS to DS, 14 November 1826, quoted by kind permission of Linda Steward.

65 MS to DS, 7 February 1830, NRO MC 144/15.

66 MSR, p. 77.

67 *Ibid*., p. 78.

68 *Ibid*.

69 Isichei, *Victorian Quakers*, pp. 7, 9, 45.

70 *Ibid*., p. 46.

71 *Ibid*., p. 44.

72 *Ibid*., pp. 9, 45–6.

73 Quoted in Bayly, p. 83.

74 *Ibid*.

75 MSR, p. 78.

76 I am grateful to Michael Metford-Sewell – who also possesses a bust, possibly from a death mask, of William Sewell – for advising me that William Sewell died in Scarborough and was buried in Malton in 1836.

77 MSR, p. 79.

78 *Ibid*.

79 *Ibid*.

80 Bayly, p. 84.

81 MSR, p. 79.

82 *Ibid*.

83 MSR, p. 83.

84 *Ibid*., p. 79.

85 *Ibid*., p. 83.

86 *Ibid*., p. 84.

87 EBB2, p. xviii.

88 AS to MS, 23 September 1835, qtd in Chitty, p. 93.

89 Cunnington, *English Women's Clothing*, p. 123.

90 Nineteenth-century statistics on age of menarche are, however, rare and suspect (in the race and class assumptions they draw).

91 Quoted in Janice Delaney, Mary Jane Lupton, and Emily Toth, *The Curse: A Cultural History of Menstruation* (New York, E.P. Dutton and Co., 1976), p. 47.

92 Postscript by Anne Wright in AS to MS, *c.* 17 February 1836, NRO MC 144/21.

93 Delaney *et al.*, *The Curse*, p. 54.

94 I am grateful to Peter Merchant for help in confirming the wearing of corsets from such young ages, see, for example, Phillis Cunnington and Anne Buck, *Children's Costume in England: From the Fourteenth to the End of the Nineteenth Century* (London, A. and C. Black, 1965), p. 199.

95 MAS, p. 2 claims that Anna 'always had a pony or horse', but this was only likely to have been true from her mid-twenties onwards.

96 Daniel Pool, *What Jane Austen Ate and Charles Dickens Knew* (New York, Touchstone, 1993), p. 143.

97 Mrs [Sarah Stickney] Ellis, *The Daughters of England*, 1842 (London, Fisher, Son, and Co., n.d.), p. 190.

98 AS to MS, 23 September 1835, qtd in Chitty, p. 94.

99 AS to MS, *c.* 17 February 1836, NRO MC 144/21.

100 MSR, pp. 81–2.

101 Quoted in Isichei, *Victorian Quakers*, p. 129.

102 *Ibid.*, p. 284.

103 MS to AS, *c.* 31 October 1836, NRO MC 144/2.

104 *Ibid.*

105 *Ibid.*

106 Quoted in *Home Life*, p. 70.

107 MS to AS, *c.* 31 October 1836, NRO MC 144/2.

108 *Ibid.*

109 *Ibid.*

110 *Ibid.*

111 *Ibid.*

Chapter Four

1 MS to AS, January 1837, NRO MC 144/3.

2 *Ibid.* and 1841 census return.

3 MS to AS, January 1837, NRO MC 144/3.

4 *Ibid.*

5 *Ibid.*

6 Bayly, p. 88.

7 Timothy Carder, *The Encyclopaedia of Brighton* (Lewes, East Sussex County Libraries, 1990), section 112.

8 John Ackerson Erredge, *History of Brighthelmston, or Brighton as I View it and Others Knew it* (Brighton, E. Lewis, 1862), p. 342.

9 I am grateful to Jackie Lewis of the Brighton Local Studies Library for help in confirming street numbering and location.

10 MS to AS, January 1837, NRO MC 144/3.

11 *Ibid.*

12 *Ibid.*

13 H.J. Dyos and D.H. Aldcroft, *British Transport: An Economic Survey from the Seventeenth Century to the Twentieth* (Leicester, Leicester University Press, 1969), p. 74.

14 *Wallis's Royal Edition: Brighton as it is, 1836* (Brighton, Wallis, 1836), p. 94.

15 *Ibid.*, p. 9.

16 *Pigot and Co.'s Royal National and Commercial Directory*, p. 659.

17 *Wallis's Royal Edition*, p. 9.

18 *Ibid.*, p. 17.

19 Clifford Musgrave, *Life in Brighton: From the Earliest Times to the Present*, rev. edn (London, John Hallewell, 1981), p. 241.

20 AS to IS, 17 October 1838, NRO MC 144/29.

21 *Wallis's Royal Edition*, p. 44.

22 *TPB*, p. 96.

23 Peter R. Jenkins, *Sussex Money: A History of Banking in Sussex* (Pulborough, West Sussex, Dragonwheel Books, 1987), pp. 62, 71.

24 MSR, p. 82.

25 AS to IS, 17 October 1838, NRO MC 144/29.

26 PS to AS, 20 November 1838, NRO MC 144/10.

27 Bayly, p. 81.

28 *Home Life*, p. 88.

29 MS to IS, 5 February 1838, NRO MC 144/17.

30 Edith Sewell, *Joseph S. Sewell*, p. 11.

31 Musgrave, *Life in Brighton*, p. 193.

32 Erredge, *History of Brighthelmston*, p. 364.

33 MS to AS, January 1837, NRO MC 144/3.

34 Carder, *The Encyclopaedia of Brighton*, sections 167d, 169a. The chapel was demolished in 1950.

35 *Wallis's Royal Edition*, p. 64.

36 MS to AS, November 1838, NRO MC 144/10.

37 MS to AS, January 1837, NRO MC 144/3.

38 Stanley Godman, 'Anna Sewell, Authoress of "Black Beauty" and Her Life in Sussex', *West Sussex Gazette* (9 January 1958), p. 4.

39 In her first edition Bayly states that 'they never definitely entered its fold' (p. 87). In later editions she states they 'became communicants at Mr Maitland's church' (6th edn, p. 87).

40 Erredge, *History of Brighthelmston*, p. 367.

41 *TPB*, p. 179.

42 Carder, *The Encyclopaedia of Brighton*, section 112a.

43 MS to AS, November 1838, NRO MC 144/10.

44 MS to AS, 27 November 1838, NRO MC 144/10.

45 Bayly, p. 94.

46 *TPB*, p. 108.

47 *Ibid.*, p. 109.

48 *Ibid.*, p. 111.

49 *Ibid.*

50 AS to PS, *c.* 17 October 1838, NRO MC 144/29.

51 This seems to have been the only chapel in Bond Street at the time. Rebuilt in 1861, it was demolished in 1974. Chapel baptismal records for the period have proved untraceable.

52 This information was added to later editions of Bayly (see 6th edn, p. 87) but does not appear in the first edition.

53 Isichei, *Victorian Quakers*, p.134.

54 ESRO SOF 52/3 (1833–1839), *Lewes and Chichester Monthly Meeting Book From 10th Month 1833 to 10th Month 1839*, 11 May 1838, p. 401. I am grateful to Dewayne Crawford for transcription of this material.

55 *Ibid.*, 15 June 1838, p. 407.

56 *Ibid.*, 20 July 1838, p. 413.

57 *Ibid.*

58 *Lewes and Chichester Monthly Meeting Book*, 17 August 1838, pp. 420–1.

59 *Philip Edward Sewell: A sketch January 14th, 1822 – February 6th 1906* (London, Jarrold and

Sons, 1910), pp. 2–3.

60 Bayly, p. 84.

61 Quoted in Bayly, p. 84.

62 AS to MS, *c.* 17 October 1838, NRO MC 144/29.

63 MSR, p. 36.

64 *Ibid.*, p. 56.

65 AS to IS, *c.* 17 October 1838, NRO MC 144/29.

66 *Ibid.*

67 A.B. Granville, *Spas of England and Principal Sea-Bathing Places. Vol. 2 The Midlands and South*, 1841 (Bath, Adams and Dart, 1971), p. 16.

68 AS to IS, *c.* 17 October 1838, NRO MC 144/29.

69 AS to MS, *c.* 17 October 1838, NRO MC 144/29.

70 *Ibid.*

71 AS to IS, *c.* 17 October 1838, NRO MC 144/29.

72 Cunnington, *English Women's Clothing*, p. 119.

73 C. Willett Cunnington, *Feminine Attitudes in the Nineteenth Century* (London, William Heinemann, 1935), p. 96.

74 MS to AS, 26 November 1838, NRO MC 144/10.

75 AS to MS, *c.* 17 October 1838, NRO MC 144/29.

76 AS to IS, *c.* 17 October 1838, NRO MC 144/29.

77 Cunnington, *English Women's Clothing*, p. 117.

78 AS to MS, *c.* 17 October 1838, NRO MC 144/29.

79 AS to PS, *c.* 17 October 1838, NRO MC 144/29.

80 *Ibid.*

81 *Ibid.*

82 Presumably Anna's stepcousins Isaac, Robert, and Elizabeth Crewdson.

83 AS to PS, *c.* 17 October 1838, NRO MC 144/29.

84 Unidentified commentator, qtd in Isichei, *Victorian Quakers*, p. 49.

85 Probably Isaac Crewdson and his brother-in-law William Boulton; see Isichei, *Victorian Quakers*, p. 46.

86 AS to MS, *c.* 17 October 1838, NRO MC 144/29.

87 AS to PS, *c.* 17 October 1838, NRO MC 144/29.

88 Isichei, *Victorian Quakers*, p. 51.

89 AS to PS, *c.* 17 October 1838, NRO MC 144/29.

90 *Ibid.*

91 AS to MS, *c.* 17 October 1838, NRO MC 144/29.

92 *Ibid.*

93 *Ibid.*

94 *Ibid.*

95 MS to AS, November 1838, NRO MC 144/10.

96 AS to PS, *c.* 17 October 1838, NRO MC 144/29.

97 AS to MS, *c.* 17 October 1838, NRO MC 144/29.

98 MS to AS, November 1838, NRO MC 144/10.

99 AS to PS, *c.* 17 October 1838, NRO MC 144/29.

100 PS to AS, November 1838, NRO MC 144/10.

101 AS to PS, *c.* 17 October 1838, NRO MC 144/29.

102 AS to MS, *c.* 17 October 1838, NRO MC 144/29.

103 AS to IS, *c.* 17 October 1838, NRO MC 144/29.

104 PS to AS, 20 November 1838, NRO MC 144/10.

105 *Ibid.*

106 PS to AS, 28 November 1838, NRO MC 144/10.

107 PS to AS, 20 November 1838, NRO MC 144/10.

108 MS to AS, 26 November 1838,

NRO MC 144/10.

109 PS to AS, 20 November 1838, NRO MC 144/10.

110 MS to AS, 26 November 1838, NRO MC 144/10.

111 *Ibid.*

112 *Ibid.*

113 *Ibid.*

114 *Ibid.*

115 *Ibid.*

116 *Ibid.*

117 *Ibid.*

118 *Ibid.*

119 *Ibid.*

120 AS to MS, *c.* 17 October 1838, NRO MC 144/29.

121 *Ibid.*

122 AS to PS, MS, IS, *c.* 17 October 1838, NRO MC 144/29.

123 PS to AS, 28 November 1838, NRO MC 144/10.

124 Bayly, p. 244.

Chapter Five

1 Bayly, p. 86.

2 *Ibid.*, pp. 244–5.

3 *Ibid.*, p. 245.

4 *Ibid.*, pp. 86–7.

5 I am grateful to Dr Raewyn Gavin for advice on Anna's ailments and for suggesting SLE.

6 In possession of owners.

7 Bayly, p. 246.

8 Quoted in Bayly, p. 246.

9 Bayly, p. 246.

10 AS, qtd in Bayly, p. 246.

11 MSR, p. 81.

12 *Ibid.*, p. 80.

13 Granville, *Spas of England*, vol. 2, p. 562.

14 MS to AS, *c.* 12 February 1840, NRO MC 144/5.

15 Unidentified friend or family member.

16 MS to AS, *c.* 12 February 1840, NRO MC 144/5.

17 MS to AS [*c.* February 1840], NRO MC 144/4.

18 *Ibid.*

19 PS to MS, 6 February 1840, NRO MC 144/22.

20 PS to AS [*c.* February 1840], NRO MC 144/4.

21 *Ibid.*

22 MS, qtd in Bayly, p. 93.

23 MS to AS, *c.* 12 February 1840, NRO MC 144/5.

24 *Ibid.*

25 *Ibid.*

26 *Ibid.*

27 *Ibid.*

28 *Philip Edward Sewell*, p. 1.

29 EBB2, p. xiv.

30 MS to AS, *c.* 12 February 1840, NRO MC 144/5.

31 MS to AS [*c.* February 1840], NRO MC 144/4.

32 PS to AS, 8 December 1843, NRO MC 144/14.

33 Bayly, p. 77.

34 Quoted in Bayly, p. 78.

35 MS to AS [*c.* February 1840], NRO MC 144/4.

36 *Ibid.*

37 *Ibid.*

38 PS to AS, 24 February 1840, NRO MC 144/11.

39 PS to AS, 4 March 1840, NRO MC 144/12.

40 PS to AS, 24 February 1840, NRO MC 144/11.

41 PS to AS, 22 April 1840, NRO MC 144/13.

42 AS to PS, 18 April 1840, NRO MC 144/30.

43 MS to AS, *c.* 12 February 1840, NRO MC 144/5.

44 Quoted in *Home Life*, p. 134.

45 PS to AS, 22 April 1840, NRO MC 144/13.

46 *Ibid.*

47 William Lucas, *A Quaker Journal: Being the Diary and Reminiscences of William Lucas of Hitchin (1804–1861), A Member of the Society of Friends*, ed. G.E. Bryant and G.P. Baker (2 vols, London, Hutchinson, 1934), vol. 1, p. 233.

48 PS to AS, 22 April 1840, NRO MC 144/13.

49 AS to PS, 30 April 1840, in the Norfolk Postal History Collection of R.E.F. Pegg, quoted with kind permission.

50 PS to AS, 22 April 1840, NRO MC 144/13.

51 AS to PS, 30 April 1840, in the Norfolk Postal History Collection of R.E.F. Pegg, quoted with kind permission.

52 *Ibid.*

53 *Ibid.*

54 *Ibid.*

55 *Ibid.*

56 *Ibid.*

57 *Ibid.*

58 *Ibid.*

59 Quoted in Bayly, p. 90.

60 Quoted in Edmund W. Gilbert, *Brighton: Old Ocean's Bauble* (London, Methuen, 1954), p. 197.

61 Quoted in Bayly, p. 91.

62 Bayly, p. 92.

63 *Ibid.*

64 Musgrave, *Life in Brighton*, pp. 330–2; Joshua J. Schwieso, 'The Agapemonites', *The Chapels Society Newsletter*, 5 (December 1991), 52–3.

65 Bayly, p. 246.

66 Probably Mary's cousin John Wright (son of her uncle Richard) and his wife Mary née Holahen.

67 MS to AS, *c*. 13 October 1840, NRO MC 144/6.

68 MS to AS, *c*. 16 October 1840, NRO MC 144/7.

69 MS to AS, *c*. 13 October 1840, NRO MC 144/6.

70 MS to AS, *c*. 16 October 1840, NRO MC 144/7.

71 MS to AS, [*c*. 1842–1843], NRO MC 144/9.

72 AS to PS, *c*. 6 December 1843, NRO MC 144/32. This may have been the teenage servant, Sarah Richards, listed with the Sewells in the 1841 census.

73 AS to PS, 9 March 1845, NRO MC 144/33.

74 Two letters survive addressed to AS at Leamington, one from Lucy Sewell dated 2 April 1841 and another undated from MS which may date from the same visit but probably dates from winter 1842/3.

75 Granville, *Spas of England*, vol. 2, pp. 218–19.

76 *Ibid.*, p. 242.

77 *Ibid.*, p. 247.

78 Quoted in Granville, *Spas of England*, vol. 2, p. 227.

79 Granville, *Spas of England*, vol. 2, p. 232.

80 *Ibid.*, p. 235.

81 Lucy Sewell to AS, 2 April 1841, NRO MC 144/1.

82 *Ibid.*

83 *Ibid.*

84 MS to AS [*c*. 1842–1843], NRO MC 144/9.

85 Anne Wright to PS, 16 November 1841, NRO MC 144/31. This letter is currently listed incorrectly in the NRO as being from Anna Sewell.

86 MS to AS [*c*. 1842–1843], NRO MC 144/9.

87 PS to AS, 8 December 1843,
    NRO MC 144/32.
88 ESRO SOF 52/4, *Lewes and
    Chichester Monthly Meeting
    Book From 12th month 1839 to
    the 10th month 1848*, 16
    February 1844, p. 238; 15 March
    1844, p. 246. I am grateful to
    Dewayne Crawford for
    transcription of this material.
89 PS to AS, 8 December 1843,
    NRO MC 144/32.
90 Bayly, p. 87.
91 Quoted in Bayly, p. 246.
92 Leslie Howsam, *Kegan Paul: A
    Victorian Imprint* (London,
    Kegan Paul, 1998), p. 16.
93 *Ibid.*, p. 17.
94 AS to PS, *c.* 17 October 1838,
    NRO MC 144/29.
95 Quoted in Bayly, pp. 246–7.
96 AS to PS, 9 March 1845, NRO
    MC 144/33.
97 AS qtd in Bayly, p. 247.
98 *Ibid.*
99 Gilbert, *Brighton*, pp. 139–42.
100 Erredge, *History of
    Brighthelmston*, p. 249.
101 Granville, *Spas of England*, vol.
    2, p. 570.
102 Quoted in Bayly, p. 88.
103 EBB2, pp. xviii–xix.
104 Granville, *Spas of England*, vol.
    2, p. 579.
105 Quoted in Musgrave, *Life in
    Brighton*, p. 243.

Chapter Six

1 Bayly, p. 98.
2 *Kelly's Sussex Directory* 1845
   (London, W. Kelly and Co.,
   1845), p. 684.
3 I am grateful to Kim Leslie of the
   WSRO for unearthing this
   information. Also see Anne

Powell and Eileen Colwell,
Fircroft House [no pub. details],
1998 who independently
established that Fircroft was
Anna Sewell's Lancing home.
WSRO Par. 118/8/1, *Lancing
Churchwarden's Rate and
Account Book for 1816–91*, lists
the rateable value of the Sewell's
home in 1845 as a comparatively
low £4 17*s* 6*d* at Miller (possibly
Miller's) House. The ratebook
entries for 1846–8 (no assessment
recorded for the parish in 1849)
give no address for the Sewells,
but their property's rateable value
is a much higher £20. This might
indicate that the Sewells before
October 1846 moved to a larger
home, or more probably that Isaac
had made his characteristic
substantial improvements to the
house or had taken on more land.
As Isichei, *Victorian Quakers*,
pp. 135–6, points out, Quakers
were not supposed to pay tithes or
church rates but ways
around this were frequently found.
Isaac certainly was not expelled
for any infringement of this
regulation. WSRO Par. 118/30/3
Poor Law Rate Book shows six
rates taken 6 December 1845 to
14 December 1848 with Isaac
Sewell recorded for £20 each time.
4 R.G.P. Kerridge, *A History of
   Lancing* (London and Chichester,
   Phillimore, 1979), pp. 115, 120,
   147–8; Powell and Colwell,
   Fircroft House, pp. 12, 22, 26.
5 Bayly, p. 98.
6 T.P. Hudson (ed.), *Victoria
   County History of Sussex*
   (Oxford, Oxford University
   Press, 1980), vol. 6, part 1, p. 46;
   Kerridge, *History of Lancing*,

pp. 51, 136.

7 Kerridge, *History of Lancing*, p. 3.
8 *Wallis's Royal Edition*, p. 86.
9 Hudson, *Victoria County History of Sussex*, p. 53.
10 *Ibid.*, p. 52.
11 Quoted in Bayly, p. 247.
12 *Ibid.*
13 Bayly, p. 248.
14 *Philip Edward Sewell*, pp. 3–4.
15 At 13 Norfolk Street, Strand, London.
16 AS to PS, *c.* 8 January 1846, NRO MC 144/35.
17 *Ibid.*
18 Thomas Hardy, *Jude the Obscure*, 1895, ed. Patricia Ingham (Oxford, Oxford University Press, 1996), p. 63.
19 AS to PS, *c.* 8 January 1846, NRO MC 144/35.
20 AS to PS, *c.* 14 January 1846, NRO MC 144/34.
21 *Ibid.*
22 *Ibid.*
23 *Ibid.*
24 This is likely but not entirely certain. Marienbad is mentioned once in MAS, p. 3 and although the implied timing may be correct, MAS seems to describe Anna's later visit to Marienberg. Bayly, p. 98 does not specify further than 'Germany'.
25 John Murray (ed.), *A Handbook for Travellers in Southern Germany* (London, John Murray, 1840), p. 375.
26 Material on Marienbad drawn generally from Murray (ed.), *Southern Germany*, pp. 374–6.
27 Bayly, p. 98.
28 John Murray (ed.), *Murray's Handbook for Belgium and the Rhine* (London, John Murray, 1852), p. 67.

29 PS to IS, 29 August 1846, NRO MC 144/18.
30 *Ibid.*
31 Murray, *Handbook for Belgium and the Rhine*, p. 73.
32 Unidentified. Perhaps a servant, friend, or cousin. It was not Anna's Uncle John Wright.
33 PS to IS, 29 August 1846, NRO MC 144/18.
34 PS to IS, 4 September 1846, NRO MC 144/19.
35 Probably her cousin Elizabeth Hunton who was Anna's age.
36 Postscript by MS in PS to IS, 4 September 1846, NRO MC 144/19.
37 MS to AS, *c.* 7 September 1846, NRO MC 144/8.
38 *Ibid.*
39 Elizabeth Wright and MS to Maria Wright, 21 September 1846, NRO MC 144/54.
40 *Ibid.*
41 *Ibid.*
42 Information on Joseph Sewell drawn generally from Edith Sewell, *Joseph S. Sewell*.
43 *Philip Edward Sewell*, p. 4; Obituary of Philip Sewell, *EDP* (7 February 1906), 4.
44 MS to PS, 21 January 1848, NRO MC 144/38.
45 Quoted in Bayly, p. 99.
46 MS to PS, 21 January 1848, NRO MC 144/38.
47 *Ibid.*
48 *Ibid.*
49 *Ibid.*
50 MS to PS, 25 April 1848, NRO MC 144/39.
51 *Ibid.*
52 *Ibid.*
53 Bayly, p. 127.
54 PS to IS and MS, 27 January 1854, NRO MC 144/27.

55 Bayly, p. 127.

56 MAS, p. 3.

57 Alfred Tennyson, 'Mariana'.

58 Elizabeth Jenkins, *Tennyson and Dr. Gully* (Lincoln, The Tennyson Society, 1986), p. 7, suggests that on his 1847 visit to Malvern Tennyson stayed with a friend, but a meeting in Malvern, which had many hotels, is a likelihood in 1848. Umberslade Hall, opened in 1846, used similar treatment and remains a possibility. If they did meet at Umberslade, Anna may have been one of the two people that Tennyson mentioned in a letter who wanted copies of his poems, see Tennyson to Edward Moxon, [?25 May 1847], in Alfred Tennyson, *The Letters of Alfred Lord Tennyson. Vol 1: 1821–1850*, ed. Cecil Y. Lang and Edgar F. Shannon, Jr (Oxford, Clarendon, 1982), p. 275.

59 Information on Gully and his treatments drawn generally from Elizabeth Jenkins, *Tennyson and Dr. Gully*. I am grateful to Marion Shaw for bringing this study to my attention.

60 Tennyson to Mary Howitt, 22 May [1947], Tennyson, *Letters*, p. 275.

61 Quoted in Robert Bernard Martin, *Tennyson: The Unquiet Heart*, 1980 (Oxford, Clarendon and Faber and Faber, 1983), p. 284.

62 Martin, *Tennyson*, p. 285.

63 *Ibid.*, p. 316.

64 MAS, p. 5.

65 *Ibid.*

66 Martin, *Tennyson*, p. 356.

67 Chitty states that Anna's annotated copy of *In Memoriam* could still be seen, p. 119. It has now proved untraceable.

68 Alfred Tennyson, *In Memoriam*, section 27, lines 15–16.

69 MS to PS, 24 December 1848, NRO MC 144/40.

70 *Ibid.*

71 *Ibid.*

72 *Ibid.*

73 *Ibid.*

74 MS to PS, 3 January 1849, NRO MC 144/41.

75 Unknown friend qtd in Bayly, p. 99.

76 *Ibid.*

77 *Ibid.*

78 Stanley Godman, 'Anna Sewell,' p. 4.

79 Lucas, *A Quaker Journal*, vol. 2, p. 409.

Chapter Seven

1 Wyn K. Ford and A.C. Gabe, *The Metropolis of Mid Sussex: A History of Haywards Heath* (Haywards Heath, Charles Clark, 1981), p. 1.

2 *Ibid.*, p. 29.

3 Chitty, p. 121.

4 *The Town Walk of Haywards Heath* (Haywards Heath, The Haywards Heath Society, 1999), p. 8; Arthur Howar, 'Haywards Heath', *Local History File: Haywards Heath*, vol. 1 (in Haywards Heath Library, no pub. details), p. 32.

5 *Town Walk*, p. 8.

6 The school has a similarly adorned set of wrought iron gates. In 2003 the school is itself under threat of demolition to make way for new housing. I am grateful to Kim Leslie of the WSRO for giving me information

about the plaque's unveiling.

7   In 1824, together with other
    Quaker proprietors, he had also
    opened Fleetwood House
    Boarding School for Quaker girls
    in Stoke Newington whose pupils
    Anna would have seen regularly
    during her girlhood there.

8   Information on 'America' taken
    generally from Margaret Nicolle,
    *William Allen: Quaker Friend of
    Lindfield 1770–1843* (Lindfield,
    West Sussex, Smallprint, 2001)
    and Debby Matthews, *America
    Lane: In the Footsteps of William
    Allen: Re-discovering America in
    the Middle of Mid Sussex*, Local
    History Series No. 2 (Haywards
    Heath, Re-discovering America
    Local History Project, 2001).

9   MSR, p. 73.

10 Ford and Gabe, *The Metropolis
    of Mid Sussex*, pp. 1, 61.

11 Nickola Smith, 'Introduction' in
    *Haywards Heath in Old Picture
    Postcards* (Zaltbommel,
    Netherlands, European Library,
    1993), n.p.

12 A few years later, in his will dated
    8 August 1861 (not his last will)
    Isaac lists his occupation as
    shipowner and refers to his coal
    works in the Forest of Dean. I am
    grateful to Charles Briscoe for
    this information. For Isaac's
    business as a maltster see
    Folthorp's Brighton Guide
    (Brighton, Robert Folthorp,
    1852), pp. 151, 237, 266.

13 Malting information drawn from
    Kim Leslie and Brian Short (eds),
    An Historical Atlas of Sussex
    (Chichester, Phillimore, 1999),
    p. 112.

14 St James's Street, Brighton is the
    address in PS to IS, 21 November

1852, NRO MC 144/20.

15 *Folthorp's Brighton Guide*, p. 266.

16 MSR, p. 3. Bayly, surely in light
    of Mary's later temperance views,
    omits this from Mary's
    'Autobiography'.

17 Isichei, *Victorian Quakers*, p.
    177.

18 Lucas, *A Quaker Journal*, vol. 1,
    p. 160.

19 *Ibid.*, p. 238.

20 Lucas, *A Quaker Journal*, vol. 2,
    p. 306.

21 Isichei, *Victorian Quakers*, pp.
    238–9.

22 *Ibid.*, p. 240.

23 *Ibid.*, p. 115.

24 *Ibid.*, p. 167.

25 Quoted in Delaney *et al.*, *The
    Curse*, p. 193.

26 Janet Horowitz Murray (ed.),
    *Strong-Minded Women: And
    Other Lost Voices from
    Nineteenth-Century England*,
    1982 (Harmondsworth, Penguin,
    1984), p. 48.

27 William Rathbone Greg, 'Why
    are Women Redundant?' (1862),
    reprinted in Murray (ed.), *Strong-
    Minded Women*, p. 52.

28 Ann Richelieu Lamb, 'Old
    Maidism!' (1844), reprinted in
    Murray (ed.), *Strong-Minded
    Women*, p. 49.

29 Florence Nightingale, *Cassandra
    and Other Selections from
    Suggestions for Thought*, ed.
    Mary Poovey (London, Pickering
    and Chatto, 1991), p. 205.

30 *Ibid.*, p. 213.

31 Quoted in Cunnington, *Feminine
    Attitudes*, p. 98.

32 Quoted in Rosemary Hartill,
    'Introduction,' *Florence
    Nightingale: Letters and
    Reflections* (Evesham, Arthur

James, 1996), p. 20.

33 Derick Mellor, *A History of the Red House Farm School, Buxton near Norwich* (Aylsham, Norfolk, Derick Mellor, 1976), p. ii.

34 Quoted in Bayly, p. 229.

35 E.H., *A Brief Memorial of Mrs Wright, Late of Buxton, Norfolk* (London, Jarrold and Sons [1861]), p. 5.

36 See generally E.H., *A Brief Memorial*.

37 In PS to IS, 21 November 1852, NRO MC 144/20, after PS had left England he asked IS if he wanted money for his house rent at Kings Road.

38 John H. Farrant, *The Harbours of Sussex 1700–1914* (Brighton, J.H. Farrant, 1976), p. 28.

39 *Philip Edward Sewell*, p. 4.

40 Carder, *The Encyclopaedia of Brighton*, section 161 d.

41 Quoted in John R. Davis, *The Great Exhibition* (Stroud, Sutton, 1999), p. 161.

42 Great Exhibition information drawn generally from Davis, *The Great Exhibition*, pp. 124–73.

43 *Ibid.*, pp. 172–4.

44 Quoted in Roy Porter, *London*, p. 289.

45 Although Bayly states Philip went there in 1850, p. 99.

46 *Philip Edward Sewell*, p. 4.

47 *Ibid.*

48 Philip owned an iron factory in Carril, a small village near Vilagarcía on the Spanish coast north of Pontevedra in Galicia, which in 1891 he made over to his son, John Wright Sewell, who was living there. I am indebted to Marcos Gago Otero for this information.

49 PS to IS, 21 November 1852, NRO MC 144/20.

50 Lucas, *A Quaker Journal*, vol. 2, p. 482.

51 PS to IS, 21 November 1852, NRO MC 144/20.

52 Bayly, p. 245. Bayly's comments do not specifically refer to 1853, but all indications are that her comments are apt for Anna's state at this time.

53 Bayly, p. 245.

54 Quoted in Bayly, p. 101.

55 Isichei, *Victorian Quakers*, pp. 145, 158.

56 *TPB*, p. 281.

57 Quoted in *Home Life*, p. 164.

58 Godman, 'Anna Sewell', p. 4.

59 Quoted in *Home Life*, pp. 165–6.

60 WSRO MP 424, *List of Lessees and Occupiers of Graylingwell Farm 1481–1854*.

61 Barone C. Hopper, *100 Years of Sanctuary: Graylingwell Hospital 1897–1997: A Social History* (Littlehampton, West Sussex, 1997), p. 9.

62 Bayly, pp. 102–3.

63 Hopper, *100 Years of Sanctuary*, p. 9.

64 Barone C. Hopper, 'The Lands of Graylingwell: Part 3', *West Sussex History*, 39 (August 1988), 30.

65 Peter Homer, 'Black Beauty Cottage is at Centre of Heritage Row', *Chichester Observer* (18 March 1999); Gill Trayner, '"Black Beauty Cottage" Should Be Restored and Opened as Museum' (1999), no pub. details. I am grateful to Kim Leslie of WSRO for supplying me with these articles.

66 Roy R. Morgan, *Chichester: A Documentary History*

(Chichester, Sussex, Phillimore, 1992), p. 27.

67 Quoted in Morgan, *Chichester*, p. 27.

68 Bayly, p. 127.

69 See generally *Kelly's Sussex Directory 1855* (London, W. Kelly and Co., 1855), pp. 868–9 and *Chichester Directories* for 1852 and 1858 in *Chichester Directories 1832–99* (Local History File, Chichester Library, n.d.).

70 PS to MS, 27 January 1854, NRO MC 144/27.

71 *Ibid.*

72 *Ibid.*

73 MAS, p. 6.

74 This has proved difficult to confirm. Thomas Parsons, 'Chichester Sixty–Sixty-Five Years Ago', *Sussex County Magazine*, 8:1 (January 1934), p. 42 states: 'The present depot of the Sussex Regiment was originally a cavalry barracks. I have heard it said that the Scots Greys went out from this barrack eight hundred strong to the Crimea, and were almost destroyed at the Alma.' It was not the Scots Greys who went out from Chichester at that time, but this story may well relate to another cavalry regiment.

75 Quoted in J.M. Brereton, *The Horse in War* (Newton Abbot, David and Charles, 1976), p. 97.

76 Anne Grimshaw, *The Horse: A Bibliography of British Books 1851–1976* (London, The Library Association, 1982), p. 23.

77 Brereton, *The Horse in War*, p. 100.

78 *TPB*, p. 259.

79 Bayly, p. 126.

80 *Ibid.*

81 *Ibid.*, p. 102.

82 May Nugent, 'Grandmother to Black Beauty', *London Mercury*, 26 (1932), p. 53, states that Anna went to Kaiserwerth, following Florence Nightingale's example but no source for or corroborative evidence of this has been found.

83 Bayly, p. 127.

84 John Murray (ed.), *A Handbook For Travellers on the Continent* (London, John Murray, 1856), p. 276.

85 *Ibid.*, p. 277.

86 MAS, p. 3.

87 MS to Mrs R, 19 April 1857, qtd in Bayly, p. 128.

88 Godman, 'Anna Sewell', p. 4 states that Isaac resigned in April 1857. This perhaps could not have come at a worse time. M. Rigby on the Sowell Family Heritage site <http://www.sowell.org/annasewell.htm> 15 February 2002 (untraceable November 2003) includes a letter by Isaac dated 12 February 1857 to his brother-in-law Thomas Nash regarding money he loaned to Nash and to his brother William Sewell.

89 MS to Mrs R, 19 April 1857, qtd in Bayly, p. 129.

90 *Ibid.*, p. 128.

91 Bayly, p. 127.

92 EBB1, p. 131.

93 MS preface to *Homely Ballads*, qtd in EBB1, p. 131.

94 EBB1, p. 132.

95 *Ibid.*, pp. 132–3.

96 Caroline Fox, *The Journals of Caroline Fox 1835–71*, ed. Wendy Monk (London, Elek, 1972), pp. 145–6.

97 MAS, p. 6.

98 John Murray, ed., *A Handbook for Travellers in Spain, and Readers at Home*, part I (London, John Murray, 1845), p. vii.

99 Richard Ford, *A Handbook for Travellers in Spain*, 4th edn, part I (London, John Murray, 1869), p. xxvi.

100 *Ibid.*, p. 83.

101 *Ibid.*, pp. 156–7.

Chapter Eight

1 *TPB*, p. 264.

2 In 1861, see William Page (ed.), *The Victoria History of the County of Gloucester*, vol. 2, repr. (Folkestone and London, Dawsons of Pall Mall, 1972), p. 183.

3 MS to Mrs R, 5 December 1858, qtd in Bayly, p. 165.

4 Quoted in Bayly, p. 169.

5 Misprinted as Liston in early editions of Bayly but by the 6th edition corrected.

6 The 1851 census entry lists the property as 'Siston Cottage or Blue Lodge', and Isaac Sewell in a will of 8 August 1861 gives his address as 'Siston Cottage'. I am grateful to Charles Briscoe for will information.

7 I am indebted to Joyce Peachey for information on the history of the house.

8 Quoted in *Home Life*, p. 205.

9 Quoted in Bayly, p. 169.

10 MS to Mrs R, 5 December 1858, qtd in Bayly, pp. 164–5.

11 Bayly, p. 134.

12 MS to Mrs R, 5 December 1858, qtd in Bayly, pp. 165–6.

13 *Kelly's Post Office Directory of Gloucestershire 1863* (London, W. Kelly and Co., 1863), p. 193.

14 *TPB*, p. 146.

15 *Ibid.*, p. 145.

16 MS to Mrs R, 5 December 1858, qtd in Bayly, pp. 165–6.

17 William Wooster (ed.), *The Post-Office Bath Directory 1866–67* (Bath, William Lewis, 1865), pp. 469, 474.

18 MS to unnamed, 30 November 1863, qtd in EBB1, p. 157.

19 MS to Mrs R, 5 December 1858, qtd in Bayly, p. 166.

20 Mrs J. Stirling Clarke, *The Habit and the Horse; A Treatise on Female Equitation*, 1857 (London, Day and Son, 1860), p. 4.

21 *Ibid.*, p. 3.

22 *Ibid.*, pp. 28–9.

23 *Ibid.*, p. 22.

24 *Ibid.*, p. 23.

25 *Ibid.*, p. 24.

26 *Ibid.*, p. 22.

27 *Ibid.*, pp. 17–19.

28 *Ibid.*, p. 30.

29 *Ibid.*, p. 48.

30 *Ibid.*, p. 52.

31 *BB*, p. 21.

32 I am grateful to Tim Ray who told me of the present-day (tenuous) connections of Anna to three hotel properties which refer to her in their advertising: Tracy Park; Glendale House in Goathland, Yorkshire, once owned by her cousin Edward Fuller Sewell; and Catton Old Hall, in Old Catton which offers an Anna Sewell room.

33 *The Gloucestershire: The Tracy Park Estate* advertising brochure, 2002. I am very grateful to the employees of *The Gloucestershire* who discussed Anna Sewell with me in September 2002.

34 Quoted in *Home Life*, pp. 205–6.

35 Quoted in EBB1, p. 135.

36 Dorothy Vinter, 'Anna Sewell and

Her Family at Blue Lodge',
Gloucestershire Countryside
(June–July 1963), p. 11.

37 Quoted in EBB2, p. xxii.
38 Quoted in *Home Life*, p. 206.
39 See *TPB*, pp. 172–4.
40 Quoted in EBB2, p. xx.
41 Quoted in EBB1, p. 148.
42 Quoted in EBB2, p. xxi.
43 Quoted in Bayly, p. 171.
44 EBB1, p. 132.
45 Howsam, *Kegan Paul*, pp. 18–19.
46 Quoted in EBB1, p. 132.
47 EBB1, p. 136.
48 Howsam, *Kegan Paul*, p. 19.
49 *Ibid.*, p. 21.
50 Quoted in *Home Life*, p. 206.
51 Bayly, p. 141.
52 EBB1, p. 150.
53 EBB1, p. 146. J.F. Meehan, 'Old
    Time Celebrities: No. VI Mary
    Sewell', *The New Album* (March
    1906), p. 312, states 1,088,000
    copies.
54 Dora Greenwell, 'Popular
    Religious Literature', in *Essays*
    (London and New York,
    Alexander Strahan, 1866), p. 154.
55 Quoted in advertising in MS,
    Village Children at Home
    (London, Jarrold and Sons, n.d.).
56 See Adrienne E. Gavin and
    Henrietta Twycross-Martin,
    'Mary Sewell' in Joanne Shattock
    (ed.), *The Cambridge
    Bibliography of English
    Literature*, 3rd edn (Cambridge,
    Cambridge University Press,
    1999), vol. 4, columns 434–5 for
    a bibliography of Mary Sewell's
    works. The series of *Church
    Ballads* listed in that bibliography
    and in the British Library
    catalogue are unlikely to have
    been written by Mary Sewell.
    They were published

anonymously (although with an
implied comparison to Mrs
Sewell's ballads on their cover),
no mention is made of them in
any Sewell source material, and
their focus is more high church
than would have appealed to
Mary. Possibly they were by high
church novelist Elizabeth Missing
Sewell who was no relation.

57 Published in at least one
    American edition as *Father's Last
    Words*.
58 EBB1, p. 152. An updated edition
    was published after Mary's death
    revised by 'some of her family'
    and no longer epistolary in form,
    EBB1, pp. 153–4. Anna's copy of
    the fourth edition, held in the
    Norfolk and Norwich
    Millennium Library, is inscribed:
    Anna Sewell
    never to be given away
    or lost
59 Quoted in EBB1, p. 147.
60 MAS, p. 5.
61 Quoted in EBB1, p. 133.
62 EBB1, p. 163.
63 Quoted in Bayly, p. 163.
64 Bayly, p. 248.
65 MAS, pp. 4–5.
66 EBB2, p. xxii.
67 Bayly, p. 248.
68 Quoted in Bayly, p. 167.
69 *Ibid.*, pp. 168–9.
70 MAS, p. 3.
71 MS to unnamed, 1861, qtd in
    Bayly, pp. 184–5.
72 Quoted in Bayly, p. 185.
73 *Ibid.*, p. 169.
74 *Ibid.*, p. 82.
75 *Philip Edward Sewell*, pp. 6–7;
    Mellor, *A History of the Red
    House Farm School*, p. 14.
76 *TPB*, p. 269.
77 *Ibid.*, pp. 263–4.

78 *Ibid.*

79 MS, 'Mrs Sewell's Paper', in *Women's Work in the Temperance Reformation: Being Papers Prepared for a Ladies' Conference Held in London, May 26, 1868.* Introduction by Mrs S.C. Hall (London, Published for the National Temperance League by W. Tweedie, 1868), p. 51.

80 *Ibid.*, p. 52.

81 MS to Mrs R, 1 April 1862, qtd in Bayly, p. 176.

82 MS, 'Mrs Sewell's Paper', pp. 51–2.

83 MS to Mrs R, June 1862, qtd in Bayly, pp. 177–8.

84 Bayly, p. 176.

85 MS to Mrs R, 1 April 1862, qtd in Bayly, p. 177.

86 Mrs F, qtd in Bayly, p. 172.

87 Quoted in Bayly, p. 172.

88 *Ibid.*, pp. 185–6.

89 *Ibid.*, pp. 170–1.

90 *Ibid.*, pp. 171–2.

91 Bayly, p. 249.

92 *Ibid.*

93 Bayly could not find this essay when in 1888 she wrote Mary's biography, and it remains untraced, p. 250.

94 MS to Mrs Williamson, undated, qtd in Bayly, p. 209.

95 AS to Mary Bayly, 1877 or 1878, qtd in Bayly, p. 250.

96 It also included appendices by Emma [Mrs G.W.] Sheppard of Frome, Somerset who ran a refuge for fallen women.

97 Bayly, p. 174.

98 MS, 'Mrs Sewell's Paper', pp. 52–3.

99 MS to Mrs R, 30 November 1863, qtd in Bayly, p. 186.

100 MS, 'Mrs Sewell's Paper', p. 52.

101 *Ibid.*, p. 54.

102 *Ibid.*, p. 53.

103 *Ibid.*

104 *Ibid.*

105 Bayly, p. 174.

106 MS, 'Mrs Sewell's Paper', p. 55.

107 EBB1, p. 156.

108 Quoted in Bayly, p. 171.

109 MS, 'Mrs Sewell's Paper', pp. 53–4.

110 *Ibid.*, p. 54.

111 Bayly, pp. 174–5.

112 TPB, p. 283.

113 Bayly, pp. 124–6.

114 Quoted in M. Jeanne Peterson, *Family, Love, and Work in the Lives of Victorian Gentlewomen* (Bloomington, Ind., Indiana University Press, 1989), p. 142.

115 *Ibid.*, pp. 142–3.

116 Vinter, 'Anna Sewell', p. 11.

117 MS to Mrs R, 5 December 1858, qtd in Bayly, p. 166.

118 *Ibid.*

119 Godman, 'Anna Sewell', p. 4.

120 *Ibid.* The bank later became part of Barclays Bank.

121 Bayly, p. 191.

Chapter Nine

1 MS to Mrs R, 4 July 1864, qtd in Bayly, p. 191.

2 *Ibid.*

3 MS, 'Mrs Sewell's Paper', p. 54.

4 Quoted in Bayly, pp. 188–9.

5 MS to Mrs R, 4 July 1864, qtd in Bayly, p. 190.

6 *Ibid.*, p. 191.

7 *Ibid.*

8 *Ibid.*

9 *Philip Edward Sewell*, p. 5.

10 EBB2, pp. xxii–xxiii.

11 Bayly, p. 192.

12   MS to Mrs R, undated, qtd in
     Bayly, p. 192.

13   R.E.M. Peach, *Street-Lore of
     Bath* (London, Simpkin, Marshall
     and Co., 1893), p. 96.

14   EBB1, p. 158.

15   Chapter 30 of Black Beauty, set in
     Bath, includes a scene in which
     Black Beauty visits a gentleman
     farmer who, like Anna, 'lived on
     the road to Wells,' pp. 110–11.

16   In 1881 a six-storey tower with
     crenellated battlements was
     added to the house. In more
     recent years The Moorlands
     served as a home for elderly
     gentlemen before closing around
     1990, after which squatters
     moved in and left with much of
     value including the impressive
     wrought-iron 'crinoline banisters'
     that in Anna's day curved
     outwards to give ease of access to
     the fashionably wide of dress
     (Chitty, 1971, p. 151, reports the
     banisters as there). The original
     brown, yellow, and black
     patterned floor tiles in the
     entrance hall still exist, but the
     pigsties, barn, and stables have
     been demolished. In the 1990s
     members of the Victory Church
     moved into The Moorlands and
     in 1996 added another wing to
     the west of the tower to house
     their school. Underneath the
     house is a maze of cellar rooms
     with narrow passages, and
     underground tunnels are
     rumoured to lead under the old
     meadow. In 2002 the house was
     converted into 'luxury
     apartments'. I am grateful to
     Mark McArdle and Barbara
     Baskerville for much of this
     information on The Moorlands'

     recent history.

17   Quoted in Bayly, p. 196.

18   *Ibid.*

19   Bayly, p. 196.

20   Frank E. Huggett, *Carriages at
     Eight: Horse-Drawn Society in
     Victorian and Edwardian Times*
     (Guildford, Lutterworth Press,
     1979), p. 58.

21   Bayly, p. 192.

22   I am grateful to Bridget Collett,
     headteacher of Moorlands Infant
     School, for this information.

23   MS to Mrs R, undated, qtd in
     Bayly, p. 192.

24   Quoted in Bayly, p. 196.

25   MS to AS, *c.* 31 October 1836,
     NRO MC 144/2. In PS to AS, 12
     May 1840, repr. in *Soul Search*
     2:9 (April 2003), p. 23, PS tells
     AS that on a visit back to Palatine
     Cottage he 'saw our old cat'.

26   EBB2, p. xxi.

27   Bayly, p. 192.

28   Wooster (ed.), *The Post-Office
     Bath Directory*, p. 537.

29   James Tunstall, *The Bath Waters:
     Their Uses and Effects in the
     Cure and Relief of Various
     Chronic Diseases* (London, John
     Churchill and Sons, 1868),
     p. 109.

30   Randle Wilbraham Falconer, *The
     Baths and Mineral Waters of
     Bath* (London, John Churchill,
     1881), p. 51.

31   Tunstall, *The Bath Waters*, p. 22.

32   *Ibid.*, p. 21.

33   MS to Mrs R, 4 July 1864, qtd in
     Bayly, p. 191.

34   Wooster (ed.), *The Post-Office
     Bath Directory*, pp. 532–6.

35   MS to 'JS', 17 August 1865, in
     possession of Adrienne Gavin.

36   Chitty, p. 155.

37   MS to Mrs Williamson, undated,

qtd in Bayly, p. 193.

38 Bayly, p. 194.
39 Bayly, p. 197.
40 Bayly, p. 194.
41 *Ibid.*
42 Quoted in Bayly, pp. 195–7.
43 EBB2, p. xxiii; Bayly, p. 195.
44 Quoted in Bayly, p. 196.
45 Mrs Charles to Mary Bayly, undated, qtd in Bayly, p. 204.
46 Anthony Trollope, 'Review of Mrs Sewell's *The Rose of Cheriton*', *Fortnightly Review* (1 February 1867), 253.
47 *Ibid.*, p. 254.
48 MS to Charles Fleet, 5 June [1867–1884] in possession of Adrienne Gavin.
49 *BB*, p. 140.
50 Quoted in Bayly, p. 196.
51 Wooster (ed.), *The Post-Office Bath Directory*, pp. 464, 476.
52 Quoted in EBB2, p. xviii.
53 AS to IS, 17 [January? 1867?]. Quoted with the consent of James Pepper from his partial transcription of the letter which appears on the www.abebooks.com website advertising the letter for sale (2001–3) at an asking price of US$6,500.
54 *Philip Edward Sewell*, pp. 7–8.
55 *Ibid.*, p. 8.
56 Baker, p. 80.
57 Bayly, p. 214.
58 *Ibid.*, pp. 216–17.
59 Including Beechwood and Woodstock. Some of these apply to subdivisions of the original property. In April 2003 Anna Sewell House, a Grade II listed building, was advertized for sale with an asking price of £575,000.
60 Robin Worden advises that the property once included 127

Spixworth Road, private correspondence 2002.
61 EBB2, p. xxv.
62 NRO MC 2241/2/1. It was bought by Samuel Gurney Buxton of Catton Hall.
63 Mrs F, qtd in Bayly, p. 173.
64 Bayly, p. 216.
65 *Ibid.*, p. 215.
66 EBB2, p. xxv.
67 Bayly, p. 215.
68 MS to unknown, 11 April 1882, qtd in Bayly, p. 317.
69 William White, *History, Gazetteer and Directory of Norfolk*, 3rd edn (London, Simpkin, Marshall and Co., 1864), pp. 599–600.
70 E.R. Kelly (ed.), *The Post Office Directory of Norfolk and Suffolk* (London, W. Kelly and Co., 1879), p. 256.
71 See generally I.M. Manning, *A History of Old Catton* (Old Catton, Norwich, I.M. Manning, [1982]).
72 Quoted in Isichei, *Victorian Quakers*, pp. 120–1.
73 Revd Benjamin John Armstrong, *A Norfolk Diary*, ed. Herbert B.J. Armstrong (London, George C. Harrap, 1949), p. 11.
74 Bayly, p. 214.
75 Armstrong, *A Norfolk Diary*, p. 183.
76 Bayly, p. 214.
77 Possibly with a second wife, but no mention of a second wife has been found, except in Chitty, p. 155.
78 As indicated in Margaret Sewell, 'Letters of Margaret Sewell' (unpublished, in possession of the owner).
79 Lorna Kellett, *The Sewell Connection: Family, Community, Theatre* (Norwich, Jarrold and

Sons, n.d.), n.p.

80　*Ibid.*

81　*Ibid.*

82　Probably Janet Bilsborough listed as a nurse aged forty-one in the 1871 census and from Gargrave in Yorkshire. In the 1851 census she is listed as Jane Boilsborough age twenty-two.

83　Bayly, p.114.

84　MAS, p. 4.

85　*Ibid.*, p. 3.

86　EBB1, p. 133.

87　MAS, p. 3. Writing in 1935 Margaret states that a small number of Anna's oil and pencil drawings together with 'Copies in oil of two of Landseer's animal pictures' were then in the Sewell family's possession. No drawings or paintings of Anna's have been traced.

88　Edward G. Fairholme and Wellesley Pain, *A Century of Work for Animals: The History of the R.S.P.C.A. 1824–1924* (London, John Murray, 1924), pp. 119–20.

89　Bayly, pp. 218–19.

90　MAS, p. 4.

91　*Ibid.*

92　*Ibid.*

93　Bayly, p. 187.

94　Quoted in Bayly, p. 78.

95　MAS, pp. 3–4.

96　Quoted in Bayly, pp. 171–2.

97　Edward John Tilt, *The Change of Life in Health and Disease*, 2nd edn (London, John Churchill, 1857), p. 45.

98　*Ibid.*

99　Tilt, *The Change of Life*, p. 126.

100　See generally Tilt, *The Change of Life*, and Janice Delaney *et al.*, *The Curse.*

101　Cited in Delaney *et al.*, *The Curse*, p. 189.

102　Bayly, pp. 225, 227.

103　*Ibid.*, pp. 238, 321.

104　*Philip Edward Sewell*, p. 6.

105　*Ibid.*, pp. 12–13.

106　Quoted in Bayly, p. 222.

107　Bayly, p. 217.

108　*Ibid.*

109　*Ibid.*

110　Bayly, p. 218.

111　EBB1, p. 146.

112　Bayly, p. 225.

113　*Ibid.*

114　MAS, p. 5.

115　Bayly, p. 226. The journal has not been found.

116　*Ibid.*, p. 227.

117　Quoted in Bayly, p. 227.

118　'Copy of Letter to P.E. Sewell' probably from his uncle John Wright, 12 January 1870, cited with permission of the owner.

119　*Philip Edward Sewell*, p. 8.

120　MS to Mrs Williamson, 8 August [1870?], qtd in Bayly, p. 227.

121　Bayly, pp. 215–16.

122　Armstrong, *A Norfolk Diary*, p. 157.

123　Bayly, p. 228.

Chapter Ten

1　E.B. Roche is the certifying doctor listed on Anna's death certificate.

2　Quoted in Bayly, pp. 228–9.

3　Bayly, p. 236.

4　MS to Mrs Williamson, undated, qtd in Bayly, p. 207.

5　I am grateful to Dr Raewyn Gavin for advice on Anna's condition.

6　MS to Mrs Williamson, undated, qtd in Bayly, pp. 212–13.

7　Bayly, p. 216.

8 *Ibid.*
9 Bayly, p. 253.
10 *Ibid.*
11 Bayly, p. 235.
12 *Ibid.*
13 Probably Anna's nieces [Mary] Grace and [Lucy] Edith.
14 Probably Anna's nieces [Helen] Ada and [Margaret] Amie.
15 Quoted in Bayly, p. 235.
16 *Ibid.*, p. 236.
17 Bayly, pp. 236–7.
18 *Ibid.*, p. 238.
19 Quoted in Bayly, p. 271.
20 Bayly, p. 271.
21 MS to Mrs Toynbee, [*c.* February] 1878, quoted in Bayly, p. 278.
22 *Ibid.*, pp. 277–8.
23 Chitty, p. 164.
24 Bayly, p. 235.
25 *Ibid.*, p. 229.
26 *Ibid.*, p. 231.
27 Mellor, *A History of the Red House Farm School*, p. 11.
28 The school continued to operate until about 1997 under a series of different owners and in 2003 operated as Rowan House, a home for psychologically challenging patients. I am grateful to Charles and Avril Briscoe for this information.
29 Mellor, *A History of the Red House Farm School*, p. 10.
30 *Philip Edward Sewell*, p. 9.
31 *Ibid.*, p. 10.
32 MAS, p. 4.
33 *Ibid.*
34 Bayly, pp. 232–3.
35 *Ibid.*, p. 233.
36 *Ibid.*, pp. 301–2.
37 *Ibid.*, p. 234.
38 Quoted in Bayly, p. 270.
39 *Ibid.*, p. 236.
40 *Ibid.*
41 *Ibid.*
42 Bayly, pp. 255–6.
43 Quoted in Bayly, p. 257.
44 MS to unknown, undated, quoted in Bayly, p. 256.
45 *Ibid.*
46 Perhaps indicative of the lupus 'butterfly rash' or a tubercular flush.
47 MS to unknown, undated, quoted in Bayly, p. 256.
48 *Ibid.*
49 *Ibid.*
50 Bayly, p. 257.
51 MS to Mrs Williamson, undated, quoted in Bayly, p. 211.
52 Bayly, p. 236.
53 Quoted in Bayly, p. 260.
54 *Ibid.*, p. 236.
55 *Ibid.*
56 Possibly 1873 or 1874, Bayly's dates are unclear here.
57 Quoted in Bayly, p. 238.
58 Bayly, p. 260.
59 Bayly, p. 259.
60 Quoted in Bayly, p. 259.
61 MAS, pp. 5–6.
62 Bayly, p. 258.
63 Quoted in Bayly, pp. 258–9.
64 Anna's eldest niece, Mary Grace, fifty-nine years later would also be buried in this grave at her own request.
65 Quoted in Bayly, pp. 238–9.
66 [Harriet Martineau], *Life in the Sick-Room: Essays by an Invalid* (London, Edward Moxon, 1844), p. 21.
67 Bayly, p. 261.
68 Quoted in Bayly, p. 254.
69 Bayly, p. 261.
70 *Ibid.*
71 *Ibid.*, p. 187.
72 Quoted in Bayly, p. 263.
73 Melvin E. Dieter, 'Hannah Whitall Smith: A Woman for All Seasons', *Holiness Digest* (Fall

1999) <http://www.messiah.
<edu/whwc/Articles/article10a.htm>
22 November 2003.

74   Bayly, p. 262.
75   Quoted in Bayly, p. 262.
76   *Ibid.*
77   Bayly, p. 265.
78   MS to Mrs Williamson, undated,
     quoted in Bayly, p. 266.
79   Quoted in Bayly, pp. 265–6.
80   Bayly, p. 266.
81   *Ibid.*, p. 267.
82   Quoted in Bayly, pp. 256–7.
83   MS to Mrs Toynbee [January–
     February] 1878, quoted in Bayly,
     p. 278. MAS (p. 5) and Bayly (p.
     239) both indicate that Anna may
     have been again dictating at this
     stage, but Mary's statement seems
     the more reliable. Mrs F records
     that Anna 'jotted down her
     thoughts in pencil on chance
     scraps of paper', Mrs F, quoted in
     Bayly, p. 170.
84   Quoted in Bayly, p. 257.
85   *Ibid.*, p. 271.
86   *Ibid.*, p. 272.
87   MAS, p. 4.
88   *Ibid.*
89   Quoted in Bayly, p. 272.
90   MAS, p. 4.
91   *Ibid.*
92   MS to Mrs R, early 1877, quoted
     in Bayly, p. 243.
93   *Ibid.*
94   *Ibid.*, p. 241.
95   MS to 'M.J.R.', undated, quoted
     in Bayly, p. 240.
96   Bayly, p. 269.
97   MS to Mrs R, early 1877, quoted
     in Bayly, p. 242.
98   MS to Mrs Williamson, undated,
     quoted in Bayly, p. 210.
99   Quoted in *BB*, p. 2.
100 MS to Mrs R, early 1877, quoted
     in Bayly, p. 243.

101 *Ibid.* Joseph's eldest daughter
     Lucy, in 1895 along with her
     husband William Johnson and
     their young daughter Blossom,
     was brutally murdered in
     Madagascar during an anti-
     Christian massacre. See Edith
     Sewell, *Joseph S. Sewell* and
     P. Doncaster (ed.), *Faithful Unto
     Death: A Story of the Missionary
     Life in Madagascar of William &
     Lucy S. Johnson* (London,
     Headley Brothers, 1896).
102 Bayly, p. 239.
103 *Ibid.*
104 *Ibid.*
105 MS to Mrs Williamson, undated,
     quoted in Bayly, pp. 240–1.
106 £40 is the sum that in 2002, Peter
     Salt, Jarrolds' former archivist,
     says was paid for the book. Chitty
     states £20 (p. 179), but changes
     this to £30 in her introduction to
     Ellen B. Wells and Anne
     Grimshaw (eds), *The Annotated
     'Black Beauty'* by Anna Sewell
     (London, J.A. Allen, 1989), p. xii.
     A.A. Dent, 'Miss Sewell of
     Norfolk', *East Anglian Magazine*
     15:10 (August 1956), p. 545,
     states £30, as does Baker, *Anna
     Sewell and Black Beauty* (p. 89).
     George Angell in 1890 claimed
     Anna was paid £20: Geo[rge] T.
     Angell, *Autobiographical Sketches
     and Personal Recollections*
     (Boston, American Humane
     Education Society, [1908]) p. 96.
     It has proved impossible to
     confirm which figure is correct.
     Dent states that in December
     1940 all of Jarrolds' book
     publishing records were lost
     during bombing (p. 545). It seems
     this is not the case as Salt advises
     that a ledger exists listing the

price for *Black Beauty* as £40. Other ledgers include references to Mary Sewell's work, and there are apparently letter-books that include occasional information on *Black Beauty* relating to its first decade of publication on matters such as illustrations and copyright issues. Salt confirms that there is no trace of the manuscript. Jarrolds' records are currently inaccessible. In 2001 their archives were donated to the NRO, but the business archivist advises that they have not yet been catalogued. I am grateful to Peter Salt for the information provided.

107 I am grateful to Peter Salt, Jarrolds' former archivist for this information. He advises that £10–20 was the norm, but that because of the excellent sales of *Black Beauty* after Anna's death Mary was given £200. A series of letters exchanged between lawyers acting for Margaret Sewell (as Anna's executrix) and for Jarrolds in 1921 concerning the Vitagraph Co.'s right to film *Black Beauty* reveal that Jarrolds almost, as MAS's lawyer put it, 'holding a pistol at us,' managed to obtain MAS's agreement not just to sell film rights, but agreement that Jarrolds owned all other rights in the book. Under the Copyright Act of 1911 rights would have reverted to Anna's executors. Jarrolds paid MAS and her surviving siblings £250 which was half of the £500 received from Vitagraph for film rights. I am grateful to the owner of these letters for granting me access.

108 Quoted in Bayly, p. 271.
109 EBB1, pp. 141–2.
110 *The House of Jarrolds 1823–1923*, p. 24.
111 The exact date has proved difficult to confirm. Bayly claims, 'near the end of the year 1877' (p. 272). Chitty states 24 November 1877 (p. 179). *The House of Jarrolds* gives the date of Thomas Jarrold's death as 24 November 1877 (p. 22). He died before *Black Beauty* was published indicating, if this date is correct, that *Black Beauty* must have been published slightly later that year. *The House of Jarrolds* incorrectly gives the date of publication as 24 November 1878 (p. 24). Jarrold's former archivist Peter Salt states that the novel was published the same day that Thomas Jarrold died (personal communication).

Chapter Eleven

1 BB, p. 3.
2 *Ibid.*, p. 190.
3 *House of Jarrolds*, pp. 24–5.
4 'Variant A' has a fully gilt decorated cover with a large gilt horse's head facing right framed by oat fronds entwining a trellis border. 'Variant B' is decorated in gilt and black with a large black horse's head facing right and a trellis border. 'Variant C' has a redesigned cover with a small horse's head in gilt framed in a gold medallion facing left, removes Anna's name, and black lines replace the trellis. Information drawn from Richard Dalby, 'Anna Sewell's "Black Beauty"', p. 25 and private

communication from Michael Metford-Sewell.

5 Held in Norfolk and Norwich Millennium Library.

6 In possession of owners.

7 Chitty in 1971 states (p. 184) that the now untraceable copy Anna gave to her cousin, Lucy Sewell, included a letter by Anna. It was possibly then in possession of Peter Edwards, a great-great-grandson of Anna's uncle, Edward Sewell, who in Bath in the mid-1970s may have sold off now untraceable Sewell-related possessions. I am grateful to Michael Metford-Sewell and Joyce Peachey for this information.

8 Unnamed cousin to AS, *c.* December 1877, quoted in Bayly, pp. 274–5.

9 Unnamed to AS, 18 January 1878, quoted in Bayly, p. 275.

10 Unnamed to AS, 24 December 1877, quoted in Bayly, pp. 275–6.

11 Bayly, p. 274.

12 Review of *Black Beauty*, *EDP* (22 December 1877), p. 3.

13 Review of *Black Beauty*, *The Nonconformist* (9 January 1878), 32.

14 Quoted in advertising in A. Sewell, *Black Beauty: The Autobiography of a Horse* (London, Jarrold and Sons, [*c.* 1895]).

15 Undated review comment included in advertising in later editions of Mary Sewell, *Patience Hart's First Experience in Service* (London, Jarrold and Sons, *c.* 1880).

16 MS to Mrs Toynbee, *c.* February 1878, quoted in Bayly, p. 277.

17 Review of *Black Beauty*, *EDP* (22 December 1877), 3.

18 Quoted in advertising in A. Sewell, *Black Beauty* [*c.* 1895].

19 Unattributed comment quoted in advertising in Mary Sewell, *A Vision of the Night* (London, Jarrold and Sons [1882]).

20 Anna, or possibly someone else, added a paragraph to the fifth edition at the end of Chapter 33 advising that a stabled horse should always have a bucket of water nearby.

21 Coral Lansbury, *The Old Brown Dog: Women, Workers, and Vivisection in Edwardian England* (Madison, Wis., University of Wisconsin Press, 1985), p. 64.

22 MAS, p. 1.

23 Dalby, 'Anna Sewell's "Black Beauty"', p. 20.

24 Angell, *Autobiographical Sketches*, p. 96.

25 *Ibid.*, p. 95. It is possible that *Black Beauty* appeared in earlier American editions but no hard evidence exists.

26 See generally Angell, *Autobiographical Sketches*.

27 *Ibid.*, p. 94.

28 *Ibid.*, pp. 94–5.

29 *Ibid.*, p. 95.

30 Susan Chitty, 'Biographical Foreword', in Wells and Grimshaw (eds), *The Annotated 'Black Beauty'*, p. xiii.

31 Angell, *Autobiographical Sketches*, p. 95.

32 *Ibid.*

33 Dalby, 'Anna Sewell's "Black Beauty"', pp. 20–1.

34 Angell, *Autobiographical Sketches*, p. 96.

35 Quoted in Gerard J. Senick (ed.), 'Anna Sewell 1820–1878', *Children's Literature Review*, vol. 17 (Detroit, Mich., Gale Research, 1989), pp. 131–2.
36 Angell, *Autobiographical Sketches*, p. 96.
37 *Ibid.*
38 *BB* early AHES editions.
39 Chitty, pp. 224–5.
40 Angell, *Autobiographical Sketches*, pp. 96–7.
41 Wells and Grimshaw (eds), *The Annotated 'Black Beauty'*, p. xxx.
42 Angell, *Autobiographical Sketches*, p. 99.
43 *Ibid.*, p. 98. In August 1891 Angell claimed the AHES itself had sent out over half a million copies in a little over a year (p. 108).
44 Angell, 'Addition to Our Autobiographical Sketches', *Autobiographical Sketches*, p. 1.
45 Wells and Grimshaw (eds), *The Annotated 'Black Beauty'*, p. xxv.
46 '"Black Beauty" in Norwegian', *Our Dumb Animals*, 41:4 (September 1908), p. 59.
47 '"Black Beauty"', *Our Dumb Animals*, 41:10 (March 1909), p. 149.
48 *House of Jarrolds*, p. 25.
49 MAS, p. 1.
50 Dalby, 'Anna Sewell's "Black Beauty"', p. 21.
51 MAS, p. 1.
52 Dalby, 'Anna Sewell's "Black Beauty"', p. 14.
53 Dust jacket of Jarrolds' New and Enlarged Edition of Marshall Saunders's *Beautiful Joe*, n.d.
54 Dent, 'Miss Sewell of Norfolk', p. 546.
55 '"Black Beauty" in Honolulu', *Our Dumb Animals*, 41:12 (May 1909), p. 184; 'Two Thousand Copies of "Black Beauty"', *Our Dumb Animals*, 41:8 (January 1909), p. 114.
56 Dalby, 'Anna Sewell's "Black Beauty"', p. 21.
57 Lansbury, *The Old Brown Dog*, p. 64.
58 Vinter, 'Anna Sewell and Her Family at Blue Lodge', p. 11.
59 'Cabmen's Dinner at Norwich', *EDP* (5 February 1880), p. 3.
60 Bayly, p. 273.
61 Vincent Starrett, '"Black Beauty" and its Author' in *Buried Caesars: Essays in Literary Appreciation* (Chicago, Covici-McGee, 1923), p. 205.
62 Dust jacket of Jarrolds' New and Enlarged Edition of Marshall Saunders's *Beautiful Joe*, n.d.
63 'A Hundred Thousand New Missionaries', *Our Dumb Animals*, 41:8 (January 1909), p. 114.
64 Angell, *Autobiographical Sketches*, p. 110.
65 Revd J.G. Wood, 'The Horse and His Owner: Part II', *Good Words*, 22 (1881), p. 639.
66 E.S. Turner, *All Heaven in a Rage* (London, Michael Joseph, 1964), pp. 159–60.
67 Huggett, *Carriages at Eight*, p. 26.
68 Edward Fordham Flower, *Bits and Bearing Reins*, 2nd edn (London, William Ridgway, 1875), pp. 6, 15.
69 *Ibid.*, p. 10.
70 Mrs Toynbee to MS, 29 January 1878, quoted in Bayly, pp. 276–7.
71 MS to Mrs Toynbee, *c.* February 1878, quoted in Bayly, p. 277.
72 *Ibid.*

73 *Ibid.*

74 Wells and Grimshaw (eds), *The Annotated 'Black Beauty'*, p. xxxii.

75 I am grateful to Claire Wigmore of the British Driving Society for this information.

76 I am grateful to David M. McDowell, Equine Veterinary Officer of the RSPCA for this information.

77 Unnamed to AS, 24 December 1877, quoted in Bayly, pp. 275–6.

78 Alfred Saunders, *Our Horses: or, the Best Muscles Controlled by the Best Brains* (London, Sampson Low, Marston, Searle & Rivington, 1886), p. 228.

79 Turner, *All Heaven in a Rage*, p. 160.

80 *BB*, p. 68.

81 *Ibid.*, p. 148.

82 Grimshaw, *The Horse*, pp. xix–xx.

83 Review of *Black Beauty*, *EDP* (22 December 1877), p. 3.

84 Unnamed cousin to AS, *c.* December 1877, quoted in Bayly, p. 274.

85 Unnamed to AS, 24 December 1877, quoted in Bayly, p. 275.

86 The fountain is now used as a planter. I am grateful to Robert Novak Jr of the Derby Historical Society, Ansonia, Connecticut, for this information.

87 W.J. Gordon, *The Horse-World of London* (London, The Religious Tract Society, 1893), p. 113.

88 Samuel Sidney, *The Book of the Horse* [1874], Classic Edition (New York, Bonanza Books, 1985), pp. 189–90.

89 Sally Mitchell (ed.), *Victorian Britain: An Encyclopedia* (Chicago and London, St James Press, 1988), p. 375.

90 Turner, *All Heaven in a Rage*, p. 145.

91 Huggett, *Carriages at Eight*, p. 58.

92 *Ibid.*, p. 60.

93 Fairholme and Pain, *A Century of Work for Animals*, p. 87.

94 Gordon, *The Horse-World of London*, p. 13.

95 *Ibid.*, pp. 183–4.

96 *Ibid.*, pp. 183–90.

97 MS to Mrs Toynbee, *c.* February 1878, quoted in Bayly, p. 278.

98 Arthur W. Moss, *The Valiant Crusade: The History of the R.S.P.C.A.* (London, Cassell, 1961), p. 92; Wells and Grimshaw (eds), *The Annotated 'Black Beauty'*, pp. xxvi–xxvii.

99 Wells and Grimshaw (eds), *The Annotated 'Black Beauty'*, p. xxvi.

100 'Dowse, the Gipsy', *Temple Bar*, 5 (1885), p. 216.

101 Angell, *Autobiographical Sketches*, appendix, p. 36.

102 In 1984 claims were made that it was the work of naturalist and writer Gene[va] Stratton-Porter, see discussion in David G. Maclean, 'An Examination into Attribution' in *The Strike at Shane's: A Prize Story of Indiana* (new edn) Decatur, Ind., Americana Books, 1991), pp. v–xx.

103 Angell, *Autobiographical Sketches*, p. 99 and appendix, p. 36.

104 'Black Beauty', *Our Dumb Animals*, 1:5 (October 1908), p. 71. The play was possibly also staged before this. Chitty notes

that in 1906 a dramatization by Justin Adams was staged in Boston billed, 'The Original Anna Sewell Production of the Great Humane Play Black Beauty' (pp. 225–6).

105 Quoted in 'Black Beauty', *Our Dumb Animals*, 41:10 (March 1909), p. 149.

106 'Play of "Black Beauty"', *Our Dumb Animals*, 41:12 (May 1909), p. 180.

107 Phyllis Briggs, *Son of Black Beauty* (London, Thames Publishing [1954]), p. 152.

108 'Publisher's Note' in Briggs, *Son of Black Beauty*.

109 Sidney, *The Book of the Horse*, p. 189.

110 Stonehenge [J.H. Walsh], *The Horse, in the Stable and the Field* (London, George Routledge and Sons, 1875), p. 164.

111 Sidney, *The Book of the Horse*, p. 189.

112 Josephine, Diana, and Christine Pullein-Thompson, *Fair Girls and Grey Horses: Memories of a Country Childhood* [1996] (London, Allison and Busby, 1998), p. 79.

113 This collection is part of the Northeast Children's Literature Collection of the Thomas J. Dodd Research Center and was purchased from a private collector in the mid-1980s. I am grateful to curator Terri Goldich for this information.

114 Dalby, 'Anna Sewell's "Black Beauty"', p. 21.

115 Harriet Fowler, 'Enduring Beauty: A History of Illustrations to Anna Sewell's Classic Story', *Equine Images* (Fall 2002), p. 35. I am

grateful to Karen Crossley for bringing this article to my attention.

116 Fourteen of the eighteen originals of Aldin's illustrations are still owned by Jarrolds and were displayed at its Norwich Department store 31 August–4 September 1982.

117 Dalby, 'Anna Sewell's "Black Beauty"', p. 22.

118 *Ibid.*

119 Quoted in Senick (ed.), 'Anna Sewell 1820–1878', p. 136.

120 *Ibid.*, p. 137.

121 See, for example, Andrew Stibbs, '*Black Beauty*: Tales My Mother Told Me', *Children's Literature in Education*, 22 (1976), pp. 128–34.

122 Dalby, 'Anna Sewell's "Black Beauty"', p. 21.

123 *Ibid.*, p. 24.

124 Filmfax Production/Universal Education and Visual Arts.

125 Paramount Pictures/Ealing Films.

126 Produced by Isambard (Black Beauty) Limited in association with The Fremantle Corporation/London Weekend Television/ Beta/Taurus.

127 Chitty, p. 235.

128 I am grateful to Louise van der Merwe and Lianda Martin for confirming the South African banning. American banning information is taken from Suzanne Fisher Staples, 'What Johnny Can't Read: Censorship in American Libraries', *The ALAN Review* 26.2 (Winter 1996) <http://www.scholar.lib.vt.edu/ejournals/ALAN/winter96> 16 November 2003.

129 Reviewed by Laurel Graeber, 'A Horse's Life: It's A Beauty',

New York Times (27 November 1998), E47.

130 Cleveland Amory, *Ranch of Dreams* (New York, Viking Penguin, 1997), pp. 35–6.

131 MSPCA website <http:www.mspca.org/news_even ts /Humane_Awards/ ahof2003.htm.> 22 March 2003.

132 I am grateful to Charles Briscoe for this grazing information.

133 Dalby, 'Anna Sewell's "Black Beauty"', p. 14.

134 Quoted in Senick (ed.), 'Anna Sewell 1820–1878', p. 137.

135 Lansbury, *The Old Brown Dog*, p. 97.

136 Unnamed to AS, 18 January 1878, quoted in Bayly, p. 275.

137 For a fuller discussion see Adrienne E. Gavin, '*The Autobiography of a Horse?*: Reading Anna Sewell's *Black Beauty* as Autobiography' in Martin Hewitt (ed.), *Representing Victorian Lives*, Leeds Working Papers in Victorian Studies, vol. 2 (Leeds, Leeds Centre for Victorian Studies, 1999), pp. 51–62.

Chapter Twelve

1 Quoted in Bayly, p. 170.
2 Bayly, p. 279.
3 As quoted in Bayly, p. 279.
4 MS to Mrs Williamson, [*c.* 1877–8], quoted in Bayly, p. 280.
5 Bayly, p. 280.
6 James J. Bane (ed.), *J.J. Hamilton and Co.'s Imperial Postal Directory of the City and County of Norwich, with Gazeteer* (Norwich, William Allen, 1879), p. 16.

7 Quoted in Bayly, p. 170.
8 MS to unknown [*c.* early 1878], quoted in Bayly, p. 280.
9 *Ibid.*
10 *Ibid.*
11 MS to Mrs Williamson, undated [*c.* early 1878], quoted in Bayly, pp. 280–1.
12 *Ibid.*, p. 281.
13 Bayly, p. 244.
14 MS to Mrs Williamson, undated [*c.* early 1878], quoted in Bayly, p. 281.
15 MS to unknown, April 1878, quoted in Bayly, p. 281.
16 *Ibid.*
17 *Ibid.*
18 Unknown to MS, *c.* early 1878, quoted in Bayly, p. 282.
19 Anna Sewell's Last Will and Testament.
20 MS to Mrs F, 23 April 1878, quoted in Bayly, p. 283.
21 *Ibid.*
22 Armstrong, *A Norfolk Diary*, p. 216.
23 Quoted in Bayly, p. 284.
24 MS to Bayly, May 1878, quoted in Bayly, pp. 284–5.
25 Quoted in Bayly, p. 333. Mary also uses the phrase 'with shining feet' to refer to an Angel's walking in *Mother's Last Words*.
26 Isichei, *Victorian Quakers*, p. 168.
27 Bayly, p. 279.
28 MSR, p. 5.
29 White, *History, Gazetteer and Directory of Norfolk*, 1864, p. 682.
30 MS to Bayly, May 1878, quoted in Bayly, p. 285.
31 MAS, p. 5.
32 MS to Bayly, May 1878, quoted in Bayly, p. 284.
33 Quoted in Bayly, p. 287.

34 *Ibid.*

35 EBB2, p. xxiv.

36 *Ibid.*

37 Although his gravestone records 8 November, his death certificate has 7 November.

38 MS to unknown, late 1878, quoted in Bayly, p. 288.

39 *Ibid.*

40 Quoted in Bayly, p. 291.

41 MS to Mrs Williamson, undated, quoted in Bayly, p. 310.

42 *Ibid.*, pp. 291–2.

43 Quoted in Bayly, pp. 292–3.

44 EBB2, p. xxv.

45 *Ibid.*, pp. xxv–xxvi.

46 MS to unknown, quoted in Bayly, p. 303.

47 MS to Mrs Williamson, undated, quoted in Bayly, p. 310.

48 Quoted in Bayly, p. 221.

49 MSR, p. 68.

50 *Ibid.*, p. 81.

51 MAS, p. 6.

52 Bayly, p. 319.

53 Quoted in Bayly, p. 306.

54 MS to Mrs Brightwen, undated, quoted in Bayly, p. 308.

55 Quoted in EBB1, p. 163.

56 MS to Mrs F, 26 November 1883, quoted in Bayly, p. 324.

57 EBB1, p. 163.

58 MS to unknown [1883], quoted in Bayly, p. 320.

59 MS to Mrs F, 26 November 1883, quoted in Bayly, p. 323.

60 MS to Mrs F, 26 May 1884, quoted in Bayly, p. 331.

61 EBB2, p. xxvi.

62 Mary Sewell's Last Will and Testament, and Probate.

63 Died 6 April 1879.

64 I am grateful to Marcos Gago Otero for this information.

65 I am grateful to Charles Briscoe for this information.

66 Mellor, *A History of the Red House Farm School*, p. 25; obituary *EDP* (7 February 1906), p. 4.

67 Philip Edward Sewell's Last Will and Testament.

68 See obituaries in *The Times* (19 November 1937), p. 22 and *EDP* (18 November 1937), p. 6.

69 '"Black Beauty" Author Remembered on Centenary', *EDP* (26 April 1978), p. 16.

70 Including her parents, her maternal grandparents, her great-grandfather Richard Wright and his three wives, her great-great-grandfather John Wright and her great-great-great grandmother Ann Wright née Seamer, together with Cousin Wright and his first wife, Anna's Aunt Maria, her Aunt and Uncle Wright and her cousin, Theodore Crewdson. I am grateful to Charles Briscoe who took transcriptions from the gravestones before they were bulldozed.

71 'Anna Sewell Grave Bulldozed', *EDP* (5 September 1984), p. 9 reports that the owner was 'Mrs Wendy Forsey'.

72 See '"No Permission" for Clearing Burial Ground', *EDP* (6 September 1984), p. 1 and 'Anna Sewell Grave Bulldozed', *EDP* (5 September 1984), p. 9.

73 '"Safe Place" for Sewell Headstones', *EDP* (1 September 1984), p. 1.

74 I am grateful to Charles Briscoe for this information.

Bibliography

Amory, Cleveland. *Ranch of Dreams*, New York, Viking Penguin, 1997

Angell, Geo[rge] T. *Autobiographical Sketches and Personal Recollections*, Boston, American Humane Education Society [1908]

Anna Sewell Country: Home of 'Black Beauty'. Norwich, Style Associates Ltd, 1990

'Anna Sewell Grave Bulldozed', *Eastern Daily Press* (5 September 1984), 9

Armstrong, Revd Benjamin John. *A Norfolk Diary*, ed. Herbert B.J. Armstrong, London, George C. Harrap, 1949

Baker, Margaret J. *Anna Sewell and 'Black Beauty'*, London, Longman, 1957

Bane, James J., ed. *J.J. Hamilton and Co.'s Imperial Postal Directory of the City and County of Norwich, with Gazetteer*, Norwich, William Allen, 1879

Barrows, Ellen A. *Four Months in New Hampshire: A Story of Love and Dumb Animals. Gold Mine Series No. 3. Sequel to 'Black Beauty'. A Prize Story of New Hampshire*, revised by George T. Angell, Boston, American Humane Education Society, 1894

Bayly, Elisabeth Boyd. 'Literary Work' in Mrs Bayly, *The Life and Letters of Mrs Sewell*, London, James Nisbet and Co., 1889, pp. 130–63

——. 'Memoir', in *Poems and Ballads by Mrs Sewell*, 2 vols, London, Jarrold and Sons [1886], vol. 1, pp. vii–xxvi

——. 'Mrs. Sewell' in Henry C. Ewart (ed.), *True and Noble Women*, London, Isbister and Company, n.d., pp. 281–304

Bayly, Mrs [Mary]. *The Life and Letters of Mrs Sewell*, London, James Nisbet and Co., 1889

'Black Beauty', *Our Dumb Animals* 41:5 (October 1908), 71

'Black Beauty', *Our Dumb Animals* 41:10 (March 1909), 149

'Black Beauty—100 and Still Going Strong', *Eastern Daily Press* (22 November 1977), 12

'"Black Beauty" Author Remembered on Centenary', *Eastern Daily Press* (26 April 1978), 16

'"Black Beauty" in Honolulu', *Our Dumb Animals* 41:12 (May 1909), 184

'"Black Beauty" in Norwegian', *Our Dumb Animals* 41:4 (September 1908), 59

Booth, Charles. 'The Rhodes Estate', *Survey of Life and Labour in London* (1886–1903), Charles Booth Online Archive <http://booth.lse.ac.uk/images/notebooks/b347/jpg/b347-055.jpg> 22 November 2003

Braine, A. *The History of Kingswood Forest: Including all the Ancient Manors and Villages in the Neighbourhood*, London, E. Nister, 1891

Brereton, J.M. *The Horse in War*, Newton Abbot, David and Charles, 1976

Briggs, Phyllis. *Son of Black Beauty*, London, Thames Publishing, [1954]

Bunyan, John. *A True Relation of the Holy War Made by King Shaddai upon Diabolus for the Regaining of the Metropolis of the World, or the Losing and Taking Again of the Town of Mansoul*, London, Newman and Alsop, 1682

Butler, David M. *The Quaker Meeting Houses of Britain*, London, Friends Historical Society, 1999

'Cabmen's Dinner at Norwich', *Eastern Daily Press* (5 February 1880), 3

Carder, Timothy. *The Encyclopaedia of Brighton*, Lewes, East Sussex County Libraries, 1990

Chichester Directories 1832–99, Local History File, held in Chichester Library, n.d.

Chitty, Susan. 'Biographical Foreword' in Ellen B. Wells and Anne Grimshaw (eds), *The Annotated Black Beauty* by Anna Sewell, London, J.A. Allen, 1989, pp. x–xiv

——. *The Woman Who Wrote 'Black Beauty': A Life of Anna Sewell*, London, Hodder and Stoughton, 1971

Clarke, Mrs J. Stirling. *The Habit and the Horse; A Treatise on Female Equitation*, 1857, London, Day and Son, 1860

Combe Down History. Material Collected by Members of the Combe Down Townswomen's Guild During the Winter of 1963/1964, n.d.

Crewdson, Isaac. *A Beacon to the Society of Friends*, London, Hamilton, Adams and Co., 1835

Cross, F.L. (ed.). *The Oxford Dictionary of the Christian Church*, London, Oxford University Press, 1957

Cullimore, Stan. *Little Joe Green*, Oxford, Rigby Heinemann, 1999

——. *The Making of Black Beauty: A Biography of Anna Sewell*, Oxford, Rigby Heinemann, 1999

Cunnington, C. Willett. *English Women's Clothing in the Nineteenth Century*, London, Faber and Faber, 1937

——. *Feminine Attitudes in the Nineteenth Century*, London, William Heinemann, 1935

Cunnington, C. Willett and Phillis Cunnington. *Handbook of English Costume in the Nineteenth Century*, London, Faber and Faber, 1959

Cunnington, Phillis and Anne Buck. *Children's Costume in England: From the Fourteenth to the End of the Nineteenth Century*, London, A. and C. Black, 1965

Daily Light on the Daily Path: A Devotional Text Book for Every Day in the Year; in the Very Words of Scripture, vol. 1 'The Morning Hour', vol. 2 'The Evening Hour', London, Samuel Bagster and Sons, n.d.

Dalby, Richard. 'Anna Sewell's "Black Beauty"', *Book and Magazine Collector* 132 (March 1995), 14–25

D'Aubigné, Jean Henri Merle. *History of the Great Reformation of the Sixteenth Century in Germany, Switzerland, &c*, tr. D. Walther, 3 vols, London, D. Walther, 1838–41

Davis, John R. *The Great Exhibition*, Stroud, Sutton, 1999

Delaney, Janice, Mary Jane Lupton, and Emily Toth. *The Curse: A Cultural History of Menstruation*, New York, E.P. Dutton and Co., 1976

Dent, A.A. 'Miss Sewell of Norfolk', *East Anglian Magazine* 15:10 (August 1956), 542–7

Dieter, Melvin E. 'Hannah Whitall Smith: A Woman for All Seasons', *Holiness Digest* (Fall 1999) <http://www.messiah.edu/whwc/Articles/article10a.htm> 22 November 2003

Doncaster, P. (ed). *Faithful Unto Death: A Story of the Missionary Life in Madagascar of William & Lucy S. Johnson*, with an introductory chapter by Joseph S. Sewell, London, Headley Brothers, 1896

'Dowse, the Gipsy', *Temple Bar* 5 (1885), 201–21

Dyos, H.J. and D.H. Aldcroft. *British Transport: An Economic Survey from the Seventeenth Century to the Twentieth*, Leicester, Leicester University Press, 1969

Edgeworth, Maria and Richard L. *Practical Education*, 1798, 2nd edn, 3 vols, London, J. Johnson, 1801

E.H. *A Brief Memorial of Mrs Wright, Late of Buxton, Norfolk*, London, Jarrold and Sons, [1861]

Ellis, Mrs [Sarah Stickney]. *The Daughters of England*, 1842, London, Fisher, Son and Co., n.d.

Erredge, John Ackerson. *History of Brighthelmston, or Brighton as I View it and Others Knew it*, Brighton, E. Lewis, 1862

Fairholme, Edward G. and Wellesley Pain. *A Century of Work for Animals: The History of the R.S.P.C.A. 1824–1924*, London, John Murray, 1924

Falconer, Randle Wilbraham. *The Baths and Mineral Waters of Bath*, London, John Churchill, 1881

Farrant, John H. *The Harbours of Sussex 1700–1914*, Brighton, J.H. Farrant, 1976

Flower, Edward Fordham. *Bits and Bearing Reins*, 2nd edn, London, William Ridgway, 1875

Folthorp's Brighton Guide, Brighton, Robert Folthorp, 1852

Ford, Richard. *A Handbook for Travellers in Spain*, 4th edn, part I, London, John Murray, 1869

Ford, Wyn K. and A.C. Gabe. *The Metropolis of Mid Sussex: A History of Haywards Heath*, Haywards Heath, Charles Clark, 1981

Fowler, Harriet. 'Enduring Beauty: A History of Illustrations to Anna Sewell's Classic Story', *Equine Images* (Fall 2002), 34–8

Fox, Caroline. *The Journals of Caroline Fox 1835–71*, ed. Wendy Monk, London, Elek, 1972

Fraser, H. Malcolm. *History of Beekeeping in Britain*, London, Bee Research Association, 1958

Gates, Barbara T. *Kindred Nature: Victorian and Edwardian Women Embrace the Living World*, Chicago, University of Chicago Press, 1992

Gavin, Adrienne E. 'Anna Sewell: A Consideration' in Hortensia Parlog (ed.), *Studii de Limbi şi Literaturi Moderne: Studii de Anglistică si Americanistică*, Timişoara, Romania, Tipografia Universităţii de Vest din Timişoara, 1997, pp. 33–43

——. 'The Autobiography of a Horse? Reading Anna Sewell's *Black Beauty* as Autobiography' in Martin Hewitt (ed.), *Representing Victorian Lives*, Leeds Working Papers in Victorian Studies, vol. 2, Leeds, Leeds Centre for Victorian

Studies, 1999, pp. 51–62

Gavin, Adrienne E. and Henrietta Twycross-Martin. 'Mary Sewell' in Joanne Shattock (ed.), *The Cambridge Bibliography of English Literature*, 3rd edn, vol. 4, Cambridge, Cambridge University Press, 1999, columns 434–5

Gilbert, Edmund W. *Brighton: Old Ocean's Bauble*, London, Methuen, 1954

Godman, Stanley. 'Anna Sewell, Authoress of "Black Beauty" and Her Life in Sussex', *West Sussex Gazette* (9 January 1958), 4

Gordon, W.J. *The Horse-World of London*, London, The Religious Tract Society, 1893

Gorges, Mary. *Mrs Sewell*, London, The Religious Tract Society, n.d.

Gorham, Mrs J.C. *Black Beauty: Retold in Words of One Syllable*, New York, A.L. Burt, 1905

Graeber, Laurel. 'A Horse's Life: It's A Beauty', *New York Times* (27 November 1998), E47

Granville, A.B. *Spas of England and Principal Sea-Bathing Places. Vol. 1 The North; Vol. 2 The Midlands and South*, 1841, Bath, Adams and Dart, 1971

——. *The Spas of Germany*, 2 vols, London, Henry Colburn, 1837

Greenwell, Dora. *Essays*, London and New York, Alexander Strahan, 1866

Gregory, T.E. *The Westminster Bank Through a Century*, 2 vols, London, Oxford University Press, 1936

Grimshaw, Anne. *The Horse: A Bibliography of British Books 1851–1976*, London, The Library Association, 1982

Gully, James Manby. *The Water Cure in Chronic Disease*, 1846, 2nd edn, London, John Churchill, 1847

Hardy, Thomas. *Jude the Obscure*, 1895, ed. Patricia Ingham, Oxford, Oxford University Press, 1996

Hartill, Rosemary. 'Introduction', *Florence Nightingale: Letters and Reflections*, Evesham, Arthur James, 1996

Hemans, Mrs. *Young Woman's Companion, or Female Instructor*, new edn, London, Virtue and Co., [*c.* 1830]

The Home Life and Letters of Mrs Ellis, compiled by her nieces, London, James Nisbet and Co., [1893]

Homer, Peter. 'Black Beauty Cottage is at Centre of Heritage Row', *Chichester Observer* (18 March 1999) n.p.

Hopper, Barone C. *100 Years of Sanctuary: Graylingwell Hospital 1897–1997: A Social History*, Littlehampton, West Sussex, 1997

——. 'The Lands of Graylingwell: Part 1', *West Sussex History* 39 (January 1988), 1–7

——. 'The Lands of Graylingwell: Part 2', *West Sussex History* 40 (May 1988), 18–22

——. 'The Lands of Graylingwell: Part 3', *West Sussex History* 39 (August 1988), 26–30

The House of Jarrolds 1823–1923: A Brief History of One Hundred Years, Norwich, Jarrolds, 1924

Howar, Arthur. 'Haywards Heath', *Local History File: Haywards Heath*, vol. 1, held in Haywards Heath Library, no pub. details

Howsam, Leslie. *Kegan Paul: A Victorian Imprint*, London, Kegan Paul, 1998

Hudson, T.P. (ed). *Victoria County History of Sussex*, vol. 6, part 1, Oxford, Oxford University Press, 1980

Huggett, Frank E. *Carriages at Eight: Horse-Drawn Society in Victorian and Edwardian Times*, Guildford, Lutterworth Press, 1979

'A Hundred Thousand New Missionaries', *Our Dumb Animals* 41:8 (January 1909), 114

Ingram, John H. *Edgar Allan Poe: His Life, Letters, and Opinions*, 1880, new edn, London, Henry Frowde, n.d.

Isichei, Elizabeth. *Victorian Quakers*, Oxford, Oxford University Press, 1970

Jackman, W.T. *The Development of Transportation in Modern England*, 3rd edn, 1916, London, Frank Cass, 1966

Jay, Elisabeth. *The Religion of the Heart: Anglican Evangelicalism and the Nineteenth-Century Novel*, Oxford, Clarendon, 1979

Jenkins, Elizabeth. *Tennyson and Dr. Gully*, Lincoln, The Tennyson Society, 1986

Jenkins, Peter R. *Sussex Money: A History of Banking in Sussex*, Pulborough, West Sussex, Dragonwheel Books, 1987

Kellett, Lorna. *The Sewell Connection: Family, Community, Theatre*, Norwich, Jarrold and Sons, n.d.

Kelly, E.R. (ed.). *The Post Office Directory of Norfolk and Suffolk*, London, W. Kelly and Co., 1879

Kelly's Post Office Directory of Gloucestershire, London, W. Kelly and Co., 1863

Kelly's Sussex Directory 1845, London, W. Kelly and Co., 1845

Kelly's Sussex Directory 1855, London, W. Kelly and Co., 1855

Kerridge, R.G.P. *A History of Lancing*, London and Chichester, Phillimore, 1979

Kingsley, Francis E. (ed.). *Charles Kingsley: His Letters and Memories of His Life*, 2 vols, London, H.S. King and Co., 1876

Lansbury, Coral. *The Old Brown Dog: Women, Workers, and Vivisection in Edwardian England*, Madison, Wisc., University of Wisconsin Press, 1985

Laqueur, Thomas Walter. *Religion and Respectability: Sunday Schools and Working Class Culture 1780–1850*, New Haven, Conn., Yale University Press, 1976

Leslie, Kim and Brian Short (eds). *An Historical Atlas of Sussex*, Chichester, Phillimore, 1999

Lucas, William. *A Quaker Journal: Being the Diary and Reminiscences of William Lucas of Hitchin (1804–1861), A Member of the Society of Friends*, ed. G.E. Bryant and G.P. Baker, 2 vols, London, Hutchinson, 1934

Mackie, S.J. *A Descriptive and Historical Account of Folkestone and its Neighbourhood*, Folkestone, J. English, 1856

Maclean, David G. 'An Examination into Attribution' in *The Strike at Shane's: A Prize Story of Indiana*, new edn, Decatur, Ind., Americana Books, 1991, pp. v–xx

Manning, I.M. *A History of Old Catton*, Old Catton, Norwich, I.M. Manning, [1982]

Martin, Robert Bernard. *Tennyson: The Unquiet Heart*, 1980, Oxford, Clarendon and Faber and Faber, 1983

[Martineau, Harriet]. *Life in the Sick-Room: Essays by an Invalid*, London, Edward

Moxon, 1844

Matthews, Debby. *America Lane: In the Footsteps of William Allen: Re-discovering America in the Middle of Mid Sussex*, Local History Series No. 2, Haywards Heath, Re-discovering America Local History Project, 2001

Matthews, P.W. and Anthony W. Tuke. *History of Barclays Bank Limited*, London, Blades, East and Blades, 1926

Mayhew, Edward. *The Illustrated Horse Management*, 1864, London, Wm H. Allen and Co., 1867

Meehan, J.F. 'Old Time Celebrities: No. VI Mary Sewell', *The New Album* (March 1906), 312–13

Mellor, Derick. *A History of the Red House Farm School, Buxton near Norwich*, Aylsham, Norfolk, Derick Mellor, 1976

Milligan, Spike. *Black Beauty According to Spike Milligan*, London, Virgin, 1996

Mitchell, Sally (ed). *Victorian Britain: An Encyclopedia*, Chicago and London, St James Press, 1988

Moon, Marjorie. *John Harris's Books for Youth 1801–1843*, rev. and enlgd, Folkestone, Kent, Dawson Publishing, 1992

Morgan, Roy R. *Chichester: A Documentary History*, Chichester, Sussex, Phillimore, 1992

Moss, Arthur W. *The Valiant Crusade: The History of the R.S.P.C.A.*, London, Cassell, 1961

Mumford, Brian W. *An Historical Walk Through Wick High Street*, Wick, Wick History Group, 1998

Murray, Janet Horowitz (ed.). *Strong-Minded Women: And Other Lost Voices from Nineteenth-Century England*, 1982, Harmondsworth, Penguin, 1984

Murray, John (ed.). *A Handbook for Travellers in Southern Germany*, London, John Murray, 1840

——. *A Handbook for Travellers in Spain, and Readers at Home*, Part I, London, John Murray, 1845

——. *A Handbook For Travellers on the Continent*, London, John Murray, 1856

——. *Murray's Handbook for Belgium and the Rhine*, London, John Murray, 1852

Musgrave, Clifford. *Life in Brighton: From the Earliest Times to the Present*, 1970, rev. edn, London, John Hallewell, 1981

A Narrative of the Grand Festival at Yarmouth, Yarmouth, J. Keymer, 1814

Nicolle, Margaret. *William Allen: Quaker Friend of Lindfield 1770–1843*, Lindfield, West Sussex, Smallprint, 2001

Nightingale, Florence. *Cassandra and Other Selections from Suggestions for Thought*, ed. Mary Poovey, London, Pickering and Chatto, 1991

'No Permission for Clearing Burial Ground', *Eastern Daily Press* (6 September 1984), 1

Nugent, May. 'Grandmother to Black Beauty', *London Mercury* 26 (1932), 52–60

Our Gold Mine at Hollyhurst. Gold Mine Series No. 1, Sequel to 'Black Beauty.' 'Duke': A Prize Story of Massachusetts. Boston, American Humane Education Society, 1893

Page, William (ed). *The Victoria History of the County of Gloucester*, vol. 2, repr., Folkestone and London, Dawsons of Pall Mall, 1972

——. *The Victoria History of the County of Sussex*, vol. 2, repr., Folkestone and London, Dawsons of Pall Mall, 1973

Palgrave-Moore, Patrick, compiler. 'Sewell of Yarmouth', *Norfolk Pedigrees Part Three: Norfolk Genealogy Vol. XIII*, Norfolk and Norwich Genealogical Society, 1981

Palmer, Charles John. *Perlustration of Great Yarmouth*, 3 vols, Yarmouth, George Nall, 1872

Parsons, Thomas. 'Chichester Sixty–Sixty-Five Years Ago', *Sussex County Magazine* 8:1 (January 1934), 42–3

Peach, R.E.M. *Street-Lore of Bath*, London, Simpkin, Marshall and Co., 1893

Peterson, M. Jeanne. *Family, Love, and Work in the Lives of Victorian Gentlewomen*, Bloomington, Ind., Indiana University Press, 1989

Philip Edward Sewell: A Sketch January 14th 1822–February 6th 1906, London, Jarrold and Sons, 1910

'Pigots 1840—Sandgate &c.'
<http://freepages.genealogy.rootsweb.com/~shebra/pigots_1840_-_sandgate_&c_.htm> 22 November 2003

Pigot and Co.'s National Commercial Directory: Norfolk & Suffolk, London, Pigot and Co., 1830

Pigot and Co.'s Royal National and Commercial Directory and Topography of the Counties of Bedford, Cambridge, Essex, Herts, Huntingdon, Kent, Middlesex, Norfolk, Suffolk, Surrey and Sussex, London, Pigot and Co., 1839

'Play of "Black Beauty,"' *Our Dumb Animals* 41:12 (May 1909), 180

Poe, Edgar Allan. 'William Wilson' (1840) in Julian Symons (ed.), *Selected Tales*, Oxford, Oxford University Press, 1980, pp. 79–96

Pool, Daniel. *What Jane Austen Ate and Charles Dickens Knew*, New York, Touchstone, 1993

Porter, Roy. *London: A Social History*, London, Hamish Hamilton, 1994

Powell, Anne and Colwell, Eileen, *Fircroft House*, no pub. details, 1998

Preston, John. *The Picture of Yarmouth*, Yarmouth, John Preston, 1819

Pullein-Thompson, Josephine, Diana, and Christine. *Black Beauty's Family*, [1975 as *Black Beauty's Clan*, 'Black Ebony', 'Black Princess', 'Black Velvet'], London, Red Fox, 2000

——. *Fair Girls and Grey Horses: Memories of a Country Childhood*, 1996, London, Allison and Busby, 1998

——. *More from Black Beauty's Family*, [1978 as *Black Beauty's Family*, 'Nightshade', 'Black Romany', 'Blossom'], London, Red Fox, 2001

René-Martin, Linda. *Sandgate: Rise and Progress of a Village*, Sandgate, René-Martin, 1998

Review of *Black Beauty* in *The Bookman* (London) 43:255 (December 1912), 134

Review of *Black Beauty* in *The Bookman* (London) 62:367 (Spring 1922), 51–2

Review of *Black Beauty* in *Eastern Daily Press* (22 December 1877), 3

Review of *Black Beauty* in *The Nonconformist* (9 January 1878), 32

Rigby, M. 'Anna Sewell—Black Beauty', Sowell Family Heritage Site 1998 <http://www.sowell.org/annasewell.htm.> 15 February 2002 (untraceable November 2003)

Ritvo, Harriet. *The Animal Estate: The English and Other Creatures in the Victorian Age*, London, Penguin, 1987

Robinson, Elizabeth. *Lost Hackney*, London, Hackney Society, 1989

Rye, Walter. *Norfolk Families*, 2 vols, Norwich, Goose and Son, 1911

'"Safe Place" for Sewell Headstones', *Eastern Daily Press* (1 September 1984), 1

Saunders, Alfred. *Our Horses: or, the Best Muscles Controlled by the Best Brains*, London, Sampson Low, Marston, Searle and Rivington, 1886

Saunders, [Margaret] Marshall. *Beautiful Joe: The Autobiography of a Dog*, 1894, new and enlrgd edn, London, Jarrold and Sons, n.d.

Schwieso, Joshua J. 'The Agapemonites', *The Chapels Society Newsletter* 5 (December 1991), 52–3

Senick, Gerard J. (ed). 'Anna Sewell 1820–1878,' *Children's Literature Review*, vol. 17 (Detroit, Mich.: Gale Research, 1989), pp. 130–47

Sewell, Anna. *Black Beauty*, 1877, ed. Peter Hollindale, Oxford, Oxford University Press, 1992

——. *Black Beauty: The Autobiography of a Horse*, London, Jarrold and Sons [*c*. 1895]

——. *Black Beauty: His Grooms and Companions. The 'Uncle Tom's Cabin' of the Horse*, ed. George T. Angell, Boston, American Humane Education Society, 1890

Sewell, Edith, compiler. *Joseph S. Sewell: A Quaker Memoir*, London, Headley Brothers, 1902

Sewell, Margaret. 'Letters of Margaret Sewell', unpublished typescript, in possession of owner

——. 'Recollections of Anna Sewell' in *Black Beauty*, London, Harrap, 1935, pp. 1–6

Sewell, Mary. 'Autobiography' in Mrs Bayly, *The Life and Letters of Mrs Sewell*, London, James Nisbet and Co., 1889, pp. 1–76

——. *The Children of Summerbrook; Scenes of Village Life, Described in Simple Verse*, London, Jarrold and Sons, 1859

——. *Davie Blake, the Sailor*, 2nd edn, London, Jarrold and Sons [1875]

——. *Homely Ballads for the Working Man's Fireside*, London, Smith, Elder and Co., 1858

——. *Mother's Last Words: A Ballad for Boys*, London, Jarrold and Sons, 1860

——. 'Mrs Sewell's Paper', in *Women's Work in the Temperance Reformation: Being Papers Prepared for a Ladies' Conference Held in London, May 26, 1868*, Introduction by Mrs S.C. Hall, London, Published for the National Temperance League by W. Tweedie, 1868, pp. 51–5

——. *Our Father's Care: A Ballad*, London, Jarrold and Sons [1861]

——. *Patience Hart's First Experience in Service*, London, Jarrold and Sons, 1862

——. *Poems and Ballads of Mrs Sewell*, 2 vols, London, Jarrold and Sons [1886]

——. 'Reminiscences', 3 vols, unpublished manuscript, in possession of owner

——. *The Rose of Cheriton: A Ballad*, London, Jarrold and Sons; London, S.W. Partridge, [1867?]

——. *Sixpenny Charity*, London, Jarrold and Sons [1884]

——. *'Thy Poor Brother': Letters to a Friend on Helping the Poor*, London, Jarrold and Sons, 1863

——. *Village Children at Home*, London, Jarrold and Sons, n.d.

——. *A Vision of the Night*, London, Jarrold and Sons [1882]

——. [published anonymously]. *Walks with Mamma, or Stories in Words of One Syllable*, London, John Harris, 1824

Showalter, Elaine and English. 'Victorian Women and Menstruation' in Martha Vicinus (ed.), *Suffer and Be Still: Women in the Victorian Age*, 1972, London, Methuen, 1980, pp. 38–44

Sidney, Samuel. *The Book of the Horse*, 1874, Classic Edition, New York, Bonanza Books, 1985

Smith, Hannah Whitall [Mrs Pearsall Smith]. 'A Word to the Wavering Ones', *The God of All Comfort* <http://www.godstruthfortoday.org/InTheGarden/HWSmith/TheGodOfAllComfort012.htm> 22 November 2003

Smith, Nickola. *Haywards Heath in Old Picture Postcards*, Zaltbommel, Netherlands, European Library, 1993

Staples, Suzanne Fisher. 'What Johnny Can't Read: Censorship in American Libraries,' *The ALAN Review*, 26.2 (Winter 1996) <http://www.scholar.lib.vt.edu/ejournals/ALAN/winter96> 16 November 2003

Starrett, Vincent. '"Black Beauty" and its Author' in *Buried Caesars: Essays in Literary Appreciation*, Chicago, Covici-McGee, 1923, pp. 205–23

Stibbs, Andrew. '*Black Beauty*: Tales My Mother Told Me', *Children's Literature in Education* 22 (1976), 128–34

Stonehenge [J.H. Walsh]. *The Horse, in the Stable and the Field*, London, George Routledge and Sons, 1875

The Strike at Shane's: A Prize Story of Indiana. Boston, American Humane Education Society, 1893

Tennyson, Alfred. *The Letters of Alfred Lord Tennyson. Vol. 1, 1821–1850*, ed. Cecil Y. Lang and Edgar F. Shannon Jr, Oxford, Clarendon, 1982

Tilt, Edward John. *The Change of Life in Health and Disease*, 2nd edn, London, John Churchill, 1857

Todd, John. *The Student's Manual: Designed by Specific Directions to Aid in Forming and Strengthening the Intellectual and Moral Character and Habits of the Student, c.* 1835, 10th edn, London, Milner and Co., 1860

The Town Walk of Haywards Heath, Haywards Heath, The Haywards Heath Society, 1999

Trayner, Gill. '"Black Beauty Cottage" Should Be Restored and Opened as Museum', no pub. details, 1999

Trollope, Anthony. 'Review of Mrs Sewell's *The Rose of Cheriton*', *Fortnightly Review* (1 February 1867), 252–5

Tunstall, James. *The Bath Waters: Their Uses and Effects in the Cure and Relief of Various Chronic Diseases*, London, John Churchill and Sons, 1868

Turner, E.S. *All Heaven in a Rage*, London, Michael Joseph, 1964

'Two Thousand Copies of "Black Beauty"', *Our Dumb Animals* 41:8 (January 1909), 114

Vinter, Dorothy. 'Anna Sewell and Her Family at Blue Lodge', *Gloucestershire Countryside* (June–July 1963), 10–11

Wallis's Royal Edition: Brighton as it is, 1836, Brighton, Wallis, 1836

Watson, Isobel. *Hackney and Stoke Newington Past,* rev. edn, London, Historical Publications, 1998

Weinreb, Ben and Christopher Hibbert (eds). *The London Encyclopaedia,* rev. edn, London, Macmillan, 1995

Wells, Ellen B. and Anne Grimshaw (eds). *The Annotated 'Black Beauty',* by Anna Sewell, London, J.A. Allen, 1989

White, William. *History, Gazetteer and Directory of Norfolk,* 3rd edn, London, Simpkin, Marshall and Co., 1864

——. *White's 1845 Norfolk,* repr., Newton Abbot, Devon, David and Charles Reprints, 1969

Wightman, Mrs [Julia]. *Haste to the Rescue; or, Work While it is Day,* London, James Nisbet and Co., 1860

Wood, Revd J.G. 'The Horse and His Owner, Part II', *Good Words* 22 (1881), 635–41

Woodfield, H.J.B. Review of *Black Beauty* in *The School Librarian and School Library Review* 4:4 (March 1949), 169

Wooster, William (ed.). *The Post-Office Bath Directory 1866–67,* Bath, William Lewis, 1865

Wright, Mrs [Anne]. *The Globe Prepared for Man; a Guide to Geology,* London, W.J. Adams, 1853

——. *Listen and Learn: A Short Narrative of a Three Day's Ramble,* London, Jarrold and Sons [1856]

——. *The Observing Eye; or Letters to Children on the Three Lowest Divisions of Animal Life. The Radiated, Articulated, & Molluscous,* 3 vols, London, Jarrold and Sons [1850]

——. *Our World: Its Rocks and Fossils. A Simple Introduction to Geology,* London, Jarrold and Sons [1859]

——. *The Passover Feasts and Old Testament Sacrifices Explained, Shewing their Typical Meaning, and their Fulfilment in Our Lord Jesus Christ, with a Slight Sketch of Jewish History, Adapted to the Instruction of Youth, By a Lady,* London, Jarrold and Sons [1849]

——. *What is a Bird? The Forms of Birds, Their Instincts, and Use in Creation Considered,* London, Jarrold and Sons [1857]

Wright, Maria. *The Anchor of Hope; or, New Testament Lessons for Children,* London, Routledge, Warnes and Routledge, 1859

——. *The Beauty of the Word in the Song of Solomon,* London, James Nisbet and Co., 1872

——. *The Bow of Faith; or, Old Testament Lessons for Children,* London, Routledge, Warnes and Routledge, 1859

——. *The Forge on the Heath,* London, The Book Society, 1873

——. *The Happy Village, and How it Became So,* London, The Book Society [1873]

——. *Jennett Cragg, the Quakeress: A Story of the Plague,* London, S.W. Partridge and Co., 1877

Index